THE UNLIKELY LAVENDER QUEEN

The
UNLIKELY
LAVENDER QUEEN

A Memoir of Unexpected Blossoming

Jeannie Ralston

BROADWAY BOOKS
NEW YORK

PUBLISHED BY BROADWAY BOOKS

Published in the United States by Broadway Books,
an imprint of The Doubleday Publishing Group,
a division of Random House, Inc., New York.
www.broadwaybooks.com

BROADWAY BOOKS and its logo, a letter B bisected on the diagonal,
are trademarks of Random House, Inc.

The opening quotation for Part One is from *The Genus Lavandula*,
A Botanical Magazine Monograph, by Tim Upson and Susyn Andrews,
Timber Press. The opening quotation for Part Two is from
Lavender: The Grower's Guide, by Virginia McNaughton, Timber Press.
The opening quotation for Part Three is from *Lavender: Practical
Inspirations for Natural Gifts, Country Crafts, and Decorative Displays*,
by Tessa Evelegh, Lorenz Books.

While this is a true story, some names have been changed to protect
the identities of those who appear in these pages.

Book design by Judith Stagnitto Abbate/Abbate Design

Library of Congress Cataloging-in-Publication Data
Ralston, Jeannie.
    The Unlikely lavender queen : a memoir of unexpected
blossoming / Jeannie Ralston. — 1st ed.
        p. cm.
    1. Ralston, Jeannie. 2. Lavender growers—Texas—Texas Hill
Country—Biography. 3. Lavender—Texas—Texas Hill Country.
4. Country life—Texas—Texas Hill Country. I. Title
SB63.R35A3 2008
2007029558

ISBN 978-0-7679-2795-6

PRINTED IN THE UNITED STATES OF AMERICA

1   3   5   7   9   10   8   6   4   2

First Edition

To my three beautiful boys, with all my love

CONTENTS

There are always flowers for those who want to see them.

HENRI MATISSE

•

*If you pass by the color purple in a field and don't notice it,
God gets real pissed off.*

ALICE WALKER
The Color Purple

THE UNLIKELY LAVENDER QUEEN

Delivery

When I stepped out the door at six o'clock that Friday morning carrying a plastic bucket and garden clippers, the world was violet-gray, the color of a storm cloud's underbelly. Shapes were black and fuzzy, as if I were wearing someone else's glasses. As I picked my way across the stone path to the driveway, I rubbed my arms against an unexpected chill, this being mid-May in Texas. The only noises besides my feet crunching on the driveway—which was composed of a substance ubiquitous in the Texas Hill Country called caliche, essentially limestone dust—were the doves cooing above the chirping crickets like the soft tones of an oboe laid over a chorus of violins.

It was the slice of the day that was not quite night and not yet morning. I watched my feet as I walked, to make sure I didn't stumble on the driveway, which was riddled with gullies from earlier rainstorms. I was wearing what Smith and Hawken had called muck boots, though they were not boots at all. They were more like slippers made from olive green wetsuit material. I'd ordered them for just this occasion. My debut as a farmer.

As I walked the one hundred yards to the field, I recalled one of the last times I was out at this hour, years earlier. It was on the other side of sleep, right after a New Year's Eve party, as I was stumbling through SoHo with my then-fiancé—right before I met the man who would become my husband and take me out here. I had watched my feet then, too. Mainly because I didn't trust them, in my champagne stupor, to contact the concrete securely. My shoes were different then: strappy high heels with rhinestone buckles. My life was too.

Passing the stone gate, I saw the shapes of the lavender rows spread before me. Twenty rows crawling over the hillside like so many purple caterpillars: 2,000 plants; 600,000 individual flowers. All surrounding a 450-year-old live oak that had the breadth and height of a big-top circus tent.

I stepped down one row of lavender and put my bucket down, with my dogs Katy and Weegee trailing behind me. Both were pound dogs—Katy a chunky and very international mix of German and Australian shepherd. Her heavy coat was fawn colored, but she had a black raccoon mask around her eyes. Weegee was part border collie; most of his lean body was white except for his own distinctive mask. His face was half black, half white—a canine version of yin-yang.

I wasn't sure where to start my task. I breathed in as I looked to the east, at a sliver of near-neon orange that was spreading out on the horizon like a just-split egg yolk. A breeze spread ripples through the long lavender spikes and delivered a rush of lavender scent mixed with the earthy aroma of chalky soil and woody undergrowth. The smell of lavender in the field is to the lavender scent in bottled cologne what eating a fresh, ripe strawberry off the vine is to the taste of strawberry jam. Nothing manufactured can compare to lavender as God made it—sweet and hearty, potent but not overbearing.

Visually, lavender rows are nature's version of a pointillist work of art. Up close, every stem, every tiny bud on the pipe-cleaner-shaped flower is discernible. At middle distance, the hundreds of flowers on each plant meld into one form that suggests a pom-pom and then even farther in the distance the plants come together to create one long uninterrupted row.

Scanning the row before me, I found a plant that looked especially prolific. My husband had estimated there were three hundred flowers on each plant, shooting out from the woody part of the plant on long graceful stems, looking like hair that had been subject to a strong dose of static electricity. This plant I bent over seemed to have four hundred blooms.

I reached into the plant and grabbed what looked to be the most perfect flower. Each flower head is made up of many calyxes, which are purple and tubular shaped. Some calyxes remain closed, others burst open into petals called corollas, which appear like tiny trumpets around the flower. On the blossom I chose, about a third of the calyxes were open, all at the bottom. My fingers slid gently down the eighteen-inch stem, as if I were preparing a thread for a needle, all the way to the spot where stem met leaves. My left hand was lost in purple. My right hand, holding the clean, never-before-used pair of clippers that I'd also bought for the occasion, dove in to cut at the place my left hand was holding. I pressed my right thumb toward my right fingers, which were curled around the handle, and the stem was freed. I put it in my bucket. Only 1,599 more to go that morning to fill our first order of flowers for a store in Austin.

I should have been serene. Everything about the setting screamed serenity, soulfulness, romance. But at the moment my emotions were at direct odds with the scene. I was thinking not that Martha Stewart might have approved of our crop, or that kneeling in a lavender field in full bloom might be somebody's idea of heaven. I was thinking about my husband and how he had done it to me again. Dragged me into something that I was supposed to embrace fully, dragged me into his dream. I snipped another lavender stem, harder than necessary.

Here I was alone out in a lavender field, doing something as unfamiliar to me as riding a bucking bronco. I had no farming experience. Before I gave up trying I sent more houseplants to their death than the state of Texas has criminals. Now he had left me to handle this whole farm alone. Alone, again, I thought bitterly as I cut more stems until the number of flowers in my bucket looked to be enough for one bouquet. I clutched the stalks in my hand; the thickness seemed to equal a serving of uncooked spaghetti. Forty stems, I guessed. In spite of myself, I admired the bouquet's loveliness, how lavender was not about each part, but the sum of them. How in numbers there was real beauty, a beauty exponentially greater than each singleton.

When my husband, Robb, hatched the idea for a lavender farm, I had resisted, just as I had resisted moving here. But ultimately I had a reason to move to the country, far from normal life as I knew it; it was part of a compromise. Tending a lavender farm, though, chopping away in a field like a migrant worker, was never part of the deal.

I had to give Robb credit. He was persuasive. Surely the most persuasive man in the world. My being in the field at this hour, when I could have been doing something truly productive like writing, was certainly proof of it. There was a time I would do anything for an article; while reporting a cover story for *Life,* I got myself arrested at an abortion protest just to find out what the evangelical activists went through in jail. Since moving to the country, I would often wonder where I might have landed if my trajectory hadn't been interrupted, if I hadn't landed here in the Texas Hill Country. But usually I had to turn my mind away from such thoughts. I had to put down the magazines emblazoned with names of onetime colleagues if I didn't want my throat and pride to burst.

When I could stuff no more flowers in the bucket, I pulled it against my body and started back to the house. I was suddenly anxious that one of my two boys, whom I had left inside, had woken up and I hadn't heard him. I imagined him roaming around the house in agony, wailing for me, feeling deserted. I walked faster. The water in the bucket sloshed on my red cotton pajama pants. I didn't even have proper farmer clothes, I thought. The tops of the lavender stems tickled my chin as I jogged up the driveway. As I got closer to the house—a two-story stone barn my husband and I had renovated—I strained to hear noise coming from the window I'd left open in their room. Any whimpers or whines. I got nearer and was relieved that it was still only the sound of the crickets and doves that filled the morning air. But I didn't really relax until I got inside the door and tiptoed with the bucket into the boys' room.

They were still in bed, still alive. Jeb, the two-year-old, was sleeping with his bottom in the air in a twin bed with a guard on the side made of plastic and nylon mesh to prevent him from rolling out. Smashed like an inkblot against the guard on the other twin bed was Gus, age four. He could choke all tangled up like that, I thought. I put the bucket down and shoved him, with some effort, toward the middle of the bed. I saw that his face bore the imprint of the nylon mesh that had been stretched across his cheek. He squirmed and mewed, then fell silent again.

I left the full bucket on the large screened porch that connected the old barn to a new stone building we designed. "The world's biggest dog trot," was how my father described the porch with its twenty-seven-foot-high ceiling when he first saw it. I picked up another bucket, filled it with water, and headed back to the field. I could already feel an ache in my back from stooping over. The sky was lighter now, light enough that the pickup that drove past the field on the main road into the nearby town of Blanco didn't have its lights on. I recognized the maroon-and-cream truck as our neighbor's and waved. Roger Felps waved back; well it was actually more of a salute off his cowboy hat. He was a sweet retiree who spent his days searching for different types of fallen trees in the Hill Country—elm, walnut, mesquite, oak—and then turning the wood on a lathe to make bowls, vases, platters. He had given each of the boys small, hand-turned wood tops when they were born. And he helped Robb plant this lavender field two years ago. Where was everybody to help me now?

I randomly chose another row and found a plant to start cutting on again. I harvested another quarter bucket and began feeling weary. It was just before seven and the boys would be waking soon. This seemed like an endless chore. I wanted to go inside and be still with a cup of tea before the boys got up, but I had to get the lavender harvested and into Austin by 11 a.m. A week earlier, I had taken a sample of some lavender bunches into a store called Central Market, an upscale grocery with a large floral department, to see if they would buy some. I felt silly sitting there in the floral buyer's office with my bucket of wares. I wanted to tell her that I don't really do this. I'm really a writer who has been published in the *New York Times* and *Conde Nast Traveler.* I felt she was looking at me as if I were desperate for the sale. Maybe she imagined that I lived on a tiny patch of land and that I needed to sell flowers to feed my family. I have immense respect for people who make their living off the land, but farming was so foreign to me it threatened the image I had of myself. To save my dignity, I wanted to reassure the buyer that we didn't need the money.

But what did we need? Robb had started the lavender farm because he needed a new project, basically. It wasn't enough that he was shooting photographs around the world for *National Geographic* or that he was clearing our two hundred acres of cedar, a weed-like, scrubby tree known to mob around oaks like paparazzi around a red carpet, or that we had two kids. He had to keep moving, keep testing himself. He was a person of infinite ideas, and for some reason, of all the ideas that wafted through his head, the one he followed through with was lavender.

Though he didn't actually ask me to take over the lavender while he was away on another assignment, it seemed assumed that I would. I stepped in because there were rows of glorious lavender in the field and something had to be done with it. I knew from being in Provence with Robb that it only bloomed for maybe five or six weeks. With Robb going away for three of them, this moment would be missed, and for me, missed moments were painful.

This was the natural dance of our relationship. When he was off traveling, which totaled about eight months out of the year, though not all at once, I would get the ball, whatever the ball happened to be at the time. Renovating our house was the same. He was the mastermind, the visionary, who could see in the skeleton of the old barn—among the cows and their poop—a spectacular, soaring home. I ended up being the one who interpreted his vision, working onsite with the contractor for months, while Robb was in Egypt, Japan, Costa Rica.

So, it was just as much my fault that right now, at the age of forty, my bones ached from this silly task.

I heard a car far off in the distance, maybe a mile away. It was first a soft swooshing of metal breaking through air, tires rubbing on pavement. Then I heard the pitch drop and knew the car was going down on the part of the road that crossed the creek bed. The tone became higher and louder. I heard gears grinding and an engine straining as it climbed the hill on this side of the creek. I looked up at the exact moment that the car became visible to the left—or southeast—of me, moving from behind a stand of skinny oaks on the edge of the property.

The car, or truck, rather—a gold Chevy—belonged to Juanita, the boys' babysitter. As I straightened up, she was pulling into our driveway to the right of me. I put my hand on the small of my back and imagined that my posture looked like every farmwoman I'd ever seen in the movies. Elbow sticking out from a bowed back like a misplaced gesture in a recitation of "I'm a Little Tea-pot." It was a few minutes after seven now. I had asked her to come two hours earlier than usual to look after the boys while I finished the harvest. I waved to her, happy for an excuse to leave the field.

The dogs took off after her car, leaping over lavender bushes as they ran. Weegee was the faster of the two; he stretched out like a cheetah when he ran. He was such a gorgeous, fleet runner that I often called him my Emmitt Smith, after the Dallas Cowboys Hall of Fame running back. Katy lumbered stiffly, trying to keep up and assert her alpha dog status. Years earlier, she'd had surgery on the torn tendons in both knees. "Joe Namath knees," is what I dubbed them, continuing the football metaphors.

"Buenos días, Nene," I called to her as I approached the house, using the name the boys had for her. *"Yo estoy muy cansada. No me gusta trabajando en el campo."* I was sure many of her countrymen from Mexico didn't like working in fields either. Nene spoke no English, which was one reason we hired her. We wanted the boys to grow up speaking Spanish. I showed her a blister that had worn on the first knuckle of my right index finger from the cutting.

"Oh Yean," she said, pronouncing the *j* as a *y*. She grabbed my hand gently to look closer. *"Necesitas guantes."* She was right. I did need to wear gloves. Maybe I would have thought of that if I had any gardening sense.

Since the boys were still asleep inside, Nene began washing dishes while I set up a place on the screened porch to prepare the flowers for the delivery. I hoped I'd cut enough to make the forty bunches the store had ordered. I pulled out a skein of raffia, which I'd bought at a floral supply store, and filled a spare bucket with clean water and a capful of some flower preservative I was instructed to use by some real farmers who lived nearby. They had greenhouses and acres of fields filled with sunflowers, ranunculus, larkspur, delphiniums. They had advanced degrees in horticulture. Fortunately, they took pity on me, the clueless cultivator, when I asked for advice on harvesting and transporting my lavender.

To make each bundle, I clumped roughly forty stems of lavender together, wrapped them in a rubber band, and tied them up in a bow of raffia. After about twenty minutes—and only six bunches—I heard one of the boys upstairs speaking to Nene. "*Quiero leche, Nene,*" Gus was saying.

As Nene retrieved his cup of milk, I called to him, "Hey, Bunny."

"Mama. Why are you out there?" he said in his husky, sleepy voice, as he came to the open glass doors that looked over the screened-in porch from the upstairs living area. The three bedrooms and two baths were downstairs, and so was the main level of the screened porch, where I was sitting.

"I've got to get this lavender to the store," I told him, as he climbed down the metal stairway to my level of the porch. He was wearing gray pajamas covered in little red baseballs and bats, and I could still see the faint diamond-pattern impression where the bed-guard mesh embossed itself across his right cheek. When he came near, he stretched out his arms for me to pick him up. I dried off my hands on my T-shirt and hoisted him onto my lap.

"Give me a *besito,*" I said, prompting him to plant a kiss on my cheek. In return I kissed his hair, which was the color of potato chips. I breathed in to get a whiff of him, but I couldn't find that familiar salty smell. My nose had been too full of lavender for the past hour and a half.

Nene brought his cup of milk, and I continued bundling the lavender with him sitting on my lap, which slowed me down. He got off later and asked to play with some lavender flowers. Even though I hated to spare even one hard-won flower, I gave him five and watched as he tried to tie them up in a bundle with a piece of raffia. When I finished my seventeenth bundle, I saw that I was going to be short of lavender. As I left Gus playing on the floor of the porch and headed back to the field, I cursed Robb again.

Out in the field it was already getting warm. I wished I had told Antonio, the young guy who helped us around the property—clearing cedar, trimming trees—to come at six, instead of his normal eight o'clock. When Robb does the harvesting, I thought, he'll have to get up at five-thirty and go pick him up.

I only had another quarter bucket of flowers when Antonio's ride pulled up at eight. Antonio was a short, mustached man with a whisper of a voice. Once I showed him how the flowers should be cut, I could tell he would be much faster than I was. With his help, there was some hope of meeting my deadline. Back at the house, I worked as speedily as someone possibly can while being interrupted at what seemed like ten-minute intervals. First, by Jeb waking up and wanting a hug, and Gus wanting to show me a cricket he had caught by the leg, and then by a request from the boys to push them on their tricycles. I noticed that Jeb looked like he had a flotation device strapped between his legs, which meant Nene hadn't changed him yet. As I swooped him off his feet to put a new diaper on him, I felt a stab of guilt for not spending enough time on potty training. Gus had been trained by this age. When Jeb was changed, the boys asked Nene to turn on TV. With Teletubbies blaring, they sat transfixed in their chairs, Jeb twisting his right index finger in the hair at the crown of his head as he drank from his sippy cup. More self-reproach followed for using TV to bring peace, but at least I could finish the flowers.

After Antonio brought another bucketful, the phone rang.

"How's it going?" Robb asked lightly.

A hundred potential responses flashed through my head, none of which would contribute to harmony in our marriage. I found one that seemed least likely to provoke an argument—mainly because I didn't have time for one. "I'm making progress, but this is *not* a one-person operation," I said firmly, as I placed another bunch in a bucket. "I got up at six and have been going full tilt ever since."

"I'm sorry I'm not there," he said sheepishly. "Hey, maybe next week what you can do is cut some in the evening and put them in the refrigerator in the garage till the morning."

"Yeah," I said. "I guess." The truth was I didn't want to cut flowers the night before. When I had visited the floral buyer at the market she had showed me some lavender that had been shipped from California. It was droopy and wan. I had made a point of telling her we could get lavender to her hours after it was harvested from the field. Even if I didn't care about the lavender, I cared that had I made a promise.

"So how many bunches have you done?"

"I'm now at thirty-four," I said. "You know it's a lot of work for four dollars"—which was the amount we were getting paid per bunch. "And I've got a blister on my hand."

"One hundred and sixty dollars," Robb said. I snorted when I heard the pitiful payoff for the morning's work stated out loud. On photo shoots for advertising clients, Robb could earn thousands in a day. I could make thousands for one magazine story.

"Now remind me why I'm doing this?" I asked.

"Because you're a beautiful, supportive wife and you're always open to trying something new."

"Ha, ha," I said.

"It's a new adventure. Farming—it's not just a job, it's an adventure. You're a pioneer, remember."

"Not that pioneer shit again," I said. "That's *your* fantasy." When Robb had wanted to move to the Hill Country, his most extraordinary logic for country living was that we would be pioneers. He always said *pioneer* with great enthusiasm, as if this was the answer I had given since age six to the question, What do you want to be when you grow up? He later gave up on pioneer and tried to appeal to my inner-New-Yorker's fondness for being ahead of a curve. "We'll be there before it gets trendy," he said. "You'll see." The Hill Country was certainly beautiful—with its rocky undulations and groves of live oaks— but in 1994, when we bought this place, trendy was its antithesis. Nobody lived here, it seemed, except old ranchers, young ranchers with the mind-set of old ranchers, and a few ersatz hippies.

But his cutting-edge rationale wasn't what finally convinced me to move. It was the compromise we made, and I thought I'd already been through all the angst—depression, isolation, scorpions—to keep my end of it. Now, there was more. There was this—these flowers in my hand. How much further from my true self was I going to have to stray?

"I'll be home in two weeks," he reminded me. "You'll be off the hook."

"You know you're going to owe me big-time," I said, relishing the leverage I would now have.

When I finished the last bundle, it was almost ten o'clock. I asked Antonio to load the buckets into the back of my white Isuzu Trooper, then ran into the house for a sponge bath before putting on a flowered skirt and a blue linen shirt. I wanted to wear something presentable, so I didn't look right off the farm—even though, of course, I was.

"Okay, I'm off," I announced as I rushed back upstairs, then kissed the boys good-bye. Starting toward the door, my mental clock took notice of how long the TV had been on. I spun and shut it off. "That's enough TV," I said. As usual, the boys moaned like mauled cows. Jeb slid out of his chair onto the floor like a glob of hot tar and accentuated his screams with a series of kicks. *"Nene, podrias traerlos afuera, por favor."* They needed to get outside and take a walk with Nene. Why live in the country if they were going to stay inside all the time?

I ran to the car, then jumped out again. I needed an invoice to leave with the flowers, and in my office, I grabbed a cream-colored piece of paper with the words *Hill Country Lavender* stretched across the top in purple. I had come up with the name for the farm, choosing it for its simplicity and the surprise it implied. No one expected to find lavender in the Texas Hill Country. I designed the stationery a week earlier, if designed is the proper word for centering 48 point Palatino font on a page.

To assuage the guilt of leaving Jeb upset, I told myself as I drove alongside the impossibly green Blanco River, that I would take them down to our creek for a picnic after I got home. The market had told me they wanted flowers twice a week—Tuesdays and Fridays. I was relieved that I only had three more days of this lunacy before Robb came home to take over.

When I got to the loading dock of the market, I wasn't sure where to park or even which door to go in, so I watched other vendors. Most of them were using dollies or carts for their stacks of crates and boxes, which they were pushing with great purpose. I had four measly buckets, one only half full. I could have carried them, but I figured I'd already exerted myself enough. Finding a spare cart, I loaded up my buckets and brought them inside to a part of the store I'd never seen before. I shopped at this market religiously, several times a week when I lived in Austin and, now that I was an hour away, anytime I was in town. Though my journalistic self was fascinated to see the backstage workings of my favorite store, it felt awkward not to be entering through the front door. If we'd never left Austin, I thought, I might be coming into the store right now in the proper way to buy flowers for a Friday night party instead of hawking them like a reverse Eliza Doolittle.

Standing on the loading dock, figuring out what to do next, I tried not to look as self-conscious as I felt. Finally, I found a woman wearing a Central Market shirt who directed me to another clerk.

"Oh, my gosh," the clerk said after she took my invoice from me. "Are these yours?" She crouched down and stuck her nose in the middle of the lavender. "Did you grow these?"

"Yes," I said uncomfortably. I hoped she wouldn't ask me anything about *how* we grew it.

"Where?"

"Out in Blanco, about an hour from here."

"You can grow lavender in Texas? I didn't know that."

"It's new," I said. "We're the first ones selling it."

The woman stood up and called to a couple of friends who came over to stroke the lavender and sniff it. They were cooing over my flowers just as other women had cooed over my babies not long ago. The three declared they were going to buy some bunches once they were put out on the floor. After signing my invoice, the first clerk showed me the doorway to the retail part of the store. Rolling the cart into the bright lights of the store aisles, I felt back on familiar territory, but was struck by a panicky thought—what if I saw people I knew while pushing this cart? I tried to tell myself not to be so proud, but I couldn't help it. I was used to people admiring my job, my work. What if someone thought I'd been reduced to slaving away as a delivery girl? Would they think this is what happens to people who move out to the country?

I sped toward the floral department up front and was relieved to make it there unnoticed. "Nice," said the florist, a young woman whose dark dreadlocks and tattoo-filled arms made her taste in something as delicate as flowers suspect. "I heard lavender was coming. I had no idea it would be this good." She picked up a bunch and breathed in. "It's gorgeous. Thank you so much. This is *so* cool."

When I got back in the car, I sat for a moment. I was exhausted; my back muscles were throbbing and my mouth was dry and pasty. I realized I hadn't brushed my teeth that morning, and tried to remember if anyone in the store had come close enough to catch my stale, sleep-and-caffeine breath. The lavender delivery lady who doesn't smell so good, I thought with a laugh. I tilted the rearview mirror to see that my looks weren't any better than my breath— long, unruly brown hair, tea-stain circles under my green-gray eyes that looked more deep-set than ever.

I thought of what I once looked like, back in the heyday that seemed to have passed too soon. I used to fit into the category of well-groomed; on good days, I may have even been considered pretty. To me, ordinary was always the worst condemnation—in looks, in work, but especially in life. But here I was on the verge of becoming ordinary in seemingly every way. An ordinary farmer. I thought I looked dangerously like a farmwoman in Blanco, who was about my age and whose skin was splotched and leather-like; apparently the straw hat she always wore was useless, no match for the hours of sun it battled against. Her hands were even scarier—callused and too wide and strong for her gender. The traces of dirt that seemed permanently embedded in the cracks around her knuckles and fingertips reminded me of the miners' hands I had seen growing up in East Tennessee.

As I did frequently, I couldn't help but question how I'd gotten to this strange spot in my life, so far from what I'd expected for myself. Yes, there had been a heady romance a few years back. Then a slew of subsequent decisions, fueled by love and yearnings I didn't even know I had. But I never, ever would have suspected that this was where the sum total of them would bring me. That afternoon a new doubt dripped into my mind. When do you know, I wondered, whether the choices you've made were the right ones?

Part One

THE FIELD

There are three essential prerequisites for healthy growth and long life—full sun, free-draining soil and good pruning. . . . Lavender in the wild grows in some fairly inhospitable soils. . . . It will thrive in very poor stony soils, even those mixed with builder's rubble or such like. . . . Lavender is always found in sunny, often highly exposed positions in the wild.

•

—TIM UPSON AND SUSYN ANDREWS,
The Genus Lavandula

CHAPTER ONE

Severed Roots

I couldn't have missed Mortimer's that night. From two blocks away I saw that the rarefied air surrounding this famous haunt of stupendous some-bodies on the Upper East Side was shuddering with flashes of light. I was reminded of the view of thunderheads from an airplane—the convulsions of lightning inside always appeared to me as if the gods were battling within the clouds, and here in the loftiest neighborhood of Manhattan, gods of another kind were waging their own type of battle. For attention. The paparazzi were out in force, focused at the moment, I could see, on Ronald Perelman, the chairman of Revlon, and his wife, Claudia Cohen, a gossip columnist. The two were standing perfectly still inside a wreath of photographers, his arm was draped around her shoulders. Their faces were frozen in a grin-gnash that barely hid the contempt for the hands that fed their celebrity.

Through the front windows, I saw swaying silhouettes in various party postures—drinks to mouths, hand on someone's shoulder, heads cocked back in an exaggeration of ecstatic laughter. Right before I crossed Lexington Av-enue, into the arc of Mortimer's halo, I checked myself. Over a black camisole and a short black lace skirt, I wore a sheer black blouse with a gold shimmer that I'd bought at a SoHo boutique. On my feet were a pair of Manolo Blahnik pumps borrowed from a friend who worked for Anne Klein. I counted my blessings that I had a fashion industry friend who was my exact size.

Once I made my way through the door and into the bright light, I grabbed a glass of wine and began to circulate. I saw socialite Anne Slater, sitting at the bar in her famous blue-tinted glasses, and thought that she must have been

Anna Wintour's role model for sunglass ubiquity. I noticed Martha Stewart and publishing executives I could identify from Page Six. Two women whose skin was pulled tightly over their yesterday's-deb bone structure were gushing over the man who was the reason for this gathering, Dominick Dunne, who I noted was much shorter than I expected. It was May 1990 and the party was to celebrate the publication of his novel *An Inconvenient Woman*.

As much as I enjoyed star watching, I was actually there to work—eavesdrop really. I was profiling the woman behind the event—a distinguished party planner named Nancy Kahan who had a track record of pulling off the most over-the-top publishing events in the city. I caught up with her and watched her in full schmooze for a while, then I had to race off to a French restaurant called Pierre's in Greenwich Village, around the corner from where I'd once lived.

This article I was writing—commissioned by a friend at *Manhattan Inc.* magazine—had caused a serious rift with my fiancé, Ben. The magazine needed the story in a week's time to fill in a hole in the lineup of their next issue, and the seven-day deadline happened to coincide with my fiancé's graduation from New York University Film School. Ben's father had come in from overseas and his mother was up from Nashville with her second husband. A man who loved good theatrics and high living, Ben had wanted to mark the occasion as if it were the Oscars. There was a week's worth of parties and dinners in his honor. He hadn't wanted me to take the assignment, but I refused to give up the opportunity to write something for Clay Felker, who had recently taken over as the editor of the magazine. Felker was a journalism legend, one of the original proponents of the New Journalism (nonfiction that reads more like a novel) I'd studied in my magazine writing class at the University of South Carolina. I had assured Ben I would sacrifice sleep to make all his events *and* my deadline.

That night I thought I would join Ben, his mom, and stepfather by the time they were ready to order their meal. But in the end, I didn't make it until dessert. Ben didn't even look at me as I slipped into a chair beside him and made my apologies.

When we got back to our Chelsea apartment, Ben finally deigned to talk to me. Well, talk isn't the right word. He was furious that I had missed dinner and cursed the story I was working on. "You're just not there for me," he said at the end of his rant.

Those words might as well have been a crank on a jack-in-the-box. Suddenly, I had sprung up out of my chair. I heard my skirt rip, but I'm not sure *how* I heard it, my voice was so loud. "Not there for you! Not there for you!" I spit. When I threw my hands in the air, as my 50 percent Italian blood pre-ordained I must, I caught my silver beaded necklace. Beads bounced all over the floor as if a gumball machine had been broken open. I tried to convey the multifaceted ways in which his charge was offensive. The truth was I had taken care of him for four years, since I met him on an airplane flying from Nashville to New York in 1986. I had let him move into my apartment with me; I had helped him write his application to NYU film school. I ran our household, paid the bills, did the laundry, cooked our dinners. He had already exhausted me.

After my eruption, I locked myself in my office. I could not expend any more energy on fighting since I had to start writing my story on the party planner. I resolved to smooth things over so that I could get through the assignment and his grandiose graduation. I had a trip to Texas coming up the following week. That would give me time to think.

•

I have always been a leg woman. I love a well-shaped man's leg. I have been known to watch a men's tennis match solely for those moments, shot from behind, when the player is bent over slightly, dribbling the tennis ball right before serving. That angle affords the best view of long, handsome legs.

Nothing, however, beats seeing nice legs in the flesh, and a week later I was in Texas, eyeing a particularly gorgeous set. Calves like sinuous interpretations of an upside-down Coke bottle. The pair belonged to a man I'd just met. He was a young photographer, single and straight, from what I could tell, and I was at a cookout at his house in Houston. We were scheduled to fly to Fort Worth the following day to start our story for *Life* magazine about B. Don Magness, the longtime director of the Miss Texas Pageant. I had met Magness once before in Houston and thought he was such an outlandish Texas character that he would be a perfect profile for *Life*.

I had not wanted a male photographer to shoot the story. A female would have less trouble getting behind-the-scenes shots. But several weeks earlier my editor had called me up to float an idea.

"I've got this guy in Texas I'd love to use, if you'll agree," she said. "He's so talented and young. And *so* cute."

"Okay," I told her after some thought. "I guess it could help to have some-one from Texas."

Maybe it was the cute part that got me to agree. But it was the word *young* that spiked my eyebrow. I was used to people commenting on *my* youth. I was an associate editor of *McCall's* at twenty-two and editor-in-chief of my own magazine by twenty-five. I'd already been published in most of the major women's magazines and reported a cover story (among other articles) for *Time* magazine while working freelance in the New York bureau. At twenty-nine, I had reported several stories for *Life*—the *Life* magazine I'd read faithfully growing up—and now was writing my first *Life* feature.

After I agreed to this photographer, named Robb Kendrick, I had an oc-casion to doubt my choice. The night after I fought with Ben, I was wearing a perky party face for a get-together at our Chelsea apartment. I was in the steamer-trunk-sized kitchen cutting up pizzas I had made myself from my mother's recipe for hors d'oeuvres when Ben stuck his head in to tell me I had a phone call. "It's that photographer for the *Life* story, Robb Kendrick."

"Oh," I said, my fingers smeared with tomato sauce, "could you tell him I'll call him back tomorrow." Ben disappeared, and as I was putting the pizzas on a platter he came back with a quizzical look on his face.

"He said no."

"What?"

"He said no, you couldn't call him tomorrow. He needs to talk to you now."

Who the hell does this guy think he is, I thought as I washed my hands and wiped them on the blue tunic and skirt I'd recently bought in Paris. I walked back to my office, away from our chattering friends in the living room. Just what I need, another fucking demanding man, I thought. I was cranky from lack of sleep—I had stayed up till three the night before trying to make headway on the Kahan profile—and was prepared to let him know that we weren't going to work together well if he couldn't be flexible.

"Hi, Jeannie," he began. "I'm sorry; I know you're having a party, but I'm working on a story in the mountains in Georgia and I don't know when I'll be near a pay phone again."

Something about his voice—a mellowness, a rich timbre—calmed me. I found all my armaments sliding away. I chatted with him for fifteen minutes while the party swirled outside my office door. In the end, we were laughing over his rendition of "Dueling Banjos," inspired by his location in the mountains of North Georgia. When he found out that I was going to be in Houston the next weekend for a *Glamour* story before heading up to Fort Worth for *Life,* he invited me to a cookout at his house.

Now that I was in his backyard with some of his Houston friends, the sight of his legs somehow put the failings of Ben in stark relief. Ben's legs were chunky, with no differentiation between calf muscle and ankle. Even Ben referred to his lower limbs as Fred Flintstone legs. Comparing the two sets of legs—the photographer's and my fiancé's—produced a stab of awareness. How could I marry a man whose legs I didn't adore?

Just before arriving at his house for the cookout, I had talked to my mother, who was pressing me to decide on a place for my wedding. Ben and I had been engaged for two years, and a long engagement is never a good sign. Dates and locations were batted around, but we could never agree. We had tentatively looked at the coming fall and my mother had sent me brochures for hotels near her in the Smoky Mountains. I had carried them to Houston, but hadn't yet looked at them.

"If we want to reserve for this October, we need to make a deposit on one of these places," she told me when I had talked to her from Houston. "It's getting a little late."

"I know," I said, but I couldn't imagine my parents putting money down on my wedding at a moment when marrying Ben seemed as appealing as a dermabrasion. "But listen, I'm really tired. I've got these two stories I need to work on here. Let me think about this when I get back to New York."

Then I met Robb Kendrick at his house. Then I noticed his legs. Then, after I settled in a lawn chair in his backyard with a glass of wine, I observed that on one gorgeous calf muscle was a tattoo. A small, discreet eye.

By the end of the party, I was taking note of other things. His lagoon-blue eyes. His impish smile. The curls that had fallen out of his ponytail. His one gold earring. I could see my editor was a reliable source. He *was* cute. Perilously cute.

The peril seemed to increase the following day when Robb and I arrived at our hotel in Fort Worth to start our story. The rooms they gave us were adjoining.

The door between the rooms stayed locked for the first three nights of our assignment. During that time, we followed around our subject, B. Don Magness, a balding man with glasses and a swell of a stomach, as he helped contestants prepare for the state pageant, a month away. With Robb and me in tow, he dished out so many outrageous comments I complained of quote overload. He described a woman he didn't like as "uglier than a she-wolf who's been shit over a side of a cliff." He criticized one contestant's lack of hair volume. "It's so flat it looks like a cat's been sucking on it." The antidote for such an affliction? Hairspray. More hairspray. He'd once given a T-shirt to a former Miss Texas that read, In Case of Rape, This Side Up. B. Don had his own T-shirt that he was quite proud of. It said, Matthew, Mark, Luke and B. Don.

On our off-hours, when we weren't laughing over this crude old man, we went out to dinner with friends of Robb's in Dallas, we drank margaritas for lunch. We were determined to memorize the words that Madonna chanted in the middle of her song "Vogue," and on the third night after we'd returned to our separate rooms, I heard it on the radio and finally figured out the missing parts. I called Robb next door and sang him the entire ditty. And though I had found little time to speak to Ben over the past few days, Robb and I talked on the phone for an hour. Awkwardly, we both knew all we had to do was unlock one door to see each other, but the phone was so much safer.

On the fourth day, we made a bet. We both tried to guess what the *B* in B. Don stood for. Of course I said Billy. Billy Don. Robb thought this was too obvious. He guessed Barry, which seemed so wrong that I wondered if he had truly grown up in Texas. The loser of the bet had to take the winner out to the most expensive restaurant in Fort Worth and *not* put it on an expense account. After dinner, Robb added, the loser had to carry the winner across the lobby of our hotel.

I won the bet—I suspect Robb knew I would with his pitiful guess. At dinner that night at a romantic French restaurant called Saint Emilion, I found myself too nervous to eat much of my roast duck. I had felt this intense, almost immediate infatuation only a few times before. I knew I was in love. My mother had once told me I would never find a man who met all my requirements, but here he was. I allowed myself to imagine a life with him—traveling, working together, laughing. I imagined the freedom, the psychic energy I would save from being with a man who could take care of himself. I was so completely besotted with Robb—sitting at the table in his crisp white shirt and purple tie with an abstract image of a chorus girl—that my stomach felt as functional as a chunk of putty.

Also contributing to my loss of appetite was the diamond on my finger. To go where I was heading with Robb was betrayal. Plain and simple. But the train was leaving the station.

"Okay," I said when we reached the hotel lobby after dinner. "Part two." Without hesitation and gratefully without any discernible grunting, he picked me up in his arms and carried me to the elevator. Our cackles echoed through the atrium. He continued to hold me in the elevator and carried me down the hall. I found myself trembling, but hid it with laughter. What was going to happen next? I thought. How could I hurt someone I once loved so thoroughly? But how could I resist? How could I let this moment pass? He deposited me at my door, and our eyes locked.

"Well," he said, backing away. "It was fun. See you tomorrow."

"*See you tomorrow?*" I exclaimed. I began to panic. I knew he was quite assertive. Maybe he didn't feel the way I did. I was determined not to miss the opportunity. "Don't I even get a kiss?" I blurted clumsily.

The words were out of my mouth before they had even passed through my brain. Robb told me later that because of the rock on my finger, he was determined not to make the first move. It was left to me to begin the dizzy, headlong dive. That night we opened the door between our rooms.

·

You wuz Robbed," my friend Kim crowed two days later back in New York when I told her I was in love with someone who wasn't Ben. We were standing at the Chanel counter at Barneys on Seventh Avenue. Kim wanted to know all the details, and even though she liked Ben, I could tell her without worrying she'd condemn me. We had lived next door to each other our freshman year at the University of South Carolina, and if anyone could understand romantic upheavals, it was Kim.

I had moved to New York first, after I'd received a summer internship with *McCall's* magazine, and knew immediately that Kim was born to live in the city. She was always racier than me, more daring in fashion and men. Even though she was short, she could pull off any look. When she came to New York, I showed her around, and she in turn helped loosen up my style and my earnest, goody-goody mind-set. She once, memorably, accused me of being too safe. "You're just not very adventurous," she told me. My offense had been refusing to return to the Milk Bar in the East Village on a Saturday night after my wallet had been stolen when I was there the night before. The gauntlet was down. Ever since I had made a point of proving her wrong.

"God, Ben's going to wish I'd never said that," Kim declared as we waited at the Chanel counter for a clerk, recalling her brutal assessment. "Because you're certainly being adventurous now."

Kim was the fashion editor for the men's equivalent of *Women's Wear Daily*, and a year earlier she had helped me put together a wardrobe for my three-day trip to Morocco to cover Malcolm Forbes's seventieth birthday party. I covered the bash for *Us* magazine and when I introduced myself to the owner, Jann Wenner, at the party, the only notice he gave me was to remark that I was the best dressed reporter there. My outfit—a black satin strapless gown under a jeweled bolero jacket, rented from an Upper East Side shop for the occasion—was sleek enough to allow me to be mistaken for a guest and ushered into an area no other reporters could enter.

Today, Kim was helping me again. I was writing a story for *Vogue* about the best consultations and makeovers at the city's cosmetic counters. Beauty stories for *Vogue* were a recent addition to my strange mix of journalism—serious reporting with an occasional relationship story for a women's magazine. It was a combination that kept me solvent and independent and prevented my getting too bored with any one topic.

I was in no condition to do the makeover research myself. That morning on the plane home from Texas, I'd noticed that the anxiety over my imminent breakup with Ben had prompted the return of my least attractive feature. Whenever I was stressed out, a cold sore would flower in the oddest place—my chin. With that glowering lesion front and center, as ignorable as a stoplight, I couldn't expect anyone to touch me. Instead, Kim would be the guinea pig.

"And the best part is, he was born in *Spur*, Texas," I told Kim, pronouncing Spur as a drawn-out purr. She was the first of many friends who would hear about Robb's origins. I loved the cowboy implications of the town's name. Only much later did I learn that the town, in the Texas Panhandle, derived its moniker from its history as a railroad spur, not from the iconographic boot accoutrements, but I would keep that to myself.

"That's so cool. Spur," Kim said, while a Russian girl at the Chanel counter began applying base to Kim's face. "So, what are you going to do?"

"Obviously I have to tell Ben right away." I had gotten home that afternoon and hadn't even seen Ben, who was reediting his student film. "It would be doubly wrong to not tell him immediately." I was looking at my engagement ring, which since a few days ago I'd been wearing turned around, with the diamond palm-side. I wasn't paying much attention to the makeup artist; I could only think of the scene to come, of ways I could soften the blow, of how I was going to start the dreaded conversation.

"Well, look on the bright side," she said. "You've lost weight."

"I know," I said, pulling up on the belt loops of my jeans. Being five foot eight and a regular runner, I'd never been overweight, but living in New York, I was always aware I could be thinner. With the barrage of emotions I was feeling—infatuation, excitement, terror—food still held no interest. Even an éclair would have tasted like cardboard at that moment.

I wanted to run away, but knew I had to do the right thing by Ben—now that I'd done the wrong thing by him. Finally, the only way to break my engagement was to say, holding my diamond in my hand, "I've met someone else." Four words that I suspect could not have delivered more pain if they were lasers. I put the ring on the sofa between us. The night that followed surely made my cold sore flare like a sunspot. There was a fist thrown into a closet door so hard that it came off its hinges and slammed to the hardwood floor. There were tears and threats and name-calling.

But then it was done. Over the next couple of weeks, Ben calmed down, and eventually decided it was a good time to move to Los Angeles, where his grandmother lived and where he already had contacts in the film business. When I waved good-bye to the taxi that was taking him to the airport, I was filled with nostalgia for the good memories of our four years together. But I was more than ready to begin the era of Robb.

•

Come on in, sluts." That was the first line of my article on B. Don Magness, who had made the pronouncement to a group of giggling contestants practicing for a number that would appear in the Miss Texas Pageant. He insisted it was a joke—but he wasn't all talk, apparently.

During the course of the week that Robb and I followed him during the pageant, several girls told me of his inappropriate advances and "creepy kisses." When I asked him about those, he dismissed the charges as sour grapes. But the same couldn't be said about a former Miss Texas who told me he made her model bathing suits at his house while they were alone. "Is this the kind of influence young girls should have!" the former Miss Texas said.

The story, which came out in the September 1990 issue, caused a tremor. It was covered by the tabloid TV shows and was mentioned even in the *New York Times*. The Fort Worth and Dallas papers turned up more girls who complained of B. Don's overfriendliness. In the newspaper reports B. Don called me a "skinny feminist from New York with greasy hair." My first reaction was to be thrilled that he considered me skinny. Then I laughed knowing why he thought my hair was greasy. Every morning during the week of the pageant, Robb and I had stayed in bed until the last possible minute. When I was due for an interview or an event, I would wash my hair in a rush and head to the auditorium with it still wet and pulled back in a ponytail.

In the end, B. Don had to resign his position, which he had held for twenty years. I had never meant to bring him down, but marveled at the fact that some people are so flattered by press attention that while they're putting on their show for journalists—trying to be interesting, funny, clever—they end up hanging themselves.

Even if B. Don had sued *Life*, which he never did, I doubt I could have been rattled. I was living in a hazy, love-soaked world at the time. The story broke right after Robb and I had returned from two weeks in the Caribbean, where he was shooting a story on romantic hideaways for *Travel + Leisure*. Robb had told the art director he was taking me along as inspiration. We jumped around like skipping stones from Martinique to St. Kitts to Nevis to St. Barts, staying in fabulous inns, swimming on private beaches, taking boat rides at sunset, dining, drinking, and doing our best impersonations of hedonists. Because we were there at the end of August—hurricane season—the hotels were almost empty, which meant Robb needed me to be in many shots. Fortunately, I was well stocked with bathing suits.

While we were in St. Barts, he had me sit on a chair on an "island" table in the middle of an infinity edge pool. I was wearing a black-and-orange-sherbet-colored bikini and a black-and-white polka dot ribbon in my hair. I was turned slightly away from the camera, gazing out to the bay far below me. The photo ended up on the cover of the December issue of *Travel + Leisure*, right in time for my thirtieth birthday. I found the issue on the newsstand around the corner from my Chelsea apartment, soon after we returned from working on a story together in London and northern France. I pulled the issue off the newsstand and began jumping around, waving it in the air. "This is me! This is me!" I announced most immodestly to the guy working at the newsstand. "Can you believe it?"

I heard from my family; my grandmother was most appalled by a photo of me inside lying on a lounge topless with just a strategically placed book covering me. I got a call from Ben, who had started making a life in Los Angeles. Robb's ex-wife—he'd been married once before at the age of twenty-three—complained that I was on subscription cards that dropped in her lap every time she opened the magazine. "Does this happen to every divorced woman?" she asked Robb plaintively. Somehow, this endeared her to me.

If Robb had not already proposed, I would have gone down on my knee to beg him to marry me. How could I not adore this man who had given me the best thirtieth-birthday present a girl could ask for? I felt with Robb life would always be this exciting. How could it not?

·

By the end of 1990, Robb had given up the house he rented in Houston and moved his things into my Chelsea apartment, somewhat reluctantly. I knew that he didn't like New York, but I had made it plain I wasn't moving to Houston. It would be the only time I would have the say-so in where we called home.

Though Robb paid rent on the apartment, we didn't quite live together. He was gone much of January, shooting in different parts of the country and also visiting *National Geographic* headquarters in Washington, DC. Robb had been an intern at *Geographic* right out of college and had shot for the book division before. Now, in January 1991, he was being asked to go to Nepal for fourteen weeks and shoot a feature on Sherpas for what was known as "the yellow magazine" to coincide with the first all-Sherpa expedition up Mount Everest.

It wasn't the first time he'd been offered a feature story for the magazine. The editors had asked him to go to the Gulf Coast a few months earlier, but he'd turned down the assignment, which was daring for a young photographer. Most wouldn't dream of rejecting a shot at making their name in the magazine. But, as I later realized, Robb had a stubborn, quiet confidence and a gambler's nerve. He felt sure he'd be asked again, and didn't want to take on an assignment that wouldn't allow him to do his best work. "I just don't want to spend three months of my life in swamps and shopping centers," he said when I worried he was being too finicky. Fortunately, he had plenty of talent to back him up. Even though they were documentary shots, his photographs were so painterly—in color, in composition, in soulfulness—that I was surprised to learn he'd never studied art.

He left for Nepal on the eve of the first Gulf War, which I wrote about for *Life*. For my story, about women in the military getting closer to the front lines than they'd ever been, I interviewed Congresswoman Pat Schroeder in DC and went to Fort Bragg, North Carolina, to talk to female soldiers coming home from the Gulf. Another reporter sent back dispatches from Riyadh, Saudi Arabia, that I incorporated in my story. I worked furiously, anxious to get the article wrapped up by March 5, which was the date of my flight to Kathmandu.

At the same time, I was reworking a story for the *New York Times Magazine,* a profile of a maverick public hospital administrator. These two major stories kept me busy enough that I had less time to mope over my separation from Robb. I was used to speaking to him several times a day, but once he left Kathmandu he was entirely off the grid. The Himalayas were almost prehistoric—no phones, no electricity, no plumbing, no roads, no cars.

Having a healthy dose of ingenuity, Robb figured out a way to communicate, however. "Are you da wife of Robb Kendrick?" a strange German-accented voice asked me one afternoon when I picked up the phone. The crackle of the connection told me it was an international call. I imagined that someone was calling to tell me Robb had fallen into a crevasse or that a helicopter crashed, or, well, I had no problem thinking up spectacular disasters.

"Yes," I answered cautiously. Even though we weren't married yet, this was no time to confuse the issue.

The woman explained that she had met Robb up at a lodge in the Himalayas. When he found out she was heading back to Kathmandu, he had written a note to me and given her money to call me. My mind was lurching to keep up with the explanation. I was still expecting the phone call to turn dark, to convey something that would crush me. Then she began reading Robb's note.

"Dear Jeannie Mo Beannie," she began, his nickname for me in her voice sounding as odd as a chirp from a bullfrog. "I'm okay, but I miss you so much. I miss . . ." Here my caller paused. "*Spooning* with you?" Her voice rose on the word *spooning,* as if she'd later be looking for the definition in the *Kama Sutra.* I cried as she continued and I imagined him scrawling the note on some rustic table by the light of a fire. When she was finished, I asked if he had given her enough money to read the note again.

"It doesn't matter," she said. "This is so romantic, I am happy to be part of it." Not only did she read it again, she mailed me the original when she got back to Germany. I got two other calls like this over the month that he was out of touch and marveled at how fortunate I was to have met a man who was not only romantic, but resourceful too.

·

When I left for Kathmandu, by way of Frankfurt and New Delhi, I had finished the fact-checking on the *Life* piece, but no researcher had been assigned to the *Times Magazine* article since it hadn't been put on the schedule yet. I left my *New York Times* editor phone numbers for the trekking service coordinating the Sherpa expedition, hoping they might know how to get me a message.

After spending the night snoozing uncomfortably on my suitcase in the New Delhi airport, I arrived in Kathmandu, where Robb met me at the airport. He was gaunt from the hiking; he'd carried his cameras all the way up to Everest Base Camp at eighteen thousand feet and into the dangerous Khumbu Icefall. He was never scheduled to go all the way up Everest with the Sherpa expedition. Instead, after his base-camp visit, he was concentrating on photos of the culture and the people, who were wonderfully warm, even if their climate wasn't.

We flew into the Himalayas on a private plane, a Pilatus Porter, Robb had chartered. On the flight up—as calm as a spin through a food processor—the pilot pointed out Mount Everest, tucked behind some lesser peaks. It was dark and chunky, with a bearing that suggested a crossed-arm, cranky monarch surrounded by minions. I noticed a white plume waving from its summit, and the image that then came to mind was a Hershey Kiss with its white tag on top.

"That's where the top of Everest hits the jet stream," Robb told me. "It's snow flying off the summit."

"Wow. If I do nothing else," I said in awe, "at least I've seen Mount Everest."

We flew onto a grass landing strip in a town called Shyangboche, almost thirteen thousand feet high. Once off the plane, I followed Robb and his guide for thirty minutes to the village of Khundi, breathing like a hoarse accordion the whole way. Khundi was a congregation of thirty-some stone buildings on the tundra; criss-crossing walls built of loosely stacked stone bisected the community like three-dimensional graph paper hatching. Women were in a field planting potatoes with babies strapped to their backs; I got my first look at yaks—shag-carpeted oxen—and a furry bovine the locals called a zopkyoke, a cross between a yak and a cow.

We were staying at a typical Sherpa home belonging to Robb's guide and translator. The animals were kept downstairs, and the humans lived upstairs where they could benefit from the heat rising off the animals. We crept through the barn, trying not to disturb the animals, and climbed the narrow ladder to the living quarters. Upstairs was one large all-purpose room, where the guide's mother cooked over a fire on a stone slab in the middle of the room and at night the family slept on pallets around the perimeter.

We set up camp in the family chapel, off the main living area, where paintings of Buddha and curing goat meat shared space on the walls. We zipped our North Face sleeping bags together and tried to keep each other warm at night. Because of the altitude I had to use the bathroom as often as a newborn feeds, which was particularly annoying at night since I had to get out into the frigid air, slinking past the sleeping family and the slumbering animals down below. Then I had to walk alone through the snow, through the walled-in "front yard" to a stand of large rocks that provided cover from any Peeping-Tom yetis up at that hour.

The only benefit of these nighttime excursions was seeing the Himalayas bathed in gleaming blue moonlight, ghostly sentries crowding the horizon. Right in front of us was the most spectacular peak, Ama Dablam, which had an unusually square top that reminded me of an emerald-cut diamond. Ama Dablam wasn't the highest peak, but in that sense it played the role of the Chrysler Building to Mount Everest's Empire State Building. Even with the stunning view, after a few nighttime outings I decided to make use of the large glass jar Robb kept by our sleeping bags, but this meant trying to act casual as I walked by the family in the mornings with a jar of cold urine.

My five weeks in the Himalayas were spent building up my lungs and calves by following Robb along the mountain trails. We attended celebrations in the high-tundra towns, which were always a good walk's distance; we browsed through markets, where traders sold goods from Tibet. We watched religious ceremonies in Buddhist temples, which always involved men in funny hats and trumpets as long as vaulting poles.

For Robb's twenty-eighth birthday, I convinced him to spend the night at an inn called the Hotel Everest View, a stone and glass structure whose angular lines gave it a modern, Frank Lloyd Wright feel that was completely out of place among the small Sherpa cottages. Tourists—mostly Japanese—flew into the same landing strip where I'd arrived, then rode yak-back up to the hotel. Because of the rapid ascent many tourists had trouble adjusting to the altitude, which is why the hotel had a hyperbaric chamber and offered tanks of oxygen via room service. In the hotel lounge, we watched Japanese sitting around the fire alternating between drags on a cigarette and drags on an oxygen tank.

I was eager to go to the hotel because I craved a real bed and a hot shower (after seventeen days with nothing more than a few sponge baths). I got a shower but the water was heartbreakingly tepid. There was a phone in the room, which raised my hopes. Maybe I could call my parents or the *New York Times Magazine* to see if my story had been scheduled. But alas, it was a tease— a line only to the front desk.

Near the end of my stay—when I'd more than had my fill of potatoes, yak butter tea, and a local alcohol called chang, made from fermented rice with the not-secret-enough ingredient of human spit—we made a two-day hike to a town called Tomo. There we heard about a Buddhist monk who lived in a mountain cave and reportedly gave advice to those who sought him out. At first I thought this might be a joke. It seemed to be right out of a movie—the sage on the mountaintop who can tell you the meaning of life.

After climbing an hour straight uphill, with frequent stops so that my increasingly feeble brain could get blasts of oxygen, we saw a door and a window in a stone wall built under a rock overhang. Inside in a corner was the monk, who was blind—his eyes as white as his long, wispy beard. I couldn't make out his legs at all; he seemed to spring forth from his waist up out of his chair, as if he were a hand puppet. It was dark and smoky; years of indoor fires had charred the glass on the only window.

To test out his sage powers, I asked the monk a silly women's magazine question: Would I ever be able to balance a career and a family? After rolling a die with yellow-nailed fingers and having his assistant read the results, he whispered something in Nepalese. "He says if you are to be truly happy," Robb's interpreter told me, "you must move from where you are now living."

Robb turned to me meaningfully. During the trip, we had been talking about where we should live. Robb was dreading his return to Manhattan and wanted me to consider moving to Austin. Thanks to his upbringing in the

Texas Panhandle, which has the color and topography of a tortilla, he wasn't comfortable unless he could see the horizon. The vertical squeeze of the city made him eager to move back to the West.

I couldn't fathom giving up New York, and with it, I assumed, my identity, which had taken so long to forge. I had arrived in the city as a quasi-hayseed, pronouncing the word *chez* in Chez Laurence to rhyme with *fez*. I had refashioned myself into something urbane, knowing, and sufficiently jaded, and had established myself in the New York magazine world. I wasn't ready to let go of all that, but here was this mountain mystic telling me I should. What would become of me in my next life, I wondered, if I went against his advice?

·

When I arrived back at the four-star hotel in Kathmandu alone, I was sad that I'd had to leave Robb behind in the mountains, but I was more thrilled than I wanted to admit to him to have a truly hot shower, sustenance other than potatoes, a toilet to sit on, a bed to sleep in, and CNN Headline News to watch over and over for hours. I immediately called my mom, who wanted to know how Robb and I had gotten along. "I was afraid the trip might be too hard on you two," she said. "I think a trip like that could really be a strain." My parents were very invested in my new relationship. They didn't want to suffer the embarrassment of their daughter's second failed engagement. The first one—with my infidelity—was bad enough.

I phoned my editor at the *New York Times Magazine* and learned that the story had been scheduled while I was gone, but because I couldn't be reached for fact-checking, it had been postponed. I was crushed. For me there was really no higher journalistic achievement than a story in the *Times Magazine*. I worried that the trip might have cost me my shot.

It turned out that it did. Soon after I got back to New York, the magazine—facing a downturn in advertising—decided to release my story and several others because they wouldn't have room to publish them. I could console myself with the fact that I had been paid and that my story had been good enough to be accepted in the first place. But the truth was that without ever getting into print, I was missing a chance for major exposure, potentially career-making exposure.

But I couldn't say that I was sorry I'd gone. I relished the adventure Robb and I had together, and even though I was keenly ambitious, I never wanted to be out of balance—all work, all whacked. I hoped for a personal life that would be as remarkable as my professional one. My emphasis on equilibrium was the difference between Robb and me, maybe the difference between men and women in general. It made me more flexible, the one more willing to adjust my schedule and goals. It soon became clear to me that two big careers in one relationship would be almost impossible to manage. If we were going to work, something—or someone—would always have to give.

CHAPTER TWO

Texas Soil

*Thank you so much for such an incredible day. The place smelled
like a great hallucination. I have lived in Texas all my life and
thought I had seen everything, but it is always fun to find
something new and spectacular.*

—TIM SMATHERS,
June 20, 2004

I knew I was going to die. Especially after Robb bought the motor-cycle. It was a gorgeous specimen of machinery—a teal blue Harley Davidson Springer Softail—that I was sure would deliver me to my death. I rode behind Robb with a smile and even bought a leather motorcycle jacket, but all the while as my helmeted head bobbed in the wind, I couldn't help but think that the end was only a wrong turn into someone's blind spot away. I was thirty now and the place that represented my twenties—my youth—was gone in my life. I mourned New York as if it were one of my limbs. Unconnected from the city, I felt old, mundane, and acutely aware of my own mortality. Leaving the city was the first major decision I'd made for someone other than myself, and though I told myself this was the kind of trade-off people made for love,

I was morose. It was as if I'd spent all these years climbing exuberantly up the ladder on a playground, looking forward to what was on the other side. But now that I was there, starting down that slide, I could see there was only one destination. Death.

I hadn't really had time to adjust to the idea of a move before it happened. When Robb came back from Nepal in early June 1991, four weeks after my return, it was clear he wasn't going to last long in the city. He brought with him three water-heater-sized duffel bags, containing photo equipment and clothes, but also an old water-buffalo-skin trunk he bought from a Tibetan trader for eight dollars and a case of large sheets of handmade paper. He said hauling the bags up the three flights of stairs to my fourth-floor Chelsea apartment was worse than lugging his gear to Everest Base Camp. He complained about the size of my two-bedroom apartment, which was the smallest place he'd ever lived, yet after a series of studios and hobbit-like one bedrooms, I felt as if I was living in the Park Avenue Armory.

Even though I had sort of agreed to move after our encounter with the Buddhist monk in Nepal, I got back to New York hoping Robb had forgotten about it. Maybe I could pass it off as a promise made under the influence of acute exoticism or oxygen deprivation. At least, I hoped I could delay the move for a year or so.

But in mid-June, Robb and I were on a plane for Austin. I thought we were going to take a sniff around to see if I liked the place, but Robb was way ahead of me. He had set up a meeting with a realtor, and the bulk of our time there was spent viewing houses—sixty-two of them. We stopped looking when we came to a stone house from the 1930s on a double lot with towering post oaks and a garage apartment. Robb made an offer the same day, and he had an agreed-upon price the next, to close at the end of July. I was blurry-eyed at the speed of it all, and my brain started a new calculus. Not how long I could delay his move, but how long *I* could put off moving without losing him. Then Robb found a pot sweetener. A classified ad for what he knew was my dream car, an old VW convertible. It was bright orange with the original paint and only 45,000 miles. Giving in to what I saw as the inevitable move, I bought it on the spot.

I returned to New York stunned by the commitments we'd made. "Well, I think I bought a whole new life," I told my friends.

In the end, I didn't put off moving. Soon after our Austin trip, I went to *National Geographic* headquarters with Robb and met a few editors and other photographers. Fortunately, I was traveling with samples of my work—Be Prepared was not just the Boy Scout motto—and I came away with an assignment to write a feature story on Appalachia, where I'd grown up. Since I would by contract spend eight weeks in the field reporting, it did't make sense for me to hang on to my expensive Chelsea apartment while I was on the road.

At the end of July, a moving crew began clearing out my apartment, struggling with sofas and boxes on the same three flights of steps that had been, I think, the breaking point for Robb.

I went out one last time the night before the move with some of my best friends—Kim, Barb, Andrea, Bill, Lila, Terry. We had a boozy dinner at a favorite restaurant in the West Village called Gus's Place, where I'd spent much time when I lived two streets away. I walked home that night and tried to absorb all the sensations—the noxious but comfortingly familiar smells of traffic, the shimmer and smolder of lights, the snippets of passing conversations, which I knew were like no other conversations in the country. Certainly, I would return to New York, but I was aware that it would never again feel the same, as relaxed and intimate, as *mine*, as it did that night.

The next morning the movers arrived to get the last of my boxes and my friends came to kiss me good-bye. Then I was off to LaGuardia. The sky was hazy that afternoon and when the plane taxied onto the runway, I could barely make out the silhouette of the skyline. I thought of the day—June 6, 1982—I had flown into New York to start my first job at *McCall's* magazine. It was the night of the Tony Awards, which has always given me a special affection for the event, a way to mark the years.

Tears tumbled as the plane picked up speed. Memories surfaced and faded like fireworks. Getting ready to go out, soon after arriving, with "Saturday with Sinatra" on the radio. Falling asleep each night at my apartment on the Upper West Side, comforted by the rhythmic blinking red lights of the skyline. Jazz at the Blue Note and the Village Vanguard. Bobby Short at the Carlyle. Pomme frites at Florent at 3 a.m. My apartment on Charles Street, with a view out the back that was right out of *Rear Window* and cherry trees in front that burst into bloom every spring. Watching old movies at Film Forum and Yankees games from a friend's luxury box behind home plate. Renting a beach house in The Pines on Fire Island with Ben and some gay friends and constantly losing bustiers and bikini tops to my housemates. I'd lived in New York for more than nine years. I'd accomplished more than I thought possible. For the first time, I felt my youth passing. I craned my neck to see the skyline as we lifted into the air and suddenly the clouds swallowed up the city. New York was gone. I had the man I wanted, but at that moment the price seemed heartbreakingly high. I was officially and irreversibly no longer young.

·

For months, the New York skyline still had the power to wring my stomach. I could hardly watch *Saturday Night Live* or David Letterman with their opening scenes of Manhattan.

I spent little time in Austin after I officially moved there. I was basing out of my parents' home in Tennessee for my *National Geographic* story. On my first flight to Tennessee, I got the question I was dreading. "Where you from?" asked the businessman next to me, a folded *Wall Street Journal* in his seat pocket. He had no idea what a crisis his query was provoking. I had always taken such pride in telling people I was from New York. To be from New York meant something—that you were a survivor. What did it mean to be from Austin?

I should have rehearsed this, because my answer was so long in gelling that I saw his eyebrows shift, like levers on a pinball machine, from polite interest to concern. "Austin," I finally blurted, "but I used to live in New York." The man nodded and retrieved his newspaper, surely happy he had somewhere else to direct his attention.

My turbulent state was only heightened at home with my parents, who suspected that with Robb I was just playing house again. When I talked about marrying Robb, they treated me like a mental patient who was planning a trip to Paris. Yeah, yeah. Of *course* you are. It didn't help that I didn't have an engagement ring. My thought was I didn't need one. I had a honker of a diamond from Ben and in the end it hadn't meant anything. Plus, I'd done an investigation for a New York publication called *Seven Days* that exposed the rampant hucksterism of the diamond trade. I tried to explain this to my parents, but I could tell I had as much credibility with them as an infomercial for juicers.

I hadn't died yet on Robb's motorcycle, but driving the mountain roads to go deep in the hollows of Appalachia was the perfect opportunity. I imagined disaster around every curve, and since there were plenty of those, I was in a constant state of panicked doom. I tried to imagine how it might feel to smash into another car. How long would it hurt before I died? What would be destroyed first, my head? My legs? Did it matter? So the day that I actually had a close brush with another vehicle, I wasn't surprised. I was trying to pass—surely tempting fate on these two-lane roads—when a coal truck of all things came barreling around the mountain. This is it, I thought, just before I swerved left onto the shoulder and the coal truck blasted its horn. I sat on the shoulder for fifteen minutes breathing hard and staring at the Ford logo in the center of my rental car's steering wheel, wondering if I could still feel alive outside of New York.

A few days later, near catastrophe found me again. I didn't think I was claustrophobic until I was down in the dirt of a Virginia coal mine, the darkness lit only by the cones of light from my headlamp and those around me. A crusty old miner whose voice carried the weariness of years in the unrelenting blackness and the scratchiness of just as long on cigarettes drove me along underground tracks in a topless, sandbox-sized cart. At one point, he stopped the cart and directed his headlamp toward a tunnel. "This is where it happened," he said solemnly, referring to an explosion probably caused by a buildup of methane gas that killed seven miners a few years earlier. Not thirty minutes later, we heard a siren, a whooping noise that almost sounded like an Indian war chant in an old Western. At first we were told that it was just a drill, but when it didn't shut off, my guide called someone on his walkie-talkie. "Get them out of there," was the command that crackled back. The fans that pulled the methane out of the mine had shut down.

Moving through the dark in that cart, I felt as if we were trying to run underwater. I thought we would never reach the elevator shaft. I turned my headlamp up to the rocky roof of the tunnel and imagined all that earth coming down on top of me, "mashing me flatter than a belt buckle," as one miner had said. When we got to the elevator, ready to make our 440-foot ascent to the surface, I breathed easier, but only for a moment. For some reason, the elevator doors wouldn't close. I pressed my body against the side of the elevator and was sure everyone else in the crammed space could hear my heart beat. I stared at the elevator doors, willing them to shut. This is how it happens, I thought to myself. I knew I should never have left New York. Finally I saw the doors move toward each other, then retreat. I caught my breath again. For two more torturous minutes, the doors teased us. Finally they relented and did their job. We were going up, and when the doors parted and I felt sunshine on my face, I stumbled out dramatically. If the miners hadn't been watching I would have kissed the ground, or better yet the air, since I had had plenty of ground down below.

Later, after I was back in Austin, I would assign great meaning to what I considered two brushes with death so close together. I had survived. Maybe I wasn't meant to die, I thought. Maybe there is life after leaving New York.

·

I finished the *Geographic* story in November 1991 and after the ordeal of filling up, then distilling sixty notebooks of research, I became aware that I needed a social life. I had met people in Austin, but if they hadn't lived in a big city before, if they didn't know the difference between Isaac Mizrahi and Issey Miyake or between sushi and sashimi, I didn't think I could relate. I'm sure many people couldn't relate to me. I was constantly comparing my life in Austin to my New York existence, and Austin didn't have a chance. Even Robb would get irritated. On a particularly stunning evening, we rode his motorcycle to a restaurant downtown—supposedly the hippest new place—and as we were getting ready to go in, Robb took off his helmet and raked his hair, which was newly cut; I suppose long hair *and* a Harley was too much the rebel, even for Robb.

"Look at the skyline tonight."

"Hmmph!" I snorted. "*That* is *not* a skyline." To me, it was a wannabe, Lego-land skyline, designed by someone who built malls for a living.

Finally, I met a woman who I could commiserate with. She had grown up in New York, worked as a retail executive there, and, like me, had recently followed a man to Austin. Judith and I could sit for hours and talk about our favorite blocks in specific Manhattan neighborhoods, the best way to navigate Grand Central at rush hour, why we liked H&H bagels over Zabar's. We were like two aging Cubans in Miami, reliving the glories of their pre-Castro Havana.

But soon the time came to face reality, which meant giving up the charade I'd been living since I'd moved. I had simply told my editors that I had a boyfriend in Austin and was often off visiting him. I was sure my assignments would dry up if editors thought I'd gone suburban. I would just fade in their minds, just another someone in the sameness of mid-America. All my mail was forwarded from a New York address to Austin, and I had found out that I could forward my phone as well. My editors would dial the local number they had always used for me, but they didn't know I was answering it two thousand miles away. God, I loved technology.

One day I was expecting a phone call from my editor at *Allure,* where I was now a contributing editor, and as I sat in the office Robb and I shared in the basement of our house, I was startled to hear thunder. I looked outside and saw a storm rolling in. I ran around the office frantically closing windows.

"What are you doing?" Robb wanted to know.

"It's about to rain; I'm getting chilly." I didn't want him to know how neurotic I had become about this pretense. If my editor in Midtown Manhattan heard the rainstorm while we were on the phone, she would want to know how it could be raining at my "Chelsea apartment," but not at her office.

After I successfully got off the phone without raising any suspicions, Robb put his hand on my shoulder. "I think it's time to tell your editors," he said softly. "I think you've got a good enough track record that they'll still hire you. Living in Austin isn't like having a contagious disease."

That Christmas I sent each of my editors a pecan pie from one of Robb's favorite Houston restaurants. The pies were packaged in wood boxes branded with a silhouette of Texas, which I announced as my new home state in an enclosed note. I waited to see what the fallout would be.

•

In early 1992, Robb was asked to do a story for *Geographic* on an expedition to restore a historic Antarctic research base. He would be gone five weeks, and like his time in Nepal, he basically would be incommunicado.

Before he left, the expedition required him to draw up a will. He named me as his beneficiary, but it became clear that our lack of a marriage license was a problem. If something did happen to him down there, would I have any trouble keeping the house, which he had bought on his own? We'd been together eighteen months and had been engaged more than a year. I was starting to worry that I was repeating my Ben experience, as I'm sure my parents suspected. I determined that counting my two-year engagement to Ben, I had spent a third of my post-college life engaged. It was starting to look bad for me. Always a fiancée, never a bride.

It wasn't that we hadn't wanted to get married, but with Robb's travels, it was difficult to pin down a date when he was sure to be standing still. With his being out of phone contact in Antarctica, I knew he wouldn't be able to schedule any work for the weeks after he arrived home. I realized that whenever we got married it was going to have to be a blitzkrieg operation. I wanted to be prepared, so I bought a dress at an Austin store that had what I deemed to be a New York–caliber collection. The short dress was made of luscious beaded lace, with an off-the-shoulder neckline and long sleeves. I paired it with some silver lamé slingbacks and a pearl necklace.

I was also ready with a place. While researching a story on the Texas-Mexico border for *Travel + Leisure*—being their cover girl a year earlier had been my entrée with the editors—I found a tool-shed-sized mission in the border town of Mission, Texas. The mission, built of white stucco in the 1880s and the source of the town's name, was so charming in its simplicity that when I saw it, I knew that's where I wanted to do the deed. Now I just needed my groom.

That ended up not being difficult, thanks to the loneliness of his five-week Antarctica excursion. I talked to him twice through a ham radio operator, which wasn't conducive to a smooth or intimate conversation. Awkwardly, each time I finished with my bit I had to say "over," so that the ham operator could throw a switch to let Robb speak. When I said something to Robb about wishing I were there to warm up his sleeping bag, his voice was sheepish when he answered me and I heard deep chuckling in the background. "Uh, Jeannie, I should let you know that there are ten other men listening to this call—all of them have been without their wives and girlfriends as long as I have."

When I met him in Ecuador, where he was shooting a story for *Travel + Leisure*—his reward after the Antarctic cold and deprivation—he was ripe. "I'm getting a lot of pressure from my family," I told him. "They're starting to wonder." We agreed to get married when we returned to Texas, but Robb insisted on two points—he wanted me to keep working after we got married and he wanted an unpretentious wedding. At the root of each stipulation was his previous marital mishap. His first wife had sucked him dry financially, he told me. She'd also made him endure a big fussy wedding, which he compared to a white monster that gobbled up money, patience, and good sense. An inn in Napa Valley had been rented out for the occasion, and a couple hundred people had swooped in from all over.

"What did you expect, falling for a socialite," I said. "She wasn't exactly your people." Robb's father was an ag equipment salesman.

We would have the anti-big wedding, the semi-elopement. On a Monday we started calling our family and friends, telling them we were going to get married on the Texas border by a justice of the peace the following Saturday, April 4. We apologized for the short notice and told them we understood if they couldn't make it. My parents came, as did Robb's. My brother Jeff showed up from Houston with his kids. Several of Robb's buddies from Texas were there, including his adored friend Katie, whom Robb declared his "best man." And Ellesor, my best friend from college, my raucous companion during our semester in London our junior year, flew in to be my maid of honor.

My older sister, Janyce, who had planned the baptism of her fourth child that same day, was wounded that I was going ahead without her. I never thought I would get married without Janyce—or my other siblings (a younger sister and two other brothers). We were close in a semi-nerdy, Brady Bunch way—what could you expect when the names of all six kids, our parents, and our dogs all started with the same letter? I was a gooey sentimentalist who loved family gatherings, but I was also pragmatic about this occasion. I was mobilizing with or without my beloved siblings.

Thanks to the no-frills edict, my mother claims it was the most relaxed of any of her children's weddings. She only had time to make two contributions—napkins that read Jeannie & Robb, April 4, 1992, and the ceramic bride and groom that had topped her own wedding cake forty-one years earlier. With only twenty guests, my father maintains it was the cheapest. He also benefited from the custom Mexicans have of decorating chapels and shrines with plastic flowers. The altar of the tiny mission looked like a floral shop, and in pictures every fake lily looked real. When my mother's friends saw the photos later, they couldn't help but comment on the impressive display. "How did Jeannie have time to get all those lovely flowers?" many of them asked. My mother wouldn't correct them. "Oh you know, Jeannie," she'd say. "She always finds a way to get what she wants done."

That was the reputation I had in my family, ever since I convinced my parents to pay for my semester in London. I had saved them enough by getting scholarships, I had argued, that they could pay for my six months in London and still be ahead. During those months in London, I had interned for *Time* magazine, and later when the bureau chief moved to New York, she asked me to work for her as a freelancer. She had connected me to *Life,* which had connected me to Robb, who I was just beginning to learn was more than my match in determination.

•

Is your dad the grumpy *National Geographic* photographer the other guys told me about?" asked the young man we met on our street; he had recently rented the house next door. Robb paused as I suppressed a laugh.

"No," he said, flashing a grin—he was used to people thinking he was too young to have his career. "*I'm* the grumpy *National Geographic* photographer."

"Oh man," said our neighbor, surely the prototype of the Austin slacker. "Well, man, what makes you so grumpy?"

I crossed my arms and waited for Robb to answer. I wanted to know, too. By then—a year after our wedding—I could say that I was truly comfortable in our new home, unlike Robb. I had found a group of friends, and when Robb was away shooting stories—in Hong Kong or the Congo, for instance—I got to live a quasi-single life, hanging out at bars, seeing movies, going to concerts. And often when he was traveling, I got to tag along—to places like Japan, Bali, and Morocco—which to me seemed like an endless stream of honeymoons. I went to New York regularly to visit editors and friends, shop, and, since I didn't trust anyone in Austin, to get my hair cut and highlighted. When people asked how often I was in New York, I replied, "Oh, about every half-inch," while pointing to my roots. We had adopted two mutts from the pound: Katy, our first, who we named after our friend, and then Weegee. They were so much the focus of our lives that we had put their photo on the front of our wedding announcement.

Despite my fears of being ostracized by the magazine world for leaving the fatherland, the pies I sent my editors seemed to do the trick. I hung on as a contributing editor at *Allure* because my stories—I specialized in irreverent pieces that looked at the lies of the beauty industry—could be compiled anywhere. Since many magazines were sending me to different parts of the country to report stories—to Buffalo to cover abortion protests for *Life,* to L.A. to write a posthumous profile of Nicole Brown Simpson for *Glamour*—it didn't matter where I lived. Plus, editors were looking for writers who could find stories in mainstream America that weren't being proposed by every other New York freelancer. I wrote one of my favorite stories for *Glamour* about the troubles between a Russian bride in Dallas and her husband, who'd found her through a catalog.

But just as I was truly embracing Austin, Robb was moving in the opposite direction. We arrived in Austin before it broke as a cool place to live, before it established itself as a high-tech mecca and the South by Southwest Music Festival became a national event. When Austin started getting some national buzz, I felt especially clever that we'd moved there ahead of the masses.

But coolness came with drawbacks. The annual property taxes on our stone house in Hyde Park, a neighborhood of Victorian homes in central Austin, were approaching five digits. The highways I used to zip along in my VW convertible were at times as difficult to navigate as a stadium parking lot after a pro football game. None of this bothered me since, compared to New York, Austin was clearly underpopulated. The change began to eat at Robb, however. Under pressure from his many *Geographic* stories and advertising clients, I began to see a different side of him. He was still goofily romantic much of the time, but more and more, he would be crusty and curt; he was mulishly clear how he wanted his life and his career to progress. And how he wanted his neighborhood to be—quiet.

So he was most disturbed when the delicate owner of the stone and brick home next to ours was moved to a nursing facility and four frat boys took her place. Our bedroom window faced the house, and the boys were fond of playing exuberant games of Ping-Pong late into the night. Robb would regularly call to complain to the guys, and if they didn't quiet down he began ringing the police. Ranting about the neighbors became part of his nighttime ritual, so much so that I accused him of being an old man in training at age thirty-one. Which is basically what the frat boys thought of him, and why they had warned the new renter about his cantankerous ways.

"I don't know if I'm grumpy, really," Robb said to the renter, in answer to his query about the source of his ill-temper. "I guess I just expect some courtesy. After ten, keep a lid on it. Unless you want me to mow my lawn at six in the morning."

Soon after meeting the new neighbor, Robb began floating the idea of moving from Austin. I was incredulous at the suggestion since I'd just made the leap from New York. But naively I assumed it was a passing phase, fueled by the bongo drums the renter insisted on playing—despite a lack of talent and Robb's repeated requests for percussion-free nights. Robb loved the house too much to consider leaving, I thought. He was about to head out on an assignment about rice-growing around the world, which would take him to Haiti, India, Nepal, Bali, Japan, China, and Madagasca, and I was sure that the urge to move would have disintegrated by the time he returned.

But time, travel, and sickness—he contracted malaria on his trip—didn't lessen his conviction that he was through with Austin. He pushed so hard that before I knew it we were driving around looking at buildings in mid-sized towns surrounding Austin—Taylor, Kyle, San Marcos. Possessing some type of Henry Higgins gene, he was fascinated with the idea of giving a commercial building a makeover. We looked at all sorts of buildings—old hardware stores, crumbling firehouses—none of them right for various reasons. This obsession will die under its own weight, I was certain. It took too much time to find a place and upend our life, and time was the one thing Robb lacked.

Unfortunately for me, one Saturday we drove into the town of New Braunfels, forty-five minutes from Austin and twenty-five minutes from San Antonio. We didn't see For Sale signs on any of the attractive buildings along Main Street. "That's exactly the kind of building I want," Robb commented, pointing to a red brick building with white limestone eyebrows over its arched windows. The date 1894 occupied a prominent spot on the cornice. I agreed that it was beautiful and really the prettiest building we'd seen in any of the towns, but too bad it wasn't for sale. I was ready to call it quits, proud of myself for being a good, understanding wife who gave her husband room to explore his dreams.

But in his typical exhaustive fashion, Robb wanted to stop at a real estate office to see if we'd missed anything. The realtor wasn't encouraging. "I think there's only one building for sale downtown," she said, as she fumbled through her file drawer. After finding the folder she was after, she called out the address, then handed us a flier for the Old First National Bank Building. It was the same building Robb had been coveting. Could I get a break here, I wanted to yell.

After looking at the building, Robb regaled me with his vision for the place. We could live upstairs, and downstairs we could have a photo gallery, and hang pictures by all his photographer friends. He painted a scene of wonderful gallery openings that all our friends would want to come to.

As delightful as all this sounded, I'd quickly determined that living in a commercial building in the center of a smallish town (population 40,000) offered the worst of both worlds. We would be living in a loft as if we were in a big city, with none of the advantages of one. We would be giving up conveniences but getting no perks—like a yard, distance from neighbors, a tree to call our own. I went with him when he worked up an offer with the realtor, but by then had recovered enough from my shock to inform Robb that he should buy the building for an investment but that he shouldn't expect me to move there.

The purchase sent me into a tizzy. He was serious. He was really serious about moving out of Austin. If I had to leave Austin, I decided, I was going on *my* terms. And I wasn't going empty-handed. That's when the deal was struck.

At the time I was thirty-three, but I could see thirty-five lurking ominously on the path ahead. I had first heard about the fearsome age of thirty-five when I moved to New York at twenty-one. I was working as an assistant editor at *McCall's*, and one of my illustrious duties—besides answering the phones and making copies—was typing edited manuscripts in those pre-computer days on special paper that the production department could scan.

The first manuscript I retyped—so earnestly, with a bottle of Liquid Paper at the ready—was called *Baby Hunger*, about savvy working women who in their early thirties became possessed with the desire to have children. The editors gave it big play, but I and other assistants my age laughed at the premise, considering it a faux trend that made a good cover line. We had that luxury. I flitted through my twenties in New York with the notion that I could have kids or not. Work, love, friendship, travel all seemed so much more engaging and important.

But when Robb started his Exit Austin campaign, I had already and suddenly been struck by the emptiness of my life. I adored our dogs to a fault, as only childless couples can; I even called us yuppie puppie parents. I once phoned my mother from Bangkok to tell her where Katy and Weegee were boarded. "If anything happens to us, please don't separate them," I pleaded.

"For heaven's sake," my mother countered, "you need to have children."

She was right. At the time my life was given form mainly by the articles I was writing or the trips Robb was taking. I wanted something more constant, permanent, and, though I hated the word, meaningful. I abruptly found myself thinking like the quotes I had read so many years before in the *Baby Hunger* manuscript. I realized most miserably that I was on the verge of cliché. I wanted children, and I wanted them now.

The route to this destination—this intense urge to reproduce—had been paved beautifully by my mother. My mother, a well-educated force of nature who could have been a CEO or a senator if she had so chosen, had devoted her life instead to raising her six children. Since I moved to New York, she would tell me cautionary tales of "career women" who had put off having children only to find that when they were ready to have them their bodies weren't. She would sigh dramatically about the wife of my father's coworker or the daughter of one of her bridge club friends. "What a shame," she would cluck. "She just waited too long."

Of course Robb and I had talked about kids. He thought I was overreacting to the proclamations that thirty-five was the end of fertility. "I definitely want kids," he would say. "I'm just not ready yet. I want to be able to completely focus on them." This was one of the perils of marrying a younger man. Time and possibilities still seemed limitless to him. A man's never ready for kids, my mother told me. You have to tell him when he's ready. It seemed to me that the time was right for me to go to the mat.

Robb's determination to leave Austin created the perfect opportunity for a compromise. I told him I would move, but I would find the place that suited me and I wanted kids. He agreed, with the stipulation that we would try to get pregnant only *after* we had moved out of Austin. We'd hire a babysitter, but he still wanted me contributing to the family finances. It felt crass to be talking about children in such a cold way, as if we were buying a new SUV. Before I agreed, I discussed our potential pact with a therapist, expecting her to be shocked or offer some gloomy forecast for our relationship. She shrugged. "Marriage is a series of compromises and accommodations," she said wearily. "If it gets you what you want, don't make it into a bigger issue."

So I made the bargain. It was a case of thinking with my uterus.

·

My original parameter was that I wouldn't go any farther from Austin than the outer limit of the *New York Times* home delivery service. But that condition soon proved unworkable. It landed me on the edge of the mindless suburbs on Austin's outskirts. They were filled with houses that were identical except for a bay window here or a dormer there, that presented garage doors to streets that went nowhere. Even the bank building in New Braunfels was preferable. At least it had history and character.

So I extended my search area to include anywhere thirty minutes or less west of Austin, into the Hill Country. I couldn't go east because to the east were towns where it was difficult to find a home that had not arrived via the highway. The Hill Country—a patch of limestone uplifts and outcroppings roughly bordered, in my mind, by Austin, San Antonio to the south, Junction to the west, and San Saba to the north—had some mystique going for it. The actress Madeleine Stowe had a place in the Hill Country, I had read. So did Willie Nelson. Luckenbach—*the* "Luckenbach" of Willie's and Waylon Jennings's anthem to sublime idleness—was in the Hill Country. But still it seemed as far removed to me as the Himalayas.

Robb was thrilled with the turn of events. He admitted that it was always his intention to end up in the country someday. He spent much of his working life on the road and wanted a home that was a glorious getaway, allowing him to vacation without ever spending a night away from his own bed. But he thought he would have to take the middle step of a city like New Braunfels first to end up there. Now, he would be achieving his desire ahead of schedule. But that's the way it always is with him: He has the knack for getting what he wants and making it seem effortless.

·

The first time I laid eyes on the barn it was in a fuzzy black-and-white photo on a strip of thermal paper. During my search for property, I had noticed an unassuming classified ad: "200 Hill Country acres, stone barn, seasonal creek." It was the stone barn that had attracted my attention. I left a message for the realtor, asking him to fax information to us. Robb and I were both working in the basement office when the fax machine began making grinding noises. The photo was the first thing out of the machine. Robb tore off the thermal paper. "Look at this," he exclaimed. "This is amazing."

It wasn't anything more than an empty stone shell, really. There were rectangular holes where doors and windows should have been. A massive live oak grew at one corner at a cockeyed angle, like a paper parasol in a frothy cocktail. I loved the lines of it; the bones, as an interior designer friend always called a well-formed structure. I was excited until I looked at the rest of the fax and noticed that it was near the town of Blanco, which was out of my range: "50 minutes to both Austin and San Antonio," the fact sheet said.

"That's too bad," I said to Robb, pointing out its disqualification.

"Too bad? It's incredible. Look, it's only $1,500 an acre."

That was a good price, I knew. Property closer to Austin was going for $3,200 to $5,000 an acre. Prior to this fax, the most promising piece of land we'd seen had a swimming hole on a lovely, clear creek near the town of Dripping Springs. It was only thirty minutes from Austin and only minutes, I discovered, from a convenience store that carried the *Times*. Then we found out that right next door to the property—and even worse, *upstream*—was a nudist camp, called the Pleasure Ranch, which hosted rowdy weekend events.

"And you thought people in the country weren't open-minded," Robb had said, clearly amused.

Even though we didn't have any other good prospects, I was reluctant to visit the barn. Giving Robb an inch was dangerous. He could squirm and push and pull until he'd managed to gain so much ground he couldn't be turned back, like a form of kudzu. But we were planning a real estate outing in that direction the next Saturday, and his determination won out. I agreed to drive a bit farther.

It was May 1, May Day, when we visited Blanco, a small town whose main square was dominated by a two-story limestone courthouse with a mansard roof built in the late 1800s, before the county seat of Blanco County was moved north to Johnson City (birthplace of our thirty-sixth president).

We met the realtor, Skip, at the Dairy Queen in Blanco, which, having studied Spanish, I pronounced with a short *a*. Skip quickly corrected me. "It's Blanco," he said, articulating the word as if it were spelled Blank-o.

"But—"

"I know, I know, it's not proper Spanish, but that's the way they say it here." The Germans, who settled in the Hill Country after the Mexicans, didn't know their Spanish, and Blanco is only one of numerous Spanish names across the state that have been massacred in the mouths of Texans.

Driving to the property, four miles west of town, I couldn't help but notice the color all around me. Grasses, fruit trees, and wildflowers—orange Indian paintbrush, yellow and red firewheels, pink phlox—seemed to have exploded in an exuberant frenzy, like New Year's Eve revelers cognizant of impending resolutions. It's grow, show, and be merry because tomorrow—summer—we'll be scorched. When we pulled up the drive that day, all I could see around me was green. Shaggy grass, gently bending live oaks, fields dense with crops. And in the middle of it all was the sixty-year-old barn, parked attractively on a rise. From two sides, where the stone walls rose up twenty-seven feet, it seemed grand and imposing. From the other two sides, where a tin gambrel roof hung low, it appeared almost cottage-like.

A herd of angora goats, looking like walking mops, skittered from the inside of the barn as we approached. The floor downstairs was dirt and covered with cow dung. When we walked inside we scared away a group of black cows and a couple of barn sparrows nesting in the wood rafters. One room had a concrete floor and a working door and windows, but was completely repellent. All I could think was that the FBI had somehow overlooked the Unabomber's southern outpost. Hunters used it for camping and the floor was littered with moldy mattresses, beer cans, half-eaten pizza, and trash. It was my first stomach-churning brush with hunters. But it wouldn't be my last.

To get upstairs we walked up a hay ramp built outside the barn and used a wooden pallet turned on its side as a makeshift ladder to climb into an opening that was once used to load bales.

On the scuffed plank floor of the cavernous, dark space were piles of moldy hay, and lying on top of one I saw a tissuey tube the texture and color of an onion's outer layer.

"Look, a snake skin," I said, stooping over to get a closer look.

"A rattlesnake skin," Robb added, pointing out the series of bumps at one end, which had apparently once encased a rattle. If he wanted me to like this place, it was entirely the wrong thing to say.

Was this an omen? I wondered.

"Great. There are rattlesnakes in the barn." I peered cautiously at the creamy limestone walls and the tin gambrel roof, which in the center rose up seventeen feet above us. The tin roof was supported by an impressive lattice of aged pine planks and the combination of metal, stone, and wood was a satisfying blend of textures, hard to soft, and colors, cool to warm.

"I think this is it," Robb whispered to me as we prepared to descend the hay-pallet ladder. I didn't like hearing this. Once his mind was set, I didn't know if I had the power to change it.

I had to agree, though, that the property was dazzling. Skip took us for a drive around the two-hundred-acre plot, which we noticed on the plat was the shape of the state of Louisiana, bordered by a small county road on one side and on another by a meandering creek that flowed, we were told, eight months of the year. The creek was not large but had many picturesque terraces of rock and a swimming hole, which was a large oval scoop that nature had hollowed out of limestone ledges. A small cascade tumbled into it on one side; cottonwood trees and live oaks shaded it. I imagined myself splashing in the pool and had a moment of something that felt awfully close to excitement.

Driving along the dirt road—made not with any special grading machinery, just years' worth of car tires following the same path—we saw a clump of deer in front of us, maybe eighteen of them, on the edge of a forty-acre field. As we approached, the deer scattered before us, as if we were the magnet and they the diamagnetically charged iron shavings.

Running north through the middle of the land was a ridge of limestone that grew incrementally steeper the farther from the barn we traveled. The summit, on the back of the property, was a horseshoe-shaped peninsula, that jutted out dramatically over three terraces of limestone fanning out below.

That first day, when I stood on what became known to us as the Campsite—because we pitched a tent there before our house was finished—I was awed by the views. Almost 360 degrees of swelling earth and clusters of live oaks and Spanish oaks, each grouping resembling a verdant thunderhead. I could only see one house on a distant hilltop and two metal windmills, which I liked to think of as tin daisies.

When we left, Robb could barely contain his enthusiasm. I admitted that it was beautiful, but reiterated that it was too far out. "How much do you think it would cost to build a place like that today?" He was forever asking me to make guesses about things I couldn't possibly know. "The walls. Did you see them? They were thirteen inches thick. They weren't veneer. They were the real thing. They don't build places like that anymore."

I held firm. It was too far.

"What's fifty minutes?" he countered. "Just think of the people who commute into Manhattan or any big city. Some people spend an hour and a half, and they're driving through crappy towns and bad traffic. This is at least a beautiful drive." Then he changed tack and introduced the pioneer strategy. "We'll be pioneers," he said excitedly. His salesman skills are seriously lacking today, I thought.

"What about me ever made you think I wanted to be a pioneer?" I asked. "When you met me, I was having my coffee and bagel delivered every morning from the corner deli. I wasn't exactly going out to milk the cow."

Robb smiled warily. "You've stuck with me. You have to be pretty brave."

•

A few days later, when Robb called Skip to ask more questions, he learned that someone had already made an offer on the barn. Robb was undaunted, accepting it as a challenge. "It's not over till it's over," he declared. The news of the offer affected me in a surprising way. I became a textbook example of the principle that desire increases in direct proportion to unavailability. Though he warned us about getting our hopes up, Skip said we could come look again. On the drive out to the property, I began imagining all the possibilities that the beautiful barn offered. If we lost it, I thought, we would surely never find anything else so distinctive.

But the offer on the property wasn't the only fingernail scratching across my psyche. I had eaten lunch the day before with a friend in Austin, the wife of another photographer. She was a year younger than me and she spent most of the two hours recounting her heartache over not being able to get pregnant yet. I felt a sensation in my chest, like an alarm clock being wound up. It was the ratcheting up of baby panic. I realized that even if we bought a place immediately, we'd still need eighteen months to two years to hire an architect and get the place built. At this rate, I would already be thirty-five before we ever began trying. I had no time to dally.

After walking around the barn and the property again, I gave Robb the go-ahead to try and snag it. Robb made an offer for full price.

"Well, if it was meant to happen . . ." he said as we drove away.

Three days later, Skip called to tell us our offer had been accepted.

"We're out of here," Robb yelled toward the renter next door.

It looked like I was going to get my family. Still, I never felt more scared in my life.

CHAPTER THREE

Rocks

I *loved discovering Hill Country Lavender. Saturday was just
delightful, seeing that huge field, your beautiful house, and that
magnificent tree. Even the dog was perfect in the scene.*

— BARBARA GREEN,
June 11, 2002

No trespassing. Survivors will be prosecuted," read the sign. Accompanying the words—hand-lettered with drippy paint—were a skull and crossbones; a visual aid for illiterate interlopers, I thought, as we passed by on a dirt road in the far northern reaches of Blanco County. Robb and I were out on a drive looking at names of other ranches, hoping for inspiration on what we should call our new purchase. Though there's no law that I know of saying Texans have to name their patch of land, it felt to us that a ranch with no name was as impersonal as calling a pet Dog.

One friend had already dubbed the place the Cow Cathedral, because of the soaring space under the barn's gambrel roof. We laughed that a sign like that on our front fence might attract a bunch of Bible-spewing buckaroos on

Sundays looking for a service. Someone else insisted the name be *Green Acres*: *The Sequel*. Indeed, *Green Acres* was the comparison people often made when they heard about our impending move. I, of course, was cast as Eva Gabor, but I at least knew better than to wear bugle-beaded gowns among the hay fields.

The only thing Robb was certain of was that he didn't want to use the word *ranch* in the name. In Texas, he said, *ranch* is reserved for a spread of at least one thousand acres. It would be unseemly and embarrassing, he said, a breach of Western etiquette, to claim the name for anything less.

While we were still debating the name, a small sign appeared on our front post, courtesy of the local branch of the Texas Farm Bureau, which provided our property insurance. Member, Texas Farm Bureau, the plaque read. But it only gave one name: Robb Kendrick. When Robb called to get my name added, the Farm Bureau representative was so flummoxed by our different last names that Robb finally gave up. She wasn't the only one we rattled. One man took the opportunity of meeting us to rail against "progressive women" who didn't change their names. "It's a travesty; it's an insult to the institution of marriage," he ranted. " 'Two shall become one,' the Bible says." Could it really be 1994? I couldn't help but wonder. I sometimes suspected the road out from Austin to Blanco passed through some sort of time tunnel.

From then on, if anyone asked about our different names, Robb chimed in: "I'm a progressive man; I kept my own name when we got married."

Robb liked to tell people we were moving to the country because of the dogs. In town, Weegee and Katy were getting into too much trouble; I called them Houdini hounds, since they always were escaping our fenced-in backyard—no matter what barricades we put up—and tormenting a whole neighborhood of felines. To me, it made sense to name our new land for them. Robb suggested Twelve Leg Farm (two of them, two of us) but I thought it sounded as if the place was home to a family of centipedes or mutants. I finally convinced Robb to go with Bad Dog Ranch—despite his feelings that we were committing an egregious Texas faux pas. I promised that we would only put the words *Bad Dog* up on our front gate, and leave off the *Ranch*. The name would perform double duty, I imagined, keeping away strangers with a promise of a slobbering, psychopathic Cujo beyond the fence. Which at times was an apt description of Katy.

The dogs' delinquency didn't end in the country; their mayhem simply took on more rural forms. Soon after we bought, when we were out at the place meeting with Leroy Behrends, who would head the renovation of the barn, and inspecting the new barbed-wire fences that were going up on our property line, Katy killed a newborn lamb belonging to a rancher named Fred who leased our land. When Mr. Behrends and the Fence Guy—like all subcontractors who worked on the construction, he was known only by his specialty—found out, they warned me that out here people shoot dogs for killing livestock.

"She might never come home one day," warned Mr. Behrends (who for some reason I could only address formally), his eyes wide behind his thick wire-rimmed glasses, as if he was telling a ghost story to a group of Cub Scouts. "She'll end up what we call here a 'Brush Pile Dog,' tossed on some trash to be burned." I was chilled. I told Robb that if anyone hurt our dogs, we were moving back to Austin.

We called Fred to offer payment for the lost lamb, but he kindly gave us a pass. "N-n-n-o. That's okay," he said in his screechy, stuttering voice. "Th-th-that lamb w-w-was a m-mistake anyhow. Some r-r-ram j-jumped over the f-f-fence and g-got my ewe pregnant."

We saw Fred often on the construction site, and his conversation was always focused on the weather, or what was wrong with the weather. We began to notice that if it was sunny, he complained there was no rain. If it was cool, he complained that it wasn't warm enough for his crops to grow. If we got rain, we didn't get enough. If we had a storm, we'd gotten too much.

"Just one day, I'd like to hear him say, 'Great weather we're having, isn't it?'" Robb said.

"Some people can't say that things are good," I responded. "I guess they think they're tempting fate."

•

When we had decided on the name, I touted its stranger-repelling qualities to my parents. My parents had warmed to Robb after we were married—relieved that someone had finally extracted me from the perils and vices of New York City. Plus, Robb and my mother had bonded over their shared maniacal obsession for cleanliness—a gene mutation that had happily skipped me.

However, both my mother and father became concerned about Robb's latest hopscotch plan. "I don't like to think that you'll be out in the country all by yourself when Robb's traveling," my mother said. "Your house in Austin is so nice."

For other reasons, my former college writing professor, a dear friend who'd first encouraged me to move to New York, was even more worried. He'd always had big plans for my career and taking myself out of the New York action to move to Austin was bad enough. Agreeing to self-imposed isolation was simply unfathomable.

"Hey, I've heard there's an island off the coast of New Zealand for sale," he joked. "If Robb really wants to get away from it all."

"No," I said. "I've told him if he asks to go any farther west it's a passive-aggressive way of asking me for a divorce."

I was in the awkward position of offering assurances—"I'll be all right; we'll have the dogs and an alarm system," or "With the Internet I can still be connected"—that I really didn't believe myself. I didn't want to feed their anxieties or risk their saying anything to Robb, who was reveling in his new hobby as amateur architect.

From the first day he saw the barn, Robb—being a visual person—was able to imagine what the place could become. He tried to describe this vision to me but the only thing I saw was a jumble of stones, tin, and wood. My head ached if I tried too hard to see them in any other arrangement than their current packaging. I was never good at the spatial concepts part of standardized tests.

Robb knew he wanted a large screened-in porch, like one we'd seen at a party we'd gone to a few years earlier. In good weather, the family had simply opened up doors onto the porch and lived quasi-outside. Robb wanted the screened porch to connect the barn to another building we would construct for our office and garage. He imagined a big sliding glass door on the upstairs of the barn that would open onto the screened porch. The upstairs of the barn, one large space used to store hay, would remain an open area for the living room, kitchen, and dining room. It was like the loft I never had in New York, only two thousand miles away. The downstairs—which had once housed the ranch hands, or "wets," as in wetbacks, as the Fence Guy so offensively put it—would be divided into three bedrooms and two baths. Better to put the bedrooms below than to chop up the airy upstairs with walls and doors.

We worked with an architect, who translated and perfected Robb's vision. He bent the screened-in porch around the large live oak beside the barn; the bend would keep the combined structures from looking too much like a three-car train, the architect pointed out. Connecting the upstairs of the barn and our upstairs office in the new building would be a catwalk that would take us along the top of the oak tree outside the screening, with views to the south, down the slope that ended at the Blanco River about a half-mile away. "Not a bad commute to work, huh?" Robb said.

•

Hey, Blanco's on the news," my friend Lori told me one April morning. Robb and I had just gotten back from Oklahoma City, where we'd gone for five days to cover the bombing of the federal building for *Life* even though it had been hard for us to break away from the construction. When Lori called, I turned the TV on and saw that the station was running a feature on militias, tying it to Timothy McVeigh's arrest. The focus of the piece was a militia in Blanco. "Watch out for your neighbors, doll," Lori said.

I was mortified. What was I getting myself into? How was I—a rabid liberal—going to make it in a place where the Republicans were not only raging but carried guns? I realized I needed to scour the town to see what my future looked like.

On my next trip to Blanco I paid more attention as I passed through the courthouse square. I saw that the hardware store was flying the Confederate flag. Did they just start doing that? How could I not have noticed that before? Surely I wouldn't have agreed to this move if I had seen that. I graduated from the University of South Carolina in Columbia, where the state used to fly the Confederate flag over the capitol building. Every fall semester, a new debate over the flag broke out—usually fueled by northerners who had just arrived on campus and couldn't believe the kind of world they'd stepped into. Even then, I felt sick at the sight of the flag. I decided never to buy even a wing nut from that hardware store. A few months later, I noticed that the owner was flying a smiley face flag along with the Rebel flag. "Oh, now he's a happy racist," I said to Robb.

The square also housed a few antiques shops and a general store in handsome stone buildings. I appreciated the old architecture of the general store, but I was worried about its contents. It had an old butcher counter in the back, and carried everything from McCall's patterns to horse feed. The only things it didn't carry, apparently, were vegetables suitable for anything other than composting. How will I ever make a meal? I wondered.

A few weeks later when my mother was visiting she sniffed out a large grocery store on the other side of the river, putting my own reporting skills to shame. This real grocery store—the Super S, or the Super Ass, as we liked to call it—was surprisingly well stocked. My basis for judging a grocery store is its selection of lettuce and the Super Ass had four different kinds. Iceberg, of course, the mainstay of millions of middle-American salads, but also romaine, bibb, and the positively exotic endive.

On the square was a blacksmith shop that had brands seared into a wooden door; I guessed this was where the blacksmith had tested his work through the years. It was run by a father and son, both named Dick. I learned that people differentiated between them by calling the father Big Dick and the younger one Little Dick. I could only imagine the emotional damage this nomenclature had caused. I told some friends from Austin about these awful nicknames. "I can't imagine calling him 'Big Dick' to his face," I said. "I just don't think I could get 'Big Dick' out of my mouth." It took me a few beats to realize my unfortunate wording. I could never drive by the blacksmith shop after that without laughing.

I was discouraged to learn that the Blanco National Bank had no ATM, nor was there one anywhere else in town. I had first used an ATM in the late seventies, in high school. A device introduced some fifteen years earlier still hadn't made it to Blanco. But what could I expect from a place that had just gone to seven-digit dialing; up until a few months before we bought, people within Blanco only had to dial the last four numbers, as if they were all on an extensive party line. Blanco didn't have a dry cleaner either, or a newsstand, or a video store. The local convenience store did quadruple duty—dispensing gas, high-fructose-corn-syrup drinks, and serving as a pizzeria and the local video rental outlet. Most of the videos, however, starred Chuck Norris and Steven Seagal and contained some conjugation of the verb to die in the title.

The Blanco Bowling Club café was just off the square and was something of a Hill Country institution. I later learned that it was one of Lyle Lovett's favorite stops when he was in the area on his motorcycle. During the week, leagues played German nine-pin bowling, where the pins are still set by hand. A lobbyist later told us that pinsetters are considered one of the highest risk occupations by the insurance industry. Who knew? Nevertheless, high schoolers risked life and limb five nights a week to keep the townspeople's targets in place.

The restaurant off the bowling alley was your basic greasy spoon where customers could pick their poison—chicken-fried cholesterol, Mexican-style cholesterol, or cholesterol in a bun. It was famous for its pies, with nine-inch meringue layers that were taller than the waitresses' hair. In the mornings, local ranchers in their Stetsons (felt in the winter, straw in the summer) gathered at the café as early as 5:30 a.m. to discuss their favorite subjects: cattle prices, rainfall, hunting, and who made a better diesel pickup truck—Ford, Chevy, or Dodge. Or at least this was what I was told; I was never up early enough to witness this myself.

The only establishments that offered peace of mind were the Pecan Street Café and the Chandler Inn. Run by a former hippie who had escaped Austin years earlier, the café featured anti-Bowling-Club fare—quiche, tofu, cappuccino, and other radical misspellables. The Chandler Inn was a formal restaurant operated by a California couple in an old farmhouse, with an organic vegetable garden out back. The menu was proof that God was still with me and my snobby palate: pork medallions with portabello mushrooms, steak au poivre, fish flown in fresh from Alaska, risotto, goat cheese galettes, and even my favorite dessert, crème brûlée. Crème brûlée in Blanco. I just might survive, I thought.

·

As much as I was scared of calling the barn home, I devoted myself to its renovation. I was on a timetable. I wanted to get on with the business of breeding. But there were many hurdles to get over first.

Because Robb was traveling—Haiti, Java, Rwanda, all in the first few months of renovation—I became the point person on the construction. This meant I had the job of making sure the crew kept on track financially, aesthetically, and time-wise. This was like asking me to substitute for a trapeze artist and expecting no one to end up in the net. Robb was the financial force—the man who could bring it in and could account for every coin that went out. My feeling about money was that, somehow, you would always make more of it. He acted as if the mint had shut down. If I didn't know better I would say that he was a child of the Depression. He just explained it with a shrug. "I'm Scottish."

He was also the design maven. When I first moved to Austin, I brought with me art deco bedroom furniture I'd proudly bought piece by piece at the Chelsea Flea Market. Robb was appalled by it and relegated it to the guest bedroom. When he found a local antiques dealer interested in art deco, he was thrilled to sell it. He was so clear on what he wanted that he once sent back boxes that had been custom-made to house his portfolios because they were an eighth of an inch off.

I spent much of the construction process in a panicked state, something I called second-guessing syndrome. I imagined it was a well-known affliction in corporate America, but I never expected it in my marriage. Would Robb, the perfectionist and the holder of the very specific construction vision, approve of the color for the mortar between the stones on the office building exterior? Would he think that light switch was in the right place? Via telephone and e-mail I had to convey the day's complex and arcane happenings. I always had a list of banal questions that tested my patience to ask and his to respond to: Where do we want our propane tank? Do we want V-groove or shiplap on the ceiling of the office? Do you want a two-plug or four-plug outlet near your desk?

And the questions that he asked in return were even more problematic. He'd press me for more details on what had been accomplished and for information I couldn't have imagined needing. I began to feel like I was sitting for oral exams after every visit to the site. Did the well guy come to check the strength of the well? he once asked. I told him yes and reported the gallons per minute flow. "Did he check the deepness of the well?" he followed up.

"I don't know," I said. "I didn't know I was supposed to ask for that." God forbid if I breathed too deeply or made any noises that could be interpreted as anger or frustration. If so, Robb would shift to lecture mode before I could let go of an entire breath.

"You've just got to be complete," he chided. "While the guy's there ask him all the questions, so we don't have to spend more money later calling him back."

Normally I'd hold the phone away from my ear till I heard the squawking stop. I'd picture myself in a yoga class, breathing deeply, calmly. It's just a house, I'd tell myself. It's just a house. At times like these, I would remind myself how lucky we were to even be able to build a house like this. In my mind this was a house that someone would build to cap off a career, as they were nearing retirement. We didn't seem quite grown up enough for the project.

And maybe we weren't, because the process exposed our vulnerabilities as nothing before—weaknesses in communication, differences in temperament and priorities. I began to appreciate why construction can lead to divorce. Energy and financial reserves are disappearing faster than water in a sand pit. With so many decisions to be made, the opportunities for conflict multiply. In our case our disaster recipe was spiked by the distance between us. Resentments began to show themselves. I felt he was delegating the dirty work to me. Each idea he had—how to make antique faucets work, where to plane and de-nail the long-leaf pine boards we'd salvaged from an old flour mill—required research on my part, which I tried to fit in among my writing assignments. He felt left out and frustrated that he had to be out on the road to pay for the project instead of being on site himself to ask the questions and see the progress.

We were saved from truly crippling strife, I believe, by Mr. Behrends, who was just as meticulous as Robb. He once read Robb's mind, or so it seemed, and capped off the top of a stone wall with cement before Robb had a chance to ask. "I just thought it finished off the wall better and would prevent little critters from getting inside," Mr. Behrends told Robb. "It was about $300 worth of cement, so it wasn't a big deal."

Robb learned he could trust Mr. Behrends, who gamely rolled along with every head-scratching project we cooked up, even though he was a simple country man, a peach and pig farmer when he wasn't hammering nails along with the rest of the crew—a chief carpenter named Lester, a few local boys, and some Mexican helpers. I thought the idea that might send Mr. Behrends over the edge was Robb's desire for a copper shower in the guest bathroom. When we described it to Mr. Behrends, I kept waiting for him to tell us it was the stupidest idea he'd ever heard of, but he just shrugged his shoulders and got someone in a few days later who could do a standing metal seam out of copper sheeting. "That's a lot of pennies," Lester said when he saw what we were doing.

Mr. Behrends probably complained to his wife every night about the absurd Austin couple, but with us he was always obliging. The crew, however, was not so circumspect. Lester, who took pride in his cantankerousness, squawked endlessly about the outlandish tasks he was asked to execute. Since we were using antique Mexican doors, every interior door had different dimensions, which meant he had to build a different size jamb for each one. There was not an inch of Sheetrock in the whole place; every wall that wasn't stone was covered with antique shiplap taken from a Victorian parsonage in Dallas. "Cain't you put somethin' new in this house?" Lester would groan.

When we asked the crew to use square nails in the long-leaf pine floor planks Lester gasped, his arms and shoulders going limp with exasperation.

"If they find this place a hundred years from now," he said later, "they won't be able to figure out when it was built. They'll think it's really old timey cuz of the square nails, but then there's electricity and all this stuff. They won't know what to think." He hiked up his tool belt on his scrawny frame. "Don't know myself to be honest wit ya."

•

Besides Mr. Behrends, our appearance in divorce court was prevented by the creativity of the project and my own sense of accomplishment, as I began to master the "knee-bone-connected-to-the-thigh-bone" nature of construction. Sometimes it was moments of sheer beauty that lifted us out of the maddening minutiae. One weekend morning after camping with our dogs and two other couples on the Campsite—and having both survived tequila-fueled wrecks while out biking the property in the full-moon light—Robb and I walked to the barn at sunrise. Scaffoldings were set up along one side of the barn, which had lost half its corrugated-tin roof. It looked semi-naked, like a sardine can partially peeled back, exposing a lattice skeleton of pine planks.

The crew was in the process of reworking the whole roof. They were taking off the original tin, so that they could build stronger trusses out of long-leaf pine beams. Then they would put back the original tin, add two layers of insulation and new corrugated tin on top. After climbing the scaffolding, we were able to look down inside the upstairs of the barn, where the lattice was casting tic-tac-toe shadows on the floor and the stone walls below. At the same time we took in the views from twenty-seven feet up—the sun floating in the east, adding a pink sheen to the patches of low fog that hung near the Blanco River to the south.

Our very best antidote to the quibbling of construction was shopping together. We shared a love of antiquing, so with a house project as a proper excuse for a major hunt, we scoured the country for unusual architectural pieces. Every time Robb was shooting in another city, he looked up architectural salvage companies in the Yellow Pages. We found the antique Mexican doors in El Paso; industrial lighting fixtures and an old railroad sink in Chicago. We bought hammered nickel door pulls from an old theater in Kansas City and turned them into towel racks in all the bathrooms. Old iron fencing from a churchyard became the balustrade around our stairwell, and a bar from a South Texas saloon, our kitchen island. In everything we bought, Robb was the arbiter—the design police, the gong ringer.

I picked up my cues from Robb and broke out on my own, design-wise. Among the pieces we had custom-made for the barn, two of the most successful, I think, were my ideas. I craved a stone sink for our master bathroom and I oversaw every step of its design and carving—I even went to the quarry and picked out the slab of limestone. We ended up with an aged limestone sink that looked like an old worn fountain basin in an Italian village.

My other creation was born of compromise—which is normally anathema to creativity. Robb wanted glass doors on the upper kitchen cabinets; I wanted them closed, having enough sense not to make a show of my untidiness. Design diplomacy led me to an artist in Austin who made the cabinet doors based on an old flour sifter I'd seen at an antique store, with baling wire strung close together where glass or wood might have gone. Rather than making out every misplaced dish or stack of junk inside, we could only see shapes and forms through the baling wire—a bit of pottery peekaboo that even Robb approved of.

·

The doubts I had about moving were diminished temporarily by a discovery in our barn one July afternoon. While Robb was in San Francisco shooting an annual report, I drove out to the site and was met by Mr. Behrends, who approached my car wearing a silly grin. "I got something for ya. We found a letter with the whole history of the barn."

I couldn't understand what he was talking about. He reached into his truck and pulled out a small clear-glass soda bottle caked with dirt and handed it to me. I saw something inside. Maybe a bug? I couldn't tell.

"Go on; open it," he insisted.

I pulled off the cork and turned over the bottle; a tightly folded sheet of paper slipped out. As I started to open the paper, Mr. Behrends, his face flushed, explained that as they were using a rock saw to cut a hole in the thick walls for a window, his grandson saw something sticking out between the rocks where the top of the hole had been cut.

"You're making this up," I said to him. "I can't believe this."

"No," he said, shaking his head. "I'm not making it up. Read it."

The letter was written by a young woman who lived on the property in September 1941, when the barn was being built. She called the barn "the new rock grainery" and she described how her father, who worked on the land earning $35 a month, had hauled the rock for the barn from a spot on the property using mules named Maude and Bawl. "World War No. 2 was going on in Europe," she wrote, "with Germany and Italy on one side, England and Russia on the other side. The United States almost at the point of war."

"You wrote this, didn't you?" I accused Mr. Behrends. "You're teasing."

His eyes crinkled up and he raised both his palms toward me. "No, no. I swear."

"But it can't be that someone put this in the one spot where we were cutting a hole in the wall. It's too weird. What are the chances?"

The window we were putting in the guest bathroom was supposed to be smaller, but at the last minute we expanded it slightly to be about the size of a coffee-table book. If we had kept to the original size, we would never have found the bottle.

I was moved by this voice from the past, this person who went to the trouble of putting the time capsule in the wall. I pictured a young girl from a different world climbing up on a ladder and slipping it in between the stones as the workers slapped down mortar. She must have loved this barn. Even though I would never have chosen life in the country for myself, a peacefulness settled over me at that moment. This structure seemed more than a barn. It seemed to be alive and talking to me. I took the against-all-odds find as a sign that the move was meant to be, that we were the right people to take care of the barn. I couldn't know then how many times—when it seemed as if the move might crush our marriage or my spirit—I would try to remember that at one point I did believe I was supposed to be living here.

•

I was so wrapped up in the daily demands of construction, that I was able to block out, most of the time, the fact that leaving Austin was around the corner. But in August 1995, when we sold our Austin house, I could no longer maintain my denial. On the day of the signing, my stomach hurt the way it used to when I was a kid and spent too long twirling on a swing flopped over the seat, backside up. The house in Blanco was still far from finished, but thankfully the new owners of the Austin house were allowing us to lease back for several months. Robb, on the other hand, turned to me after we signed all the papers and said, "I don't think there has been a time that I've been out to Blanco that there hasn't been a smile on my face when I've turned onto our road." I was glad one of us was excited.

By this time, we had already realized that we would have to live in the office first, since the barn—a more challenging construction project—wouldn't be done until months later. I had once told Robb I wouldn't live in a construction zone, but as reality set in I held as firm as a sponge. I scaled back my demands, insisting only on telephones and a bathroom. On the eve of the twenty-first century, I didn't think that was asking too much.

When it was time to leave our Austin house, I crouched in the corner of our basement office and cried. The new owner was upstairs waiting for us to hand over the key, but I didn't think I would be able to move. Finally, with Robb's encouragement, I rose zombie-like and walked to the car. Robb drove a U-Haul packed with our things and I followed in his truck, which was stuffed with boxes and the dogs—Weegee, who hated cars, drooling and puking the whole way. I played David Bowie's "Changes" over and over, trying to convince myself that change was good, even though what I had changed into, essentially, was a nomadic neurotic.

Because the office wasn't finished, we parked the U-Haul on the back acreage and moved into a cabin at a nearby bed and breakfast, sneaking the dogs in. I came unglued when I found out that the phones hadn't been hooked up, as they were supposed to be. I couldn't fathom life without a phone. Our cell phones didn't work because we were so remote; we were totally cut off. I imagined editors trying to reach me with assignments. If the *New Yorker* were ever going to call me, now would be the time, I was sure. I had been accommodating enough to change my no-construction-zone edict, but now I didn't even have the requisite phone and a place to poop.

To calm me, Robb called the phone company from a neighbor's house the following Monday and lied to them, telling them we had an invalid in the house and must have our phones set up immediately. *Invalid* was an apt description of my general state. Going from New York to Austin was like an addict going from heroin to methadone. Moving out to the country felt like going cold turkey, with all the expected withdrawal symptoms.

Once the phones were hooked up, I set up my office in our unfinished bedroom—bare concrete floors, no shiplap on the walls, power tools in the corner, sawdust thick in the air, like parade-day confetti. The bright spot in those first few weeks was finding out that, incredibly enough, we received our *New York Times* in the mail on the same day it was published. This was because the southwest edition of the *Times* is printed in Austin and as long as it got on the mail truck heading to Blanco before 5 a.m., I would have it in my mailbox on the same day. The only day that this didn't happen, of course, was Sunday. The impact of this discovery was profound. It was like learning that there's oxygen on the moon. I still had a tiny tether, however frayed, to cling to.

While we stayed in the cabin, our main mission was to get the office ready to inhabit. We had to move in by Thanksgiving because the cabin had been rented out for the holiday. On the Tuesday before Thanksgiving, with the bathroom still not done, I entered raving zone. "I must have a toilet by tomorrow night," I said to a skittish Mr. Behrends. I imagine his putting out the alarm to every plumber he knew: "Mayday, mayday. Yuppie woman on the verge. I repeat, yuppie woman on the verge." When he couldn't find a plumber to do the job (I'm sure no one was brave enough to take me on), he said he would handle it himself. "I do know a thing or two about plumbing," he told me, as I mopped my bugged-out eyes and hugged him in thanks.

The septic guy stayed till 2 a.m. on Thanksgiving morning to finish his part of the job. "My wife told me I couldn't come home until I finished," he said the next day. "She told me, 'You can't leave that poor woman without a toilet!' " I will meet her and I will kiss her, I said to myself.

The first thing I gave thanks for that holiday was my working bathroom, and second, that we were actually moved into the house, however untidily, which meant that we could start trying to get pregnant. I felt as if I'd dragged myself across the finish line, just under the wire; it was two weeks before my thirty-fifth birthday.

For the next two months, the office was our makeshift home by night and construction central during the day. Every morning, I had to be up and showered before seven, when the heavy-booted, power-equipment-toting platoon would land at our doorstep and swarm the building. If Robb had to go out of town, I scurried back to Austin or persuaded friends to come out for a sleepover. I couldn't bear the thought of being alone in the house.

Right before Christmas, the crew put up Robb's two prized neon signs on an expanse of stone in the upstairs of the barn. One was a calf salvaged from a meat packing plant in Artesia, New Mexico; the neon on its feet shifted back and forth to give the impression it was running (*away* from the slaughterhouse, if it had any sense). The other was an eleven-foot-high cowboy on a horse with a moving lasso, which originally hung in front of the El Corral Bar in Vaughn, New Mexico. They had never hung together but they were perfectly proportioned, perfectly synched. Cowboy swinging rope, calf trying to escape. The story of the West.

On the Friday the crew hung them, we handed out bottles of Shiner Boch as thanks. When we turned the neon on, Mr. Behrends set down his beer and nodded. "Oh now I get it. You want to live in a bar," he said, referring to our house. "For the longest time, I couldn't figure out what you were doing."

•

Oh my God," I whispered to Robb at the sight of the woman.

"She's the one I've seen cutting cedar with a chain saw near the road," he murmured back, equally incredulous.

At the end of the rutted road, we saw a partially skinned deer carcass hanging next to a rust-splotched single-wide trailer and an old woman for whom the word *crone* might be too nice a description. Her hair was gray-streaked and seemed slick like seaweed. She was missing three of her top teeth. Wearing a blood-splattered apron and holding a knife, she watched us slide out of the car.

It was the end of December and we were visiting our neighbor to discuss a disagreement that had been brewing over our shared fence line. I thought it would help our cause if I played the good neighbor and arrived with an apple pie. The only problem was the oven wasn't hooked up yet. That and I couldn't make a piecrust. In New York, however, I had become a master of the if-you-can't-make-it-fake-it school of entertaining, passing takeout food off as my own, and I remembered the café and bakery in Blanco. I had brought my own pie dish and asked the owner to bake me an apple pie in it.

When I offered the apple pie to the old woman, she invited us into the single-wide, where her husband—who had recently had a heart attack, we were told—lounged across a lumpy sofa the color of an avocado slice that had begun to turn. On a small Formica table were stacks of bloody deer steaks she had been cutting. The heat was turned up, and the combination of heat and the smell of blood was suffocating. This woman was claiming that the swimming hole on our creek belonged to her, not us. Having fallen in love with this charmed spot on the property, we were determined not to give it up.

With a headache coming on, I could barely keep up with the conversation except to register that she was boasting about killing the deer herself and that she was adamantly refusing to accept any of Robb's evidence, such as a legal survey, that the dividing line between our property was through the middle of the swimming hole. As we were about to leave, frustrated, I noticed a Chihuahua, as scruffy as its owner, in the corner wearing a hand-knit blue sweater. She picked him up and nestled him under her bosom. The dog curled back his upper lip and growled at me.

The visit was disastrous for my psyche, not a good start to my new life in the country. The woman, the deer, the single-wide hit too close to home. It was a bad déjà vu trip to places I'd seen in East Tennessee. I wasn't really *of* the mountains—my parents were graduates of Big Ten universities and had moved from Chicago to Tennessee for my father's job soon after they married—but I had always feared getting mired there, physically or mentally. I had worked too hard at getting out and becoming someone sleeker to find myself back where I had started.

A few days later, I got a call from another neighbor—a young man in his twenties—that made me feel sicker still. He had seen the No Hunting signs we'd put out along the fence line we shared. Naturally, we had the signs facing toward the adjoining property. "You trying to tell us we can't hunt on our own property?" he demanded to know. I stuttered and handed the phone to Robb.

"No, we're not saying you can't hunt on your own property," Robb explained in a slow, measured tone he usually reserves for particularly dense airline ticket clerks. He wisely left off the implied "stupid idiot." He paused.

"Well, we didn't turn it to face our side of the fence because people on our side of the fence would already know not to hunt. I know it, for instance. My wife knows it. We turned it out your way so that in case you've got some friends out and they approach the fence, they won't fire at a deer that's nibbling on grass over on our side of the fence and accidentally hit one of my dogs or my wife, say. That's why we turned it to face your side."

When he got off the call, Robb told me the neighbor had concluded with, "Oh. Uh, so you're saying it's okay to hunt on our side of the fence."

"Oh my God, Robb," I responded. "These people are running around on our fence line with guns. God help us."

•

As January began, we had to quickly prepare a bedroom downstairs in the barn. Robb and I had told some of his friends who were moving out of New York that they could stay with us for a few months. "Early January, everything will be done," I had assured them. Of course, I was wrong. The crew was still laying the wood floor upstairs in the barn, and putting up shiplap on the walls. We had a semi-functional kitchen and one working bathroom for them, but not much else. Despite the added stress of welcoming someone into our madness, I had insisted they come anyway. I knew Robb would be traveling and the idea of sleeping alone in the house—in the middle of nowhere, in a place where no one could hear me scream—filled me with such dread, I would have chosen to live with our deer-skinning, creek-coveting neighbor to avoid such a fate.

Brian and Beverly, our friends, were amazingly unruffled by the construction zone. "The traffic and the roadwork outside our apartment were noisier," Beverly said gamely. They'd gone to college at East Texas State University with Robb and though I'd met them only a few times, our months spent with a soundtrack of nail guns and circular saws bonded us forever. They kept my spirits up and the four of us kept the local liquor store in business. "Drink past it" became our motto.

Through them, I felt I still had a connection to New York. We talked about New York incessantly, since they were going through the same acute separation anxiety I had already experienced, the difference being they *wanted* to leave and live in the country. As soon as the barn was fully electrified, we put in a satellite dish on which I could receive New York stations. Watching local New York news—*Live at Five,* Ernie Anastos—put me in a geographic warp. Where was I, actually? Couldn't I just pretend, with the help of my subscriptions to the *Times,* the *New York Observer,* the *Village Voice,* the *New Yorker,* and *New York Magazine* that I was in a huge apartment on the far, far West Side? Couldn't I just pretend to be anywhere but where I was? I realized that this was the first time in my life I was not fond of the place I lived. But thinking I'd inherited my father's roll-with-the-jabs genes, I assumed things would look up as soon as I got knocked up.

In late January I traded in my virtual Manhattan for the real thing. Arriving in the city, I was both relieved to be in "high" civilization again but also dismayed by the extreme contrast between what I loved and where I lived. The city fed me, filled my cravings. I felt as if I'd finally found my way back to an ice cream shop after I'd been force-fed gruel for months. As I walked on Fifth Avenue, I had some corny, gleeful moments, envisioning the opening to *That Girl* or the beret-tossing moment in *The Mary Tyler Moore Show* credits.

Even more disquieting was my strange vacuity during my meetings with editors. My life seemed so sparse and dull in comparison to their lives and jobs in the city I couldn't think of much to say and, anyway, speaking in articulate sentences seemed to have become a lost art form. Discussing a story I was supposed to write for *Glamour* about life for female sailors on an aircraft carrier, I paused mid-sentence searching for the word for the surface planes land on. The gap grew uncomfortable.

"On the . . . uh, uh. Oh, what do you call the place?" I started trying to act out a landing—one hand skimming onto the other.

"A tarmac?" my editor finally suggested.

"Tarmac! Yes," I said, cringing.

I knew I wasn't pregnant yet, so I didn't have that as an excuse. But I wondered if living in the country was having the same mind-numbing effect suffered by moms who are around babies all day. Instead of mommy brain, I had developed Bubba brain.

My poor cerebellum barely made it through dinner with a writer I had worked with at *Time* years earlier. We had had a flirtation but I was living with Ben at the time; then I met Robb. He was eleven years older and handsome in a Waspy, squash-playing way. I was fond of him, but was always put off by his condescending attitude toward my work for women's magazines, especially my *Allure* connection.

At dinner—in a restaurant in Chelsea, not far from my old apartment—he told me he was thinking about getting remarried; he was on the verge of proposing to someone.

"That's great," I said, suddenly feeling otherwise. "Tell me about her."

Instead of giving me the expected details—her age, her profession, her hair color—he looked at me significantly for what I knew was too long. "Jeannie, you should have known that I wanted to marry you." I bit my lip and looked down at my poached Chilean sea bass. It was a shock for him to be so direct about our relationship, when all had been oblique. I actually had never known such a thing. I knew he liked me, but I assumed it was a get-in-my-pants kind of like. Plus, it was such an odd thing to say. I mean, we hadn't ever dated. I'd never kissed him. How could he know he wanted to marry me?

"Uh," I stammered, my articulateness at a low ebb. "You never said anything like that."

"Did I need to? I thought it was pretty obvious."

I was surely the color of his cabernet. "Wow," I said too many times in a row. That was the best I could do. The waiter arrived just in time to ask if we wanted more wine—for once a welcome intrusion by a New York waiter. I was eager for another bottle and the chance to deflect the conversation from the subject of "us." "You still haven't told me about this woman you're dating," I finally said, which turned out to be a good diversionary move.

I couldn't sleep that night, having become aware of another route I could have taken. In my gorgeous alternative life I had stayed in the city with this well-connected, Ivy League writer. I envisioned the brownstone apartment on the Upper West Side. Hordes of media friends. Two children, blond like him, who were already in toddlerhood, not merely a desperate desire. Maybe even power couple status. I was sure I had a crush on him, as unseemly as that was for a married woman. I saw then that I hadn't needed to leave New York after all.

My heart having relocated to my esophagus, I went back to see the writer at his office the next day. I had a fantasy of shutting the door and, in the cramped quarters, finding myself in his arms. I chided myself momentarily at the idea that I could be a serial betrayer, the type of woman who goes from one man to the next, looking for a better deal, always hoping to get it just right. Oh well, I thought, as I opened the door to his office. Here goes.

He stood up as I entered. I could tell he was happy to see me and maybe had sensed a shift when I called him earlier that morning asking to come by. But the sight of him stopped me like a stun gun. There he was in navy blue slacks and a light blue shirt. His suit jacket was draped over his chair. Around his neck he wore the most libido-chilling accessory ever created—a bow tie. A yellow and blue striped one. My heart found its proper place and my mental movie—the kids, the apartment, the making out—all came to a screeching halt, as if someone had just shot up the DVD player. I made up an excuse for my visit—I wanted to give him my new address—and left as soon as possible.

I returned home two nights later, pulling up the driveway in the dark. The house was still a month away from being finished, but at night the missing details weren't noticeable. It looked stupendous, lit up like a yacht at sea. I was nervous, feeling guilty about my flirtation, about the few hours I'd spent in an imaginary affair. I wondered how I'd feel to be back. Would I feel as sure as I did in the bow-tie moment?

As I approached the house, I saw a blob of light under an oak tree by the driveway. I stopped the car and saw that a leftover string of Christmas lights had been arranged in the shape of a heart. I was flabbergasted. With the construction Robb and I had both been too irritable to be very nice to each other. It was an amazingly well-timed gesture. I smiled and thought, Yes, I am sure. He might be a demanding perfectionist, but he was never boring. I felt an acute moment of certainty that I was really supposed to be with anything-but-staid, non-bow-tie-owning Robb. Wherever that may be.

CHAPTER FOUR

Fertilizer

I am a lavender enthusiast and have been dreaming of lavender for two years now. I am very eager to get my hands into the planting, care and harvest of the lavender. I am willing to apprentice (free of course), doing any menial job you will have me do, as I learn best when I can get my fingers into the soil.

— MARIANNE MACKENZIE,
September 16, 2005

The goat's blood on the snow reminded me of my own blood I'd seen earlier that February day, 1996. A rare snowstorm had blown through the Hill Country and left a dusting over the live oaks and the rigid brown grass. In the afternoon, I bundled up in a plaid fleece jacket and went out on the property with Robb and the dogs. As we walked, I noticed why the tall, slender plants that grow under the oaks are called ice plants. In the cold, the stems had split open and the sap that poured out had frozen, giving the area under the trees the look of an abstract ice sculpture garden. We made our way down to the creek, by the bed of flint shavings that we were told were left from the time Tonkawa Indians used to make tools near our creek. With the spread of snow, the bed of rocks looked like a plateful of lumpy grits.

The snow was a happy distraction from the sad discovery I had just made. Snow always made me feel that normal rules had been suspended. Growing up in the East Tennessee mountains, we often got dumpings of snow, enough to shut down school and prompt my mother to bring out the Russian tea, a blend of Tang, tea, and spices that we made with boiling water. On snow days in high school I used to spike my Russian tea with rum without my parents knowing. The snow gave me permission, the world already being a little off-kilter.

Texas snow was even more mind-bending. "If it can snow here," I told myself as Robb and I picked our way over slippery rocks and down to the dry creek bed, "anything can happen." I was trying to talk myself out of a mood that I could feel descending, an unattractive, desperate mood, the kind I wasn't used to enduring for long. Lately, it had been hovering around at the edges of my consciousness. I had felt it pressing even closer starting two days earlier when one of my best friends from Austin had visited, and only that morning it had swooped in and almost suffocated me. But the novelty of the snow was helping me beat it back.

As we left boot prints along the creek bed, Katy suddenly took off running. She disappeared around a bend in the creek and, knowing her predatory ways, we both started after her. When we saw her again, she was grabbing an animal by the neck and in one spectacularly awful, World Wrestling Federation move, she threw it up in the air and slammed it to the cold, white rocks.

"No, Katy, *no!*" Robb screamed, as terrified as I'd ever heard him. "Noooo!"

Katy backed off and Robb slipped on the creek bed as he approached. We found a full-grown goat, about seventy pounds, on its back, bleating and bleeding.

"Oh God," Robb wailed. "Katy!" He grabbed Katy by the collar and pushed her face next to the goat's. "No! No! No!" He then shoved her away.

I looked at the blood on the snow and suddenly the mood seeped into every crack of my body. The goat was dying, I knew. Something had died in me that day too, or that was how I was choosing to think of what happened.

When I agreed to move to the country, the understanding was that we would begin trying to get pregnant as soon as we left Austin. So as of November, when we were living in the office, I had started following Robb around the house, reminding him of his duty. Our first two attempts had fizzled, but I wasn't overly concerned—just enough to wonder what had gone wrong and to acknowledge that it would be more than a little awful if I ended up being infertile with all the marital maneuvering I'd done to get a baby. When my friend, Lori, from Austin had spent the night two days earlier, she informed me that she was pregnant. It was quite by accident, she said, and though she was happy, she was worried about the effect it would have on her marriage. I mustered up the energy and empathy to say something about how if anyone could manage an unexpected baby she could.

The next day another Austin friend, Cathy, visited. The two friends barely knew each other, but they bonded immediately when Cathy announced *her* pregnancy—news that prompted a sudden need for a chair on my part. She and her husband were just toying with the idea of having a baby and had sex without her diaphragm. "Bingo!" she said. "Who knew it could happen so fast?" At that point neither friend knew how desperately I wanted to be pregnant, and as the two chatted, comparing their due dates—two weeks apart—I couldn't help but become totally obsessed with my own pregnancy status. I knew that if I was going to have a period it would arrive soon, and I was already feeling the tell-tale pains in my lower back. In the type of delusion a woman who wants to be pregnant allows herself, I imagined the pain might be the embryo attaching to my uterus wall. It was the only hope that remained.

As much as I wanted to be happy for my friends, I felt a profound and unexpected envy. Will I ever get to talk about my sore nipples and compare the depths of my morning sickness? For the first time, after my friends left that day, I allowed myself to cry over my longing for a baby. I cried harder still the next morning, when I woke up and discovered blood on my underwear. Then the snow started to fall and I found something else to think about, something that might make me cheerful.

Now the goat lay before me, and I began weeping again. Robb crouched down beside me, aware that I was upset about my period but thinking at the moment that my tears were entirely for the goat. He put one hand on my knee, and petted the goat's head with the other. "What do you think we should do?" he asked as the goat's eyes darted wildly and its body twitched. "I've got my old twenty-two; maybe it would be best to put it out of its misery." I wept even harder at the thought of the gun.

Robb wrapped his arms around me and let me dampen the shoulder of his

Carhartt jacket. "No, we can't sh-shoot it," I wailed. In my mind, which was in high soap-opera mode at the moment, I was thinking that something had to live that day.

I walked back to the house and drove the car as near to the hyperventilating goat as possible. Robb carried it to the car in a blanket and I took it directly to the vet in Blanco. For the next two days, the goat was my focus—anything to keep me from thinking about the fact that I had lost another month. I was determined that the goat was going to survive.

The vet stitched up the goat's slashed neck and gave it IV and antibiotics. The total cost of its treatment was $200. Robb gently informed me that healthy, full-grown goats could be bought for $75. But the money wasn't the point. At least not to me. The goat was saved, which I took as a personal triumph. I made some calls to try to find out who owned the goat so I could return it. It wasn't Fred's nor our scary neighbor's to the north. It didn't belong to our neighbor to the west—an old woman who lived in a small stone house and had just lost her husband—nor to the family to our east, who owned a barn made of multicolored pieces of scrap metal, which we unfortunately could see from certain vantage points on our property.

I ended up giving the goat to Mr. Behrends, whose grandkids were in 4-H and would know how to take care of it. Retrieving the goat from the vet, Mr. Behrends tied it up in the back of his white Dodge Ram pickup and stopped by the house so I could say good-bye. While the truck was parked outside, our housemate Beverly took a Polaroid of the goat and presented it to me. "Thanks for everything," she had written across the bottom, which made me laugh for the first time in days.

•

With my pregnancy drama heating up, I had less patience for the construction than ever. I wanted people out of my house. I wanted to be able to cry or scream or throw myself on my bed in a fit of despair without worrying that a workman putting up trim would wonder what kind of maniac I was.

After finishing the screened porch, the last job was painting the barn and the office-garage building. Because all the walls were either stone or long-leaf pine shiplap—which were simply varnished—the only areas that required paint were the window and door trims and the eaves. With this limited amount of paint, Robb and I should have made our color decisions easily. But instead the paint became the most contentious part of the project. We couldn't agree on the colors, or whether the paint should be oil or acrylic, or whether Mr. Behrends's crew or an outside crew should do the work. In some part of my mind, I realized this was what would be classified as a nice problem—finishing out a stupendous house like this—but still our brains had passed their maximum decision capacity. Everywhere we looked were swatches of sample colors, reminding us there were still battles left to fight.

Adding to our irritability was the fact that we were now facing a deadline. At the first of the year we had decided to throw a big barn-warming party. Or rather, I had decided to throw a big barn-warming party and Robb had acquiesced. The date was April 13, and there was so much left to do—both to finish the house and make it presentable for a party. People were coming down from all parts of the country—Tennessee, South Carolina, Seattle, New York, Ohio, Virginia. I had begun thinking of it as the wedding reception I never had, and in the back of my mind I harbored a fantasy of announcing my pregnancy in front of this group of friends and family.

But such an announcement wasn't shaping up. March's opportunity had ended the same way my cycle had ended for twenty years. In bloodshed. I started sliding into despair and began burdening my friends with teary phone calls. Listening to me, they exhibited the quality they kept urging me to find—patience. The books I read said it could take six months to a year. But I had too much at stake for it to take that long. I'd turned my world upside down to have a baby. I had to have affirmation that I hadn't done it for nothing.

I didn't say much to Robb at this point. I told him when our attempts had gone awry and he would comfort me as best he could. "I know it will happen," he'd say. "Just give it time." I still had my dignity and didn't want him to think I was completely pathetic. I needed him to perform at the right time of the month. Plus, this felt like my journey.

•

That spring, among the abundant wildflowers on the property, we discovered bushes covered with small pink pom-poms that we could always smell before we could see. On our walks, we would pass through a cloud of fragrance, as if we had entered the spritzing zone on Bloomingdales' first floor, and know to look for the bush, which would normally be found towering over a patch of fuchsia wine cups or a mob of bluebonnets, the state flower, which were really more purple than blue, with white on top, like daubs of whipped cream.

The spring flowers brought more friends from Austin, and I felt compelled to push food on anyone who had come all the way for a visit. It could have been partly in my genes. My Italian grandmother measured success by the amount of food consumed at her house. But I also knew food would delay their inevitable departure. I wasn't a natural chef, but I mastered a few good dishes—leek and goat-cheese tarts, cilantro-marinated pork tenderloin, chicken cacciatore. I even learned how to make a halfway decent piecrust.

But even with the extra company, spring offered little comfort. Living in the country and not being fertile is a monstrous cruelty, especially in springtime when animals all around were rampantly reproducing—from the hapless armadillo to the squirrel that had taken up residence in the tree near our screened-in porch with her three skittering babies. Every time I drove by the roan mare down the road with her new, bamboo-legged foal, which was almost every day, I would avert my eyes. It hurt too much to witness their apparent joy and the evidence that procreation was a fundamentally simple process for everything but me.

One night I heard the cows that Fred kept on our place wailing inconsolably. The next morning on my run, I noticed they were scattered on the property; one roaming near the Campsite, two down near the creek, three near our windmill. Normally, they hung together, which is why I guess they're called herd animals. "You might want to see if something is wrong with your cows," I told Fred. "They've been acting strange. They wailed through the night like I've never heard before."

"Oh, I know wh-what's the matter with them," he told me. "It h-h-happens every year. I took their babies to market y-y-yesterday. They've been out c-calling for them." His report was crushing as much for its matter-of-factness as for the idea of the mother-baby separation. The thought of these cows—childless now like me—brought on some bovine bonding and made me more bereft than ever.

In the middle of March I got an assignment from a friend at *Texas Monthly* to write a story called "Stress-less Texas." God knows what I did to deserve this dreamy assignment just as my stress levels were peaking; my job—if you could call it that—was to try out the best spas and refuges in Texas. I soaked in a thermal spring in Big Bend and lolled at a lakeside retreat in East Texas; I was kneaded more than pizza dough, getting massages, sometimes more than one a day, in Dallas, Houston, Austin, and San Antonio. The last place I visited was a monastery in South Texas, which you couldn't enter without the head monk's permission. It was a silent monastery, meaning no talking allowed, which was a challenge for me.

By the time I drove up to the monastery, housed in a grand Victorian building on land that used to belong to one of Texas's great cattle families, I was convinced I was pregnant. It was early April and my period was six days late. My period was never six days late. I was elated and walking among the gardens and palm trees on the monastery grounds that afternoon, I thanked God that it had finally happened.

But that night, holed up in a meager closet of a room I discovered I had started my period. At first I thought I might be spotting—just a bit of blood women sometimes lose during pregnancy. Then it was a gush. I was thoroughly crushed, and spent the night lying on the scratchy sheets, trying to cry silently.

I got home a few days before the party, and I tried to lose myself in the excitement of the event. That Saturday, 120 people—including all my family, except for my brother from Houston who was traveling—ate ribs and brisket catered by a famous BBQ joint outside Austin and danced to a band that set up on a wide section of the catwalk in the screened-in porch. I wore a gold lamé jacket heavy with gemstones, as glittery and flashy as anything Las Vegas Elvis ever wore because actually it was made by the same man who had made many of Elvis's outfits. The tailor, nicknamed Nudie, also made suits for country stars like Conway Twitty. Robb had gotten the glorious jacket from a country music radio host we had met while working on the Miss Texas pageant story. I had been appalled that he had accepted it, since it violated every journalistic ethic. His argument was that as the photographer he couldn't influence the course of the story. Though I disapproved, I had secretly coveted the jacket and for the Valentine's Day that had just passed, Robb presented it as my gift. I figured enough time had passed that I could wear it with a clear conscience.

The jacket attracted everyone's attention as Robb and I walked over to the band's microphone on the catwalk. "We're here to celebrate the completion of our house," I said, looking down at the people gathered below me on the stone floor of the screened porch, "and the continuation of our marriage. There were many days in the past eighteen months when it seemed we would accomplish neither."

Later during the party, my mother pulled me aside. "I think if you can make it through a project like this," she said, as I played with my pendant, a tribal fetish I had bought in Morocco that like most tribal fetishes symbolized fertility, "you can make it through anything." Like not getting pregnant, I wanted to ask, but I didn't dare. The last thing I needed was my mother hounding me every month for progress reports.

There were plenty of reasons to be content that day and in so many ways I was. But I felt the absence of the one thing that I thought would make me completely happy—a pregnancy. Many friends commented on our "dream house" and "dream life," but the fuss made me feel worse, emphasizing how ungrateful and self-absorbed I was being and how far apart appearances and reality were.

•

After the misfortune of the monastery, I decided to take a different tack—a more spiritual mindset. Anything to try to quell the feeling that a noose was going around my neck, and to steel myself for what seemed to be an epidemic of pregnancies around me. Everywhere I looked, or so I felt, I spotted women with bulging bellies. I winced whenever I saw one, wondering what she knew that I didn't, what she had done right in a former life. My younger sister called to tell me of her pregnancy, as did an Austin acquaintance and a friend from Ohio, who thought she had conceived at our housewarming party. It was a virus that everyone but me was catching. Or it was a conspiracy to drive me mad.

My new approach led me to a nondenominational church in Blanco. I had been raised Catholic but wasn't willing to try it again. I needed a gentler God in my life and I found one through my tiny congregation, led by a man who called himself more of a teacher than a preacher. I immediately took to his sermons, which were filled with hope—just what I needed to scratch my theological itch.

"I feel I'm being punished," I confessed in a private meeting with the preacher, unable to shake my Catholic notion of a lightning-bolt-tossing God.

"That can't be. God is loving and forgiving," my minister insisted.

"Well, you must be right. I mean, if Madonna can get pregnant, I should be able to, right?" He looked at me quizzically, probably unaware that Madonna had recently announced her pregnancy. "God knows, I've never published a book on sex or anything." When I could tell my minister had no idea what I meant, I felt compelled to explain. "I mean, she did this God-awful book with all these photos of her supposedly having sex with Vanilla Ice and Sandra Bernhardt's former girlfriend and, well, Vanilla Ice is so pathetic. That's a sin in itself." My minister cocked his head to the side, like a schnauzer wondering if I had a Milk-Bone in my hand. "Uh, anyway, so maybe I have a chance."

Every morning I made my way to the huge live oak in the field in front of our house. When we first saw the property we thought the large clump of foliage in the field was a group of trees; in actuality this one tree had a drip line seventy feet in diameter. An arborist we hired to assess the health of all the major trees on the property had estimated that this one was a seedling when Columbus landed. The branches were so thick and long that the tips touched the ground. To get to the clearing under the tree I had to duck beneath or around the branches, which was like passing through a scrim. The roots of the tree were gnarled and bent, flattening out in places to make natural seats. I found a favorite spot and sat for at least a half hour every morning in what felt like my own botanical bubble. I soon began calling my meditation spot the Thinking Tree.

As the branches bent in the breeze and I breathed in the smell of hay—which is what Fred grew in the field around the tree—I prayed. I knew I wasn't supposed to ask directly for what I wanted; instead I was supposed to request the strength to get through whatever happened—including if nothing happened. But still, every morning I was asking for a baby.

"Jeannie, you need to just relax about all this," Robb told me, when he found me lying on the bathroom floor in tears after the pregnancy test I took in May came up negative. "It's not helping you to get pregnant to be so stressed out."

I knew he was right. All the books said that stress could make it harder to conceive, but telling a woman who wants to be pregnant not to worry is about as productive as spanking a child for hitting his brother. The problem simply accumulates. I cursed myself for setting up this situation. Of course, with so much riding on the outcome—my whole reason for moving to the country—I was going to be anxious. I never knew it was going to be such agony. I'd only been trying for six months; I wondered how women go years doing this.

I began pushing myself harder in my morning runs trying to keep up with

Robb, hoping to deplete my stress. As I ran, my mantra was, Mind over body. Mind over body. I was saying this to get myself up the hill faster, but I was also willing my body to listen to my mind's desires.

I frequently resorted to a relaxation tape. Sometimes I drove back to the Campsite with a yoga mat and lay outside, looking at the clouds merge, rupture, and reassemble themselves, a kaleidoscope without the colors. I'd tense up every part of my body then release, as instructed by the wistful, vaguely accented male voice that I was sure I'd heard before pitching sitar stars on obscure cable channels. I'd try to let my mind go blank, but it was stuck in an ovary-obsession rut. I became a big fan of a tea called Calm and went for regular massages with a masseuse in Blanco. On the occasions that a sense of humor found me, I could manage a laugh at my predicament. I never had to work this hard or needed this many accoutrements to relax when I lived in New York. Where, I wondered, was the peace people talk about in the country?

•

To coincide with my gynecological struggles, I was having an existential crisis too. Alone in a place from which I could see no neighbors and few signs of human life, I couldn't help questioning my relevancy. If a writer falls into the middle of the boondocks, does anyone ever hear her again? With no environmental sparks to fire my imagination, with no community of creative people to feed off, how could I ever have anything new or important to say? I feared I was being put out to pasture mentally in my mid-thirties. I had been able to continue my writing using fax, FedEx, and the Internet to tie me into the world, but I still felt like an island surrounded by hostile waters.

My sense of isolation grew worse when Robb traveled, and particularly when he and our housemates Brian and Beverly were gone at the same time. I knew that the downside of getting occasional trips to Thailand and Cuba was enduring the times Robb went to such places without me, but I'd never had to do so when I felt as needy. Our move to the country took place a few years after the publication of *The Bridges of Madison County,* and Robb and I had started joking that instead of the lonely farm wife taking up with the *National Geographic* photographer, in our case it would be the lonely *National Geographic* wife taking up with the UPS man, who was, I couldn't help but notice, quite adorable.

My mood hit its nadir when it turned hot and the scorpions started coming out. Out of the walls—literally—where they hid in cracks between the stones. I'd break into a sweat whenever I saw one, which was sometimes twice a day. Scorpions are the crawdad's evil cousins. They have pincers and pin-like eyes, but what makes them so menacing is their tail with its stinger. When I saw one, my Pavlovian response was to sweat profusely, as if I'd done one hundred jumping jacks. I'd scream for Robb, if he was home, or scream for the sake of it, if he wasn't. If my shrieks didn't send the creature scurrying into a crevice again, I'd throw a shoe at it with my eyes closed so that I wouldn't see the splattering. But most often, my blind state prevented me from hitting my target at all and the scorpion would go off to terrorize me again another day. There may have been only one family of scorpions, but because I rarely knocked any of them off, it seemed like hundreds.

Then suddenly—even with the perceived scorpion invasion—something shifted in me. One morning I was stepping out of the shower and allowed myself to go to the worst place I could think of: I would never conceive. On prior occasions when I'd imagined this scenario, I'd become distraught. But on this morning, a voice said, "We'll just adopt." Never mind that I was hearing voices, the thought soothed me. A wiser version of me spoke again. "It's not *whether* you'll become parents; it's just *how* you'll become parents."

Later that day, I left for Austin, where I would be a hostess at Lori's baby shower. I'd been dreading the event, wondering if all the procreation merriment would push me further into despair. With the car idling, I jumped out to open the front gate, and I looked out across the county road at the gathering of sheep, their heads bowed over the green slope, and felt a surge of calm, as if I'd been hypnotized. I told myself that God, the universe, something had gotten me this far in a happy, lovely life; I needed to trust that the same force would take care of me from here. As I swung open the gate, I felt lighter than I had in months. Lori's baby shower was a joy rather than a burden.

In June I followed Robb to Switzerland since my fertile period, which I took great pains to estimate, would likely fall during his trip there for *Geographic*. Somewhere over Iceland I began worrying about the effect of the long flight and the time-zone skipping on my cycle. It may not work this month, I told myself with a shrug and tried to enjoy the trip, during which we visited a small lakeside town called Zug, between Lucerne and Zurich, where I lived for four years as a child while my father was based there for Eastman Kodak.

I played the sidekick again in July on Robb's trip to Santa Fe. He was shooting for a FedEx campaign and was traveling with an art director and an account executive, who both learned from Robb why I was there. Over the four days, whenever we'd excuse ourselves from the dinner table early to return to our hotel, the women would titter knowingly.

At the end of July, my period was a couple of days late, but I wasn't feeling anything that could be construed as a pregnancy. Just in case, I bought a pregnancy test, but before I got to use it, Robb and I had a vicious fight—over a leftover construction matter, not surprisingly. I can barely recall the details; I only remember thinking during the three minutes that I needed to wait for the test results that maybe it was better if I wasn't pregnant since we obviously had such a shaky marriage; then I considered whether I would have time to meet someone else before my reproductive organs shriveled.

At the prescribed time, I looked at the little plastic stick and saw two blue lines. I checked the box to make sure that was the correct sign for a positive. I hyperventilated. It was happening. It was happening to *me*. I screamed for Robb, who was upstairs. He bounded down the stairs, irritated, thinking I was going to continue our fight.

"Look, look!" I cried, waving the pee-stained stick in his face. He grabbed my hand to hold it still and looked at the stick, then me.

"What does it mean?"

"I'm pregnant! I'm pregnant!" I began jumping around the bathroom, hugging him and kissing him, having no sense that I had wanted to swing him by his hair a few minutes earlier. Robb recalled that when he was shooting in Santa Fe he had gone to a mission called Santuario de Chimayo, which is known for its healing dirt. He had thrown some of the dirt down the front of his pants, making the women he was working with squeal at his raciness.

"That's what did it," he said. "Magic dirt."

I was ecstatic at what seemed like my miraculous conception. I took particular pleasure telling my friends who'd carried me along so good-naturedly during the months when surely they'd been tempted to screen out calls from their vampire friend who sucked energy instead of blood. On a trip to Napa Valley I met up with my older sister, who understood immediately what I meant when I said at the first vineyard, "I'm not drinking." While she blathered with joy, her husband stood by befuddled. Once the bizarre argot of childbearing women was decoded for him, he was visibly relieved. "Oh, I thought you were telling us you'd joined AA."

I reveled in every aspect of pregnancy. My aching boobs, even the pit of nausea that was a constant reminder that I was now part of a sisterhood. But as with any obsession, I wrongly believed that the fulfillment of it would negate all my problems. Now new worries arose. When I was eight weeks along, I began spotting and was convinced I was about to lose the baby and be sent back to square one as if this were a cruel game of Shoots and Ladders. Each time I had to go to the bathroom, I dreaded what I might find.

The baby hung on, but mixed with my joy, I felt a new vulnerability. Our New York friends, Brian and Beverly, finally moved out for good, so I was alone more often. Having accomplished his impregnation mission, Robb was free to move around the world without me. One day I saw an eight-inch-long centipede crawl across our upstairs floor. It was black and gold, had large pincers, and made the scorpions look as threatening as the Seven Dwarfs. Our construction crew had warned me that these creatures were poisonous. I grabbed a can of Raid and tried to douse it, but it escaped into a fissure between the wood floor and the rock wall, right above my bedroom. I knew I wouldn't sleep that night imagining centipedes dropping from the ceiling. Then I remembered I wasn't supposed to expose myself to bug spray. I was sure my baby was wheezing in a cloud of multisyllabic poisons, and called Robb in Manila to snivel.

"Jeannie, I think you'd have to lock yourself up in a room filled with that stuff and breathe it for hours before it could harm the baby," he said calmly, even though it was 3 a.m. his time. "Please tell me you're not going to be this neurotic when the baby arrives." I could guarantee him no such thing.

·

When I was four months into my pregnancy, I decided to sell my VW convertible. When we moved to Blanco, I had bought a real car—an Isuzu Trooper—and Robb suggested then that I sell the VW, since in his mind it was only a pleasure car anyway, something I only drove when the weather warranted a perfect 10. He had reminded me that the house was overbudget, which was one reason he had sold his cherished motorcycle. Despite his good example, I had resisted. I felt I had sacrificed enough just by moving here. What more did I have to give up? Robb continued to prod me, and suddenly the convertible became the manifestation of all our differences. He thought it was impractical; I thought it was fun and quirky and completely worthwhile because it made me happy. I liked what the car said about me—that I hadn't sold out completely. It was during the battle over the car that I came to realize that the thing I feared most about moving to the country was that I might turn into someone completely ordinary.

As a middle child among six, I had worked hard to stand out. I was a child who made a lot of noise and demanded attention, which is why I was drawn to journalism, I believe—to see my name in print. To me, my convertible was a hedge against convention. I would tool around on the two-lane roads near our place and feel sure that I looked like the New Yorker I was at heart who had brought her eccentric ways and taste to the country. In my convertible, I couldn't be mistaken for a woman who was on the path to becoming like my deer-hunting neighbor. To sell my car meant letting go of that safeguard, meant letting go, it seemed, of that dream of an interesting life.

But after I got pregnant and we really did need the money—our medical insurance didn't cover pregnancy—I did see that it was best to sell. But I ached. Fortunately, my dear mother, who was so delirious that I was pregnant, rescued me by agreeing to buy my car. She graciously granted me visitation rights and told me I could buy it back from her whenever I wanted; at least I knew that if I got too deep in ordinariness, my bulbous orange lifesaver was not out of reach.

·

When I was almost eight months pregnant, an ice storm hit while Robb was in Japan shooting a story on sumo wrestlers—dimensions I was approaching myself. At about 11 p.m., the electricity cut out. I went to the garage and lifted Robb's eighty-pound generator into a wheelbarrow, which I pushed to the bedroom door. I was afraid my heavy hauling would send me into labor, but when I was at the house alone, I had to take some risks. A couple months earlier, for instance, I had to play the part of reluctant matador. I had heard the thumping of hooves outside the house, and when I peeked out the window, I saw that Fred's herd of eighteen cows had gathered around the barn. Somehow they had jumped over the cattle guards we'd installed to prevent such a foray.

With Weegee, a border collie and natural herder, I began chasing away the cows. All but one jumped back over the cattle guard. The one left behind was the bull, naturally. He kept his head low as he watched Weegee and me approach. Weegee may have been afraid of thunder and shivered most of the two months of deer season, but he wasn't intimidated by the bull. This was what he was born to do. I was terrified, however. Nonetheless, I waved my arms over my head, something I had seen Fred do when approaching the bull. I felt like I was making myself more of a target than I already was with my large belly, but after freezing for an instant longer than I thought I could stand, the bull swung his head to the left and his body followed. Weegee chased him until his back hooves had left the ground to clear the cattle guard, which was apparently of little use.

The power outage was more problematic than the wandering herd. If I were to go into labor after lifting the generator, who would take me to the hospital? I wondered. Who could I call? I didn't know any of my neighbors well enough, and worse, the phone lines were down.

I pushed the wheelbarrow through the bedroom door and was about to yank the pull string on the generator when I read a warning that said, "Do not operate indoors." I was going to put it outside and string a wire through a cracked window when I realized the whole project was moot. The machine was out of gas. I would have to stay in the dark.

While I was lying in bed later, one of the thoughts that kept running through my head was: what you give up to get what you want. I realized this sentiment was dangerously close to "be careful what you ask for," but I wasn't prepared to think that—yet. I had finally achieved the Big Bird silhouette I so wanted, but in the process I had given up companionship, neighbors, and security.

The other thought that kept my brain busy during a night spent listening to the groans of ice-laden branches and the desperate, unsettling grinding of our windmill: This is when the twisted man with the Home Depot accessories appears.

I wondered if the alarm system would still work without power and contemplated my escape route if someone were to break in. Would I run to a neighbor's? Could I even run in my condition, and if so, which neighbor would I go to? The closest one was a quarter mile away. She was an eighty-five-year-old diabetic and would probably have a stroke if I were to show up at her house in the middle of the night. Should I just run outside and hide on the property? Maybe it was time to rethink my positions on guns. I remembered what a clerk at a gun store told me when I was researching a story on the NRA—that the cocking of a shotgun was universal language for "Get the Fuck Out of My House."

My feelings of helplessness were foreign and frightening to me. I had once thought toughing it out in the New York magazine jungle was a challenge. I thought the coal-mine incident in Virginia and getting stranded on the streets of Harlem at night while reporting for *Life* were scary. But I realized clearly on that night that living in the country was going to require a kind of resilience I'd never had to pull out of myself before. Could I do it? And more importantly, was it worth the effort?

•

Around my due date in early April, we had a long spell of thunderstorms. Whenever it rained that much, the creeks around us rose and we were flooded in for a few hours, until the water receded again. During an extended stretch of rain, they might go up and down several times, and one creek always ran over the road slightly during these wet times. I was panicked that the creeks would be up when I went into labor.

Normally, the sound of rain on a tin roof is delightful; it's sometimes found on CDs of soothingly rhythmic tracks, along with an ocean surf or a babbling brook. But after it had been raining for days, especially when you were praying for a break, the drops on the tin roof of the barn began to sound as if the Kentucky Derby was being run over head.

My parents arrived a week before my due date to wait for the baby. Because of the constant rain, we were all stuck in the house together, trying not to jangle each other's nerves. Every morning, when I came upstairs to the kitchen, my parents looked at me expectantly, if they didn't come right out and ask, "Any changes? Any pains?"

"If there were," I'd roar back, growing increasingly temperamental the bigger I got and the longer I hung on, "you'd be the first to know."

When I finally resorted to a spoonful of castor oil to bring on labor, the skies were clear and the car was packed and filled with gas. In the middle of the night labor pains woke me. I tried to rouse Robb so he could help me monitor my progress, but—an extremely sound and efficient sleeper—he kept nodding off between contractions. At 5:30 a.m. we headed out, with my mother rubbing my shoulders in the back of the car.

Though he fell asleep on the job earlier, Robb couldn't have been a better labor coach. I've always thought he is the ideal person to have around in a crisis. When awake, he's clearheaded and unflappable. He let the nurses know when he didn't think they were taking care of me well enough. When I wasn't progressing through labor, he advised me to do squats with each contraction.

"I've seen women in Haiti and China do this," he told me as he did deep knee-bends along with me, my face contorted in pain as I lowered myself. The squats seemed to work; afterward, my labor sped along. It wasn't till much later that Robb admitted that he'd made up the part about seeing laboring women do the squats. "I was just trying to help," he said. "It made sense to me to let gravity work for you."

I had never intended to have a baby without drugs, but I did with the encouragement of my mother, who had five of her six drug-free, and Robb (later I joked that his "just say no to drugs" cheerleading was because he didn't want to spend the money on the epidural). I think I surprised Robb and maybe made him think I was closer to an earthy, pioneer woman than I ever let on. During our Lamaze classes, the instructor had asked for the men's assessment of their wives' pain tolerance. Robb gave me a five out of ten, but I objected. "I beg to differ," I announced to the group. "I've been having bikini waxes for years." Actually during the waxing I had just before my due date, my Eastern European torturer told me that waxing was more painful than childbirth. That buoyed me, even if it turned out to be untrue.

Delivering on my own made me feel like Woman with a capital W. The kind you can hear roaring—or screaming, in my case. Which is what I did to finally get Gus Hawkins Kendrick—named for Robb's favorite uncle—out into the world. My screaming quickly dissolved into tears of joy, and surprisingly, Robb had a bigger cry than even I did. I was sure I had never loved Robb more than to see him weeping over his new son, the child I had gone to such lengths to have.

•

What are you doing on the floor?" I asked Robb on my first night home. He had put a pillow and blanket next to a bed he'd made for Weegee, who seemed completely distraught that he wasn't being allowed to take his normal spot on the foot of our bed. Gus would now be sleeping between Robb and me.

"I'm going to sleep down here tonight," he said. "I don't want Weegee to be too upset."

"You're a nut." People had told us that as soon as we had children, our dogs would become just dogs again. I was already feeling this distinction, but Robb was trying to forestall it, I could tell.

For the first couple days after we got home, I was feeling strong and confident. After delivering naturally, I felt I could do anything, and my mother, who had been through this before with six kids and eleven other grandchildren, was there to teach me all the intricacies of caring for this tiny being—bathing, diapering, and cleaning his umbilical stub.

Then, on the third day, I was getting into bed to nurse Gus when I saw—right on the paisley Ralph Lauren sheets where I was about to lay him—a scorpion, its tail arched like a lethal pincurl, ready to strike. I shrieked and, breathing like an injured bird, I swept Gus in my arms. Robb came running and gallantly removed the scorpion in one swipe with only a dab of toilet paper in his hand.

Thinking of what a scorpion sting could have done to a newborn kept me agitated all night, and that meant Gus was, too. My invincible pose evaporated. I suddenly felt more susceptible than ever in this unruly place. I realized that love as huge as I felt for Gus came with an equal amount of worry.

And there seemed to be plenty of potential disasters waiting. When Gus was a month old, tornado warnings were issued for Blanco, as several had been spotted in the area. It was the day that an F5 tornado flattened the town of Jarrell, north of Austin. I took Gus into my walk-in closet on the ground floor of the barn, put pillows all around us and thought of Dorothy. Robb, on the other hand, was upstairs in the barn, watching the lightning and the violent sweep of the clouds. "You should see it," he yelled down to me. "It's beautiful. It's like a Pink Floyd concert." That's when it became clear that my husband was a hopeless weather junkie.

"Get down here! You're a father now," I screamed, but he couldn't hear me.

He may have still risked his life for a good weather show, but fatherhood did change Robb in other ways.

"I'm going to miss a third of his life," Robb said, as I stood holding two-month-old Gus in front of the jetway that would take Robb to the Bulgarian rose harvest and to civet cat farms in Ethiopia for a *Geographic* story on perfume making. I was shocked to see tears in his eyes—something that had never materialized at any of our previous good-byes—just as I'd been astonished when he'd cried during Gus's baptism a few days earlier. We'd gathered some friends from Austin, my brother from Houston—his godfather—and members of my church to baptize Gus up at the stock tank, an old stone cistern that had 1937 chipped into the rock. While Robb held Gus, who was in a delicate lace christening gown that had been worn by all the family since my mother's father, our minister trickled water from the stock tank over his tiny head. After the minister gave a blessing, both Robb and I said some words.

"I will try to be the father I know you should have; I hope there will never be one day when you doubt . . ." Robb began before sobs strangled his words. ". . . my love for you," he continued in a voice I didn't recognize, small and scratchy. I looked at Robb as if he was someone I'd never known, and I could tell my friends—who knew Robb as quintessentially composed, sometimes cool—were exchanging glances. "He does have emotions," one friend whispered to me later. Yes, it seemed he did and our new son had tapped directly into them.

Robb and I both knew that leaving was part of his job, but it didn't make it any easier for me—or him. I tried to buck up and be strong, but I soon learned that there is something worse than being in the country alone. It's being in the country alone with a helpless baby.

•

A week after Robb left, I took Gus to the doctor's office in Blanco for his first set of vaccinations. The waiver I signed saying I understood the risks, which included coma and death, put me on edge. Should I really be doing this to him? I wondered. It was raining lightly when I left for the appointment, but began pouring like an open fire hydrant while I was at the office. By the time I headed home, the creek between town and our house was churning like a hurricane-fed surf. The pole marked off in feet to signal the depth of the creek had been washed away in the last storm. But I knew I wasn't supposed to go over low-water crossings in Texas. That's how people got a one-way ticket to the Gulf of Mexico.

I went into town and called a neighbor, Edythe, an older woman I had met at church, who was once the head nurse in a hospital pediatric unit. I had started relying on her for questions I would have asked my mom if she were close—how to take a baby's temperature, how much Tylenol I could give an infant.

Edythe said she'd gotten to her house by another, safer route. I took her suggestion and held my breath as I went over a different creek that was swollen but not yet roiling like the other one. It kept raining for hours after I made it home, which meant I was completely cut off, even from Edythe. I became frantic with fear that Gus was going to have a reaction to the vaccination and I wouldn't be able to get him to the hospital. Spinning this worry out to its worst possible end, I imagined him dying because I was marooned on this side of Bumfuck.

I was so agitated that when a friend called from Austin—a friend who had spent a lot of time helping Robb clear cedar on the property—I slid into sobs at the sound of his voice. "I'm all alone and there's no one who can help me," I bellowed, hating that I sounded as pitiful as a coyote howl. But the isolation any new mother feels was magnified by the reality that I was, in actual fact, isolated. I knew no one else with a child in a forty-mile radius. My friend Dan calmed me down and an hour later, as I was in the kitchen jiggling Gus in my arms to soothe his tears, I heard a car pulling in the driveway. It was Dan. He'd gotten across the creek in his big Suburban and had brought my favorite treat—chocolate chip cookies.

"My savior," I cried out, not entirely exaggerating. Appropriately, Dan would later go on to earn that description for real as an EMT. It was a blessing that he came because Gus did have a slight reaction; his temperature rose and he cried for hours straight. We took turns holding him from three o'clock in the afternoon until midnight, when Gus finally went to sleep on my stomach. I spent the night on my back, not daring to move for fear of waking him.

I tried not to regale Robb with all my worries when he called—just the Cliffs Notes version of every near disaster. "He doesn't need to hear every awful thing that happens," my mother would tell me, imparting wisdom gained raising six kids while my father was constantly half a world away as an international salesman. "He can't do anything about the problems anyway. Be cheery, or he won't want to call." I was never able to put on the mask my mother had.

A week later, when I was in Austin for my checkup with my obstetrician, Lori thoughtfully met me at the office to watch Gus while I was in the examining room. The next day while some neighbors were visiting, Lori called me from the hospital to report that she had contracted meningitis. The doctors were still trying to determine if it was viral or the even-worse bacterial kind. Lori was a notorious practical joker; she had called me before our housewarming party impersonating an agricultural official to warn me that planes would be crop dusting in the area that day. I thought her call from the hospital was one of her usual antics, and I didn't believe her until she put her doctor on the phone.

Luckily, when I heard the news another friend, Judith, was with me in Blanco. She was all calmness as I began pacing—or more correctly, walking in a tight circle—already imagining Gus, limp and blank-eyed, in the NICU. Judith advised me to call my sister-in-law, a nurse. When I got her on the phone, Judith took Gus to his room to change him. Suddenly I heard a shriek that wasn't Gus's. When I reached Judith, she was holding Gus, who was crying. Judith was frantic, her eyes darting wildly. She was flapping one hand in the air. I expected to see foam coming out of her mouth at any moment.

"What? What?" I cried.

"He just got stung by a red wasp. It came out of nowhere," she said, as she searched for the vicious dive-bomber. With my sister-in-law on the phone wanting to know what happened, I fell on my knees. Quite literally. I have a witness.

"Where can I turn in my mother badge?" I cried. "I don't know if I can do this." My sister-in-law, mother of three, gave me a tough-love pep talk, a verbal snap-out-of-it smack-down. Get your shit together was her general point.

Judith agreed to stay with me for a few days so that we could watch Gus together for any signs of infection, which blessedly never developed.

Besides such acts of kindness, three things got me through my first three months of motherhood. One, a visit from my older sister, a professional mom if ever there was one (four kids of her own, and plenty of experience raising her youngest siblings).

Two, the sheer joy and wonder of being a mother. Sometimes when Gus slept, I would simply stare in awe at this cherubic creature: round faced with a point at the bottom—the nub of a robust Ralston chin, I was sure. I often shot thirty-six frames of film of him in one pose, such as lying on his back, pedaling his legs and jerking his arms as if conducting a Rachmaninoff concerto. I wanted to capture every gesture, every nuance of expression. My heart would sigh with contentment when, while nursing, he would clutch my pinky as if he wanted to be even closer to me.

And throughout that month Robb was gone, I kept my eye on the prize, the trip I had planned for Gus and me: joining Robb in Provence for a month. Surely the break would do me good.

Part Two

THE SEEDLING

Traditionally grown cuttings, once rooted and
transferred to their new pots, need to be hardened
slowly. Sudden temperature changes can shock young
plants. They need to be watched carefully as they can
be susceptible to fungal and bacterial conditions if the
environment is not suitable.

•

—VIRGINIA MCNAUGHTON,
Lavender: The Grower's Guide

CHAPTER FIVE

Greenhouse

When I first saw the lavender fields in Provence, I wanted to let loose with a shirt-spotting drool, just like the type that regularly left the mouth of three-month-old Gus, who was sitting in the back of a rental car with me. From a distance, the puffy, perfectly aligned rows reminded me of a violet version of the corrugated tin on the roof of our barn. I loved the mélange of Van Gogh colors—the purple appearing more stark and brilliant against the taffy-colored soil and the wheat fields that often pushed up against their more showy neighbor. In some fields a lone almond tree offered a vertical counterpoint to all the horizontalness.

"Ooooh, look at that. Just look at that!" my mother-in-law, LaNell, shouted. We were driving toward the centuries-old town of Moustiers Sainte-Marie, which was built under a rock cliff and was famous for its delicate, glazed china. LaNell was in the back with me on the other side of Gus's car seat, and my father-in-law, Richard, was next to Robb, at the wheel. Though I didn't see any saliva dripping from LaNell's lips, the lavender fields animated her more than anything else on the trip. "It's the most beautiful thing I've ever seen!" she declared.

My in-laws had flown over with Gus and me to meet Robb in Paris. A late-June cold front had been passing through Paris and even though I hadn't brought enough warm clothes for myself or Gus, the chill couldn't have made me happier as we rode a boat along the Seine or walked from Notre Dame to the Louvre. People back in Texas were deep in their annual hell, but not me. I was layered up like a veritable onion. Sweaters in summer were a novelty I hadn't enjoyed since the last time I sat on a sand dune watching the moon over the beach in Montauk, before I left New York. I was feeling especially smug that I had escaped the Texas summer, which was perfectly heinous, I had found over my five years of living in the state. In summer, the sun in Texas hurts. It sears and stabs and pokes at your eyes and brain. To live in Texas in July is to know how a worm feels when you lift a rock. Or how it would feel to be a film-noir interrogation subject. All right, you want to scream. I confess, just turn off the damn light.

Living in Blanco made me even more heat and sun averse. The sun was magnified by the pale caliche dirt roads that make glancing down as painful as looking to the skies. Days would pass without a solitary cloud drifting by to run interference. Or at times clouds would hug the horizon timidly, like seventh-grade girls at a sock-hop clinging to the gym bleachers.

With few places to retreat, I grew cranky during Texas summers. I cursed the sun as it made me flush and warmed the crown of my head until it was almost hot to touch. I could feel the wrinkles forming around my eyes as I kept my lids scrunched together like an ornery child.

But I got blessed relief in Paris—from the heat and the provincialism that plagued me in Blanco. Having been to Provence before, I remembered coolness and sophistication there, too. After speeding through the countryside on a TGV, we found that the weather was a bit warmer in Provence, but I could still find justification for a cotton sweater even in the middle of the day. We had rented out part of an eighteenth-century stone olive mill, called Les Baumes, that a British couple had renovated. We obviously had something for stone buildings with a utilitarian history. Our section of the olive mill was once a storage area and had a large arch between the kitchen and the main room, which served for both living and sleeping. The roof in the main room was vaulted and left me wondering—and sometimes worrying—how all those stones overhead stayed in place. From our terrace, we could see the olive grove plus a collection of oaks, pines, and ash trees; beyond the slope down to the Bresque River, fierce stone cliffs rose up on the other side.

In all ways, but particularly climatically, the first week in Provence was blissful. After his parents left, Robb actually would be spending time *in* the lavender fields on the Valensole Plateau, which we skirted on our way to Moustiers Sainte-Marie. We were all here because Robb was working on his assignment for *Geographic* on perfume-making, and his main objective in Provence was to photograph lavender harvest.

I couldn't think of a more perfect vacation for a new mother. The olive mill was within walking distance of the town of Sillans la Cascade, which was in a remote part of Provence, far from the crowds in Aix or Nice. I lapped up the antiquity of Sillans, with its crumbling stone steps from the main road up to the plaza. The narrow streets were lined with old three-story buildings, either stone or stucco, accented by flowers bursting from boxes beneath shuttered windows, and by lamps that looked like gas lanterns from the last century. Twice a week a farmer's market offered pastries, bread, sausages, fresh cheese, a stunning array of leeks, tomatoes, eggplant, melons, blackberries. At a nearby winery we bought rosé wine by the jug, and we returned often to refill the jug from a tap on a wine barrel. I diligently followed almost every baby book directive but drew the line at giving up drinking while nursing (though I never overdid it). Going without wine in France to me was as illogical as not having sex on your honeymoon.

Our favorite restaurant in Sillans was Les Pins, where we went for steak frites and bouef en daube. We were there often enough that the waitstaff began to know which wine we liked best and to even tolerate my French. While we ate on the outdoor terrace, I'd often lay Gus on a blanket below our table, where he'd flail his arms and legs happily looking up at the sky and the comings and goings of waiters and other guests.

Gus could be transported everywhere with us, mostly in his Snugli that attached him firmly to my chest or to Robb's. Remembering earlier vacations in St. Tropez and Nice, when I'd gone topless on the beaches, I felt completely comfortable nursing Gus at any time—at restaurants while I ate or at the farmer's market. I'd often plop down on a bench right next to the chickens roasting on a spit and unzip my shirt.

At least three times a day, I would let Robb know how thrilled I was to be out of Texas. I would comment on the temperature, noting the coolness of the breeze, the number of clouds, the scarcity of the sun. I didn't even mind that it was too chilly to use the inviting swimming pool that came with our rental.

Robb received each comment about the weather like a head-butt. A typical Texan, his pride in his state was out of all proportion to its virtues. On the eve of my move from New York to Austin in 1991, my New York friends and I had an argument over who was more arrogant: New Yorkers or Texans. Soon after arriving in Austin I saw a college student walking down the street wearing a T-shirt that read: Fuck You, I'm From Texas. I called my New York friends and informed them that Texans won.

During our first week, Robb endured my comments silently but then the weather got warmer. It's amazing how you can trick yourself. As the temperature climbed, I pretended to still need a cotton sweater. I tied it around my waist or over my shoulders; sometimes I stubbornly wore it even though I was sweating underneath. I kept Gus under blankets in his stroller—partly out of a new mother's natural oversensitivity but mostly to convince myself it was still cool. At one restaurant we visited for lunch, the owner took the liberty of removing Gus's blankets. *"Trop chaud. Trop chaud,"* she scolded me.

Robb enjoyed this reversal and took as much pleasure pointing out the heat as I suppose I did emphasizing the temperateness. "You could have stayed home for this weather," he said one afternoon as we walked into Sillans. "And at least had air conditioning." Indeed the temperature climbed to nearly one hundred for a stretch of days and any clouds that were with us in the morning seemed to evaporate by noon like ice in boiling water.

He also took to needling me that my fondness for Provence was pretentious. He suspected that Provence—even a boiling hot Provence—met with my approval because it was a celebrated region of the world and because my mentioning my month's vacation here in an old olive mill could incite envy even in my most jaded New York friends.

In his mind, the Hill Country was just as beautiful, and he began pointing out other similarities besides the weather. The terrain in Provence was rocky limestone, just as it was in our part of Texas. Provence was hilly, the vegetation sparse. The air was dry, and fig trees grew near the olive mill, as they did on our property in Texas. Many of the buildings in both places were made of stone, he noted, though I countered that the difference was that the buildings in Provence were *hundreds* of years old.

He came across the similarity that gave him the most delight one morning in the bathroom of our rental. I heard a chuckle and then Robb asked me to come into the bathroom with a tone of someone who is about to deliver a comeuppance. "Jeannie," he called. "You're not going to believe this." I followed his finger to a spot behind the toilet. Parked there was a scorpion. A scorpion, here? To make my shock worse, this scorpion was not the caramel color I was used to in Texas, but a more menacing black. I staggered back as if he'd just shown me a photo of himself with another woman. Nowhere in my Provence guidebooks did I find mention of scorpions. As he disposed of the creature, I was crestfallen. Texas seemed to be following me.

•

Once Robb started photographing, I spent many days in our rented olive mill alone with Gus. Sometimes I'd push Gus's stroller into town and watch the old men play boule or wander down a wooded path to the stupendous column of water that poured into a turquoise pool below—the cascade for which the town was named. Or I'd lie in a lounge chair on the terrace surrounded by an herb garden that scented the air with thyme, rosemary, and fennel and read Peter Mayle's *A Year in Provence.* Why couldn't Robb have wanted to move out to *this* countryside, I'd think, contrasting my month in Provence with my life in the Hill Country. I also read about the lavender fields in my travel books and tried to decipher the French in the pamphlets Robb had brought home from his trips around the Valensole Plateau.

Lavender in the Valensole region "provides the world with 80 percent of its needs," an *Eyewitness Guide to Provence* told me. "These days the cultivation of a hybrid called lavendin has overtaken traditional lavender."

In a book Robb had brought along for research called *Lavender* by Tessa Evelegh, I learned that lavender was especially well suited for heat and dust because the oil throughout the plants protected them from drying out. "Originally brought to [Provence] by the Romans," the author wrote, "lavender took a liking to the southern slopes of the Alps with their well-drained soil, and began to grow wild in the region." At the beginning of the twentieth century, farmers cleared out almond orchards, according to the book, and in their place, began cultivating lavender to supply perfumers in Grasse. I couldn't wait to get closer to the lavender fields.

My languorous routine was broken by the arrival of my old friend Kim, who came to visit for four days after a business trip in Paris. Kim, Gus, and I went exploring on our own—to the factory that produces the L'Occitane body care line, to antiques stores in a nearby town called L'isle-sur-la-Sorgue. Kim fussed over Gus—and my appearance.

I kept my hair swept up in a clip at the back of my head, mainly so Gus couldn't tear at it when I was holding or nursing him, but also because there was nothing else to be done with it. I hadn't had it cut or highlighted in more than a year—since my last visit to New York when I'd had the flirtation with the bow-tie man. I still didn't trust anyone in Austin, and certainly not in Blanco, to do my hair. "You're definitely two-toned," assessed Kim, with her glorious sand-and-sunlight locks, perfectly colored and kept. "I could call someone and find a good salon in Nice." But I protested that I didn't have time.

"Well, we certainly can do something about your clothes," she said. With all the extra post-baby skin, my body was lumpy like a sharpei's, which made long elastic-waist skirts and loose cotton or linen shirts most comfortable. I didn't mind my frumpiness, since I had such a good excuse, but Kim was horrified.

"This is the time to emphasize your boobs," she said. "Your boobs are amazing right now."

She went through my suitcase and found two sleeveless, close-fitting tops I had planned to wear under big shirts. "There," she said when I tried on a moss-colored one with a fairly low square neckline. "You look boobilicious now." She also made me wear shorter skirts. "You've got legs and boobs going for you now. Show those gorgeous ankles. Be *adventurous*," she joked. I had to agree that I looked more presentable in her prescribed outfits, and since I didn't have to be discreet here about nursing, the long, flowing blouses I wore in Texas to hide my bare boob weren't necessary. Not being overly modest, I didn't mind flashing the French.

One day while Kim was visiting, we drove out to meet Robb and his interpreter, a young French college student named Ariane, while they were shooting the lavender harvest forty minutes from the olive mill. We'd gone to the market in town that morning and put together a picnic basket with an onion tart, goat cheese wrapped in chestnut leaves, salami, *pain de campagne*, sun-dried tomato spread, olives, pistou, couscous salad, and naturally, wine. We met Robb and Ariane in the afternoon at what turned out to be Robb's favorite field to photograph. The amethyst stripes of the field were interrupted by the ruins of a stone shed, and in the distance to the north were the Haute Alps, their profile reminding me of dog molars. Kim and I were both delirious at the view as we sat on a blanket next to the field. After our late lunch, while Kim and Gus each took naps, I ventured closer to the lavender plants, which were bubbling with color and that intoxicating scent.

The field belonged to a farmer named Daniel. Through Ariane, Robb learned about Daniel's family history of lavender growing. For three generations they'd been working the earth, producing plots of heaven that had been celebrated in books and thousands of tourist photos. On one of Robb's visits to Daniel's home, he learned that he grossed about $280,000 a year from his two hundred acres.

I had at this point given up the charade that it wasn't hot. For our picnic, I was wearing a red sundress I'd just bought with Kim's approval, but still was sweating profusely. Earlier that day, Robb had called a friend staying in our house in Texas and told me that it was only 92 degrees there. No one but a Texan would use the word *only* anywhere near the term 92 degrees. To my irritation, our rental car came equipped with an outdoor thermometer. That afternoon, it had registered 36 Celsius, or 98 Fahrenheit.

"It looks like we'll have to go home to get out of this heat," Robb said during our picnic, needling me once again.

"Hey," I said pretending not to be bothered. "Texas doesn't have lavender." I was spreading goat cheese on a slice of bread. "Look at this." I swept my arm over the variegated purple and cream landscape. "You can't beat this."

Robb didn't offer a retort, and I foolishly thought I'd scored a dunk shot. He was in fact unusually quiet the rest of the day, which I should have known meant he was up to something.

As it got closer to sunset, Robb wanted to photograph me in Daniel's lavender field, so while Ariane and Kim entertained Gus, I waded out into the middle, my red dress brushing against the flowers on either side of me and releasing spurts of scent. From behind his camera, Robb asked me to bend over the flowers, and as I brought my face closer to the bushes and all those wand-like flowers I felt the urge to keep going down. To actually plant my whole face in a bush and leave it there, inundating myself in lavender. I might have done it too but as I got over the bushes I noticed hundreds of bees drunkenly drifting from one blossom to the next, only slightly happier than me to be there, and together filling the air with a steady drone—the only sound except for the *schwick* of Robb's camera opening and shutting and occasionally Gus's cries or giggles. This photo appeared on the cover of a book entitled *Perfume,* published by *National Geographic* after the magazine story. (My second cover—not that I was keeping track or anything.)

As the light was seeping from the sky, a gust of wind rippled through the lavender plants, carrying with it a fresh surge of lavender aroma. The yellow Hermès scarf I'd bought on a visit to Paris years earlier fluttered over my face. The photo I like best from that evening is a blurred shot of me from behind running through the field, holding my hat on my head with one hand and trailing the dancing scarf with the other. For me, it perfectly captures the dreamy, hypnotic quality of a lavender field.

·

The next day, Kim left for the airport and while we were having breakfast on our terrace, Robb delivered the idea that had been rolling around in his head for several days. "You know, the Hill Country is really a lot like Provence," he said as he spread apricot *confiture* on his croissant. He was not saying it in a taunting way, however. He was reflective and serious. "Why couldn't we grow lavender at home? In that big field in front of the house with the Thinking Tree."

He then reiterated the comparisons that in his mind almost guaranteed success: the same rocky soil, the dry climate, the summer heat. He added the latter with a wink. "I checked and it gets about as cold here in winter as it does at home." He then excitedly moved to the financial potential. "Daniel makes $280,000 a year. That's just from the lavender oil, but there are so many things we could do with lavender. We could sell lavender sachets. We could make soap and candles."

He went on, but my mind couldn't get past the *we*. We? As much as being in the middle of a lavender field was a profound sensual experience, I would be very happy to be in someone else's lavender field. I did not need my own.

I reminded Robb that we both had careers that paid quite nicely.

"But just think how beautiful it would be in front of the house, all those rows," he countered. Then he began to do some mathematical computations. Robb is unusual in that he is tremendously creative but also has an incredible math mind, which he likes to exercise. He can run numbers almost faster than I can punch them in a calculator. He likes to play games like figuring out how much Michael Dell or Bill Gates earns per week, per day, per hour, per minute. "Five hundred and seven dollars a second!" he would exclaim when he had reduced a figure as far as possible. "Imagine making more when you sneeze than the average person does in a day!" I often told him it was not only unfair that his right and left brains worked at equal capacity, it was weird. He let me know that Daniel's take on his lavender was $1,400 an acre. He started making notes in the margin of the *International Herald Tribune*.

I didn't offer any objections that day. I let him have his revelry, and merely nodded as I shook a wood rattle that our neighbor Roger had made for Gus.

Occasionally I rolled my eyes, which I had learned was about the only way to deal with Robb's profusion of ideas. There was always some building he was considering buying and fixing to turn a profit. He once had an idea to start a business putting ads on the cardboard shields people in southern climates put on their windshield to block out the sun. Another idea was to put the logo of the archrivals of various universities in the plastic filters in all of the school's urinals. I finally figured out that many of his ideas were just diversions he contemplated for his own enjoyment—the way he calculated a mogul's pay scale. Even though I'd just been through the move to the country with him, I still was dense enough to believe that if I humored him and offered no resistance, the idea would be pushed aside by the demands of his career.

What I should have known at this point in our marriage is that any humoring I did early on in the process only served to strengthen his resolve. He was a dreamer, that was certain, but not an idle dreamer. When he got behind an idea, he had enough will, ambition, and resources to make it happen.

·

The lavender idea morphed from wild-eyed lark to serious business proposition over the rest of our time in Provence. When he was out photographing the farmers, he would ask through Ariane specific questions about growing lavender, harvesting it, distilling it, and took careful notes. In the evenings he would come back to our olive mill and tell me that you could harvest from the perennials for ten to twelve years. He was encouraged to learn that lavender didn't require lots of herbicides or fertilizers, nor much water, which reinforced in his mind its suitability for the dry Texas weather. I would yawn inside, but I was becoming a little alarmed at how fervent he'd become about the whole affair.

A few days later, in the nearby town of Salernes, I found a fabric store that sold a selection of the famous Provençal textiles, characterized by their small quasi-paisley patterns of flowers or fruits found in the countryside. I had decided I was going to get a tablecloth made for our long table at home, and found a gorgeous bolt of fabric in blues and yellows that featured a recurring pattern of lavender bunches. Given Robb's assignment here and the amount of time we'd spent with lavender, I decided it was the perfect choice.

"We'll think of lavender every time we bring it out," I said as I showed him my purchase.

"Oh, we'll be thinking of lavender more than that," he said ominously.

In the middle of July, we went to a lavender festival in the hillside town of Valensole—the center of the lavender-growing region. At the market there, we saw lavender arranged in dried wreaths and pressed into the sides of fat candles. We bought soaps at almost every stand, marveling at the many different scents lavender combined with—orange, lemon, vanilla, mint. Images of lavender—either singly or in bunches—adorned T-shirts, dishcloths, salt shakers. One vendor told us that the most important ingredient of the famous Herbes de Provence was lavender, which prompted Robb to buy a jar. We had our first taste of lavender honey—the tongue-tantalizing manifestation of the ethereal scent. Robb pointed out that a jar of the lavender honey sold for seven dollars, while the same-sized jar of regular honey in the farmer's market near our olive mill sold for four dollars. "We could have beehives and have our own lavender honey . . . Honey," he said with such exuberance I got a glimpse of what he must have looked like as a kid on Christmas morning.

"Robb, you don't know anything about beekeeping! You don't know anything about farming," I said with exasperation, trying to enjoy my spoonful of honey as I waited in line for lavender ice cream.

"We can learn," he said. "We're smart." Again with the *we* business. I had learned that in our marriage *we* usually meant the other person. I would say, "Maybe we should move the car inside the garage," and, I admit, I was just trying to suggest nicely that he could take care of that for me. It seemed especially likely that Robb's *we* had a second-person implication because I was normally the one who did the research for our various projects around the house.

"Have you ever thought that if you could grow lavender in the Hill Country someone would have already done it?"

His eyes narrowed to small blue dashes and he shook his head. "You can be such a killjoy. Once, just once, could you trust me? You never trust me. Could you embrace one of my ideas instead of fighting it?"

He walked off before I could vocalize my retort. Gus was sleeping in the Snugli on my chest, or I would have shouted it across the queue that had formed behind me: "I've fucking gone along with everything already!" Instead, I looked down at Gus's small bald head resting on my left breast. I've already moved twice for him, I thought. I've got a three-month-old, for God's sake. What more does he expect from me?

•

We didn't speak about the lavender idea for several days. We went into Grasse so he could photograph "noses" at work in Givaudan Roure's School of Perfumery. While he worked, I toured the International Perfume Museum with Gus. I learned about the different ways that raw materials can be transformed into perfume. Robb had told me that the lavender farmers used steam distillation to produce the essential oil, and at the museum I read that steam distillation was developed by the Arabs. "The object is to allow the steam flow to trap the raw material's volatile constituents," an exhibit informed me. This technical museum only held my attention briefly; I ended up spending much more time at the museum at the Fragonard Perfumery, which had a room full of exquisite perfume bottles dating back to the sixteenth century.

Too soon, it was time to leave France. Robb was excited as he packed up. Because he was on the road so much of the time, the real treat was being at home. Vacationing in your own backyard is a fine idea if you're the one always leaving, but if you're the one mostly staying, it's the old equation of familiarity and contempt.

Contempt was exactly the feeling that was burbling inside me as I contemplated going back to the house, back to Texas and the sun.

At the end of other extended trips, the thought of returning home after weeks away warmed me. The comfort and security of home were compensation for giving up the adventure. Many return flights were spent imagining the relief of walking in the front door and smelling the singular melange of aromas in my own home. But that was when I lived in New York or Austin.

On this flight home, I was struck by the complete absence of such sentiment. When I imagined opening the door to the house, the only thing I felt was a tugging in the middle of my chest. Dread. I could feel the heat, the dryness, the sameness of what I had left and blocked out temporarily. I resolutely did not want to go home, but knew at some point I had to.

Robb, on the other had, kept enumerating the things he couldn't wait to do. He'd check on the creek to see if it was still running. He couldn't wait to jog on the property in the morning. He'd go to the Campsite and watch the sun rise. He would put Gus in a sling and take the dogs out to roam.

Nothing on his list sounded the least bit enticing—except seeing our dogs.

The closer we got to the San Antonio Airport, which was the most convenient airport for us, the bleaker I became. On the drive home, I could not contain my despair any longer. "You know, I am not excited at all to be home," I said.

I could tell my comment stung Robb as much as it pained me to say it. I was caught between wanting to pretend to be happier than I was for all our sakes, versus the need to be honest about how unsettled I felt. I was used to thinking of myself as adaptable, as someone who could be happy anywhere. But after a year and a half, I had little affection for Blanco. I thought I would have calibrated myself to country life by now, but I felt like a skipping LP that needed a good whack to get on with the song. What was taking so long?

"I'm sorry you feel that way," Robb said with a heaving sigh. He was quiet the rest of the drive, my words squelching his joy at returning home. He was imagining, I was sure, how much better life would have been with some rugged, outdoor type with callused hands and a pioneer spirit, or someone who would have already been designing sachets in her head. Instead, he ended up with a wife who felt more at home among concrete and people than grass and trees. A thankless spouse who meshed with his dreams as gracefully as a boulder meeting Steuben Glass. I wasn't quite sure, though, who was the boulder and who was the glass.

As we drove into the town of Blanco and saw the courthouse and the Bowling Club Café with the convention of pickups parked out front, I was even more depressed. Compared to rural France, rural Texas seemed more desolate and artless than ever. We turned left at the stoplight and made our way past the doctor's office, the fertilizer store, and past a small dam in the Blanco River where maybe twelve people were swimming in the deep water. As we drove west, we came upon a large John Deere tractor, with black smoke snorting from a pipe behind the driver and huge back tires that looked like life preservers for an elephant. With traffic coming in the other direction, we were stuck behind the pokey tractor for half a mile, increasing my annoyance.

We took the right-hand turn onto the county road that led to our house. Gus was fussing in his car seat and I reached back to stroke his head. We passed the grass airstrip used by the itinerant preacher who made his rounds by airplane, and another neighbor's entryway, where a sign for Santa Gertrudis cattle hung. As we followed the road down across the creek bed, we saw that it was dry, another disappointment for Robb. As the road climbed up again it bent to the left. Looking to the right at the top of the hill, I got my first glimpse of the house. Just flickers of it, really, through a knot of skinny live oaks. It appeared and faded rapidly, as if it were a slide in a stuttering projector.

That day, as the house came into full view across an expanse of the dried-out field Fred leased for his hay, I contemplated it glumly. It was an impressive building, more stunning than any home I'd imagined for myself. The tin of the gambrel roof was gleaming in the sun, the screened porch a light and airy conjunction between two stone masses. I had put untold hours into its construction; I had just written a feature story for *This Old House* magazine about the renovation. It was the place Gus had come home to after leaving the hospital. Everyone who came to the house—no matter if they were locals or friends from New York—had a jaw-sagging moment when they first stepped into the screened-in porch, our entryway into the house. I thought of all the people who had admired our house and our life and I felt like a spoiled ingrate.

As we drove up our driveway, churning a geyser of dust in our wake, past the Thinking Tree, which I obviously needed to visit, the house looked to me at that moment like a prison. A glorious prison. Years earlier, when I was a freelance reporter in the New York bureau of *Time*, one of the seasoned correspondents warned me against working at the magazine full-time. The pay and perks were so bountiful they encouraged complacency while the bureaucracy savaged the creative spirit. She'd called the magazine a velvet coffin. Velvet coffin. Glorious prison. Now I understood.

You couldn't have told me then that I would soon feel the exact opposite, and I would never have believed the part lavender would play in my about-face.

CHAPTER SIX

Rain

*I'm trying to locate lavender honey for a friend who
fell in love with it in Provence. Braggart that I am,
I swore that Texas lavender would be far superior and that I'd find
and send her ours. Can you help?*

—DONNA TAYLOR,
July 1, 2004

That's exactly how I feel," I told Robb, pointing at two lavender plants that looked to be entirely composed of used matchsticks. The plants were among fourteen Robb had put in the ground around the base of the barn the previous March as part of a test. He wanted to determine which variety of lavender would fare best in the Hill Country. There were more than thirty-nine varieties and four hundred subspecies, he reported, and he had planted two of each of the seven varieties he could find in nurseries in the area. One of the varieties was English lavender, or *lavandula angustifolia,* and we were looking at their charred skeletons outside the door to our bedroom—all that was left by mid-August of 1998, a year after we'd returned from France.

"They just couldn't take the heat," Robb said, slipping his hands in his front pockets.

"Yeah, who can?"

"These look good." Around the corner, Robb showed me two thriving plants about the size of gallon milk jugs. "Look at these. They've been blasted by sun here on the west wall and they're doing great. Even with the sun baking the stone wall behind them." The sun survivors were *lavandula intermedia,* or "Provence" variety, Robb said, which meant nothing to me. "Daniel grows a lot of this," he explained, referring to his French farmer friend.

The two *lavandula intermedia,* or lavendin, plants were surely the only things in Texas that were flourishing that summer. The grass around the house was scorched and stiff, the hopeless color of a broom. The leaves on the live oaks around the property were thinning or acquiring a brownish tinge. We'd gone months without rain, with a string of 100-degree days added into the mix for maximum suffering, and I was particularly unable to endure the heat that year. I was pregnant again, and thrilled to be so—blessedly this feat only took two months to accomplish. But it would have been obvious to no one that I was happy. I was having a horrendous case of morning sickness, which, combined with the heat and the general weariness I felt chasing after a toddler, made me want to hiss at anything that crossed my path.

My twentieth high school reunion in early August hadn't done much for my disposition either. Of course everyone wants to be the most fabulous person in the room at these gatherings, but I felt my sparkle had faded since the previous reunion ten years earlier. I hadn't been able to make that event, but I had a glamorous reason—I was in St. Tropez with Ben—which was better than any appearance I could have made. Now, I had to tell people I lived in the sticks of rural Texas, and on top of everything else, my mother had mentioned upon my arrival home, "I think your accent's coming back."

Like my dad, my mother grew up in the Chicago suburbs and took many speech therapy classes while getting her education degree at Northwestern University. She had been appalled to hear me talk when I was a child. She spent hours trying to get me to pronounce words such as *nice* and *leg* without stretching them out to the middle of the Atlantic.

"Nice ice," she'd say as a drill; her words were as crisp as a snap of the fingers.

"Nay-ce iay-ce," I'd answer, which always made her groan. Surely she was wondering how a good Yankee from Italian stock had bred such a hillbilly child.

When I moved to New York at twenty-one, I soon realized my twang, which by then was topped by a layer of South Carolina gooeyness from my college years, could be a career killer. With my accent, many people I called for work were reluctant to believe I was who I said: "Jay-nee Ralston from MayCall's Maygazine in Noow Yahwk." I got the nickname "Tennessee" from the Lebanese guy at the deli near my office because he couldn't understand my orders at first. I worked hard to tame the accent and was proud that soon no one could detect my southern origins. But now my mother was telling me it was sneaking back. My regression had surely begun.

Maybe even worse were the signs of my conspicuous fashion deterioration. It was one thing to be a frump in rural Texas, but in New York, quite another. The previous March, before Gus turned one, before I was pregnant again, I had gone to New York with my mother along to aid and abet. I decided to be a grown-up and spring for a hotel rather than stay with friends.

Through Mary Ellen, Cathy, and Lori—who thankfully were my same size—I assembled some presentable outfits since I had few stylish clothes of my own, thanks to my post-baby fat and the low sartorial standards in Blanco. But I had forgotten about shoes, which would have been an unthinkable oversight in my New York days. The evening before I was to leave, I went through my closet and found a pair of Cynthia Rowley suede loafers with a thick, two-inch heel. They were scuffed and dusty from too much time in the bottom of my closet, but were fairly stylish, I thought. Or at least they had been recently enough. I had other more flashy shoes but I knew I could never wear the higher heels for four days in the city. My feet had spread unattractively from the pregnancy and had grown accustomed to sneakers and hiking boots—anything low and roomy and borderline butch.

I cleaned up the Cynthia Rowleys the best I could, and thought they would do in New York until I could buy a new pair. Unfortunately I was two days into my four-day New York spree before I could get by the shoe department in Saks. With Gus in his stroller and my mom in tow, I was examining sample shoes when a snappily dressed black man with white patches at his temples approached. "Are you looking for replacements for *those*?" he asked by way of a greeting. I was taken aback, then looked down at the Cynthia Rowleys, which next to the shiny samples looked like they'd just barely survived the dust bowl.

My face flushed and I managed an assent. When he went off to get my sizes in styles I had weakly pointed to, I asked my mom if my shoes were that bad.

"Well they're a little mangy but I didn't want to hurt your feelings," she told me. This from a woman who doesn't miss an opportunity to tell me how I should be wearing my hair. I thought of all the places I'd already been in those shoes. I flushed deeper still realizing that I'd actually been in the Conde Nast building—Shoe Snob Central. I cringed to think of how far I'd fallen, from someone who'd once owned a pair of glittery Prada sandals to someone who wasn't even cognizant enough to know what a fashion fool she was making of herself.

At that moment, I would have bought any shoe the salesman placed before me. How novel, but effective—the insult-your-customer school of salesmanship. I ended up with a pair of Donald Pliners that were gorgeous but truly too high for my out-of-practice legs. I wobbled out wearing them, after the salesman had pinched my Cynthia Rowleys together with two fingers and held them at arm's length. "Do you want me to dispose of these?" he asked, not even bothering to assume I might still wear them someday. I spent the next two days teetering through Manhattan with sore calves, repeating the sadistic saying a famous Texas drill team director—who I once included in a story—always told her leather-fringe-skirted troops: Beauty Knows No Pain.

The day before I could get on a plane and take off the offending shoes, Robb made a surprise appearance in New York. He had been in London for one of the last shoots of his perfume story and, finishing early, he stopped in Manhattan to photograph the release party of Christie Brinkley's new perfume. That evening, as we walked out of the Helmsley Palace onto Madison Avenue, I breathed in the exhaust of the buses and taxis clogging the street, mixed with the distinctive sugary smell of honey-roasted peanuts. Just as I was reveling in the aromatic brew that brought up memories of leaving work late to scoot to some party or another, Robb began coughing. "Jesus, I hate this place," he said. "I don't know how people live here." How different we were, I thought. I chose to ignore that most of the time, but our perfectly opposite, simultaneous thoughts that night couldn't be overlooked. Sometimes I wondered how we'd made it this far.

·

That August, with my morning sickness and fears of reemerging hickdom I was in no mood to work, but I had a story—on sleep habits—due for *Allure,* where I was still hanging on, barely, as a contributing editor. While our babysitter Juanita—whom we had hired full-time the previous year after returning from Provence—took care of Gus, I would sit at the keyboard in my office and stare at the screen, too drained to make my fingers move or come up with a coherent sentence. I spent most days sitting in the writing position, but not writing, until I finally gave up the sham and slid over to the sofa in the office for a nap with the two cats—Josie and Diego—we'd gotten a year earlier to combat a mouse infestation.

But despite the convenient excuse—"I'm doing research"—I never could manage much snooze time. Outside, a crew was installing a rainwater collection system on our house. This meant putting up gutters along all the eaves, including the precariously high and odd-shaped roofline of the screened-in porch, directing all gutters to various downspouts and then putting in piping from each downspout to a central collection spot about a football field away. The accumulated water would be stored in two silo-sized tanks that could hold eleven thousand gallons each. The crew would install a pump and a thorough filtering system, so that anytime we flushed a toilet, turned on a tap or a shower the water would be pulled from one of the storage tanks.

Robb was determined that we were going to use all our water from these tanks. He was almost pathologically concerned about water use, fearing that we, not to mention all the other inhabitants of the Hill Country, were taxing the water table with our wells. He was sure that if we just collected water from our roof during the rainy spells, we would have plenty of water to make it through any dry times. But in August in Texas, it's easy to convince yourself that it will never rain again.

Outside the crew was climbing on ladders and banging hammers and using something called a ditch witch to make a trench for the pipes in soil baked hard as plaster. Whenever they woke me up from a nap, I felt like the sleep witch—and I was embarrassed later when I saw the crew around town, worrying that they'd come up with a nickname for me that was even worse. But in my state that summer, I wanted them away from the house. Really, *I* just wanted to be away from the house. "I don't think I can spend another summer here," I told Robb. "We've got to have a plan for escaping this."

I actually had something of a plan already. Going from France to the Hill Country was such a letdown that I was sure I couldn't last. At every turn, it seemed, I was confronted with what to my newly Francophile self seemed backward and brainless. Soon after our return from Provence, while I was in an antiques store in the town of Fredericksburg—the tourist capital of the Hill Country—Gus began crying, needing to nurse. I sat down in the corner and fairly discreetly pulled up my shirt for him to latch on. Two older women walked by and their mouths were as big as manhole covers as they studied me. I knew that none of my actual bosom was visible, but I might as well have been a streaker. How awful for other women especially to act as if breastfeeding were fornication

I had also found something worse than the threat of scorpions and poisonous centipedes. The previous May, soon after Gus turned one, I was sitting on the screened-in porch, enjoying the rarest of pleasures—a Sunday *New York Times* on a Sunday morning. Robb had just flown in from San Francisco on a red-eye flight and had picked up the paper for me in the airport. As far as small tokens of love go, the Sunday *New York Times* topped almost everything. Gus was sitting on the stone floor of the porch playing with a tower of blocks, and suddenly I heard Robb overhead on the catwalk.

"Jeannie get Gus upstairs. *Now!*"

Without even thinking to ask why or to worry about the state of my Arts & Leisure section that just hit the floor, I snatched up Gus and ran up the metal staircase. "What? What?" I screamed once I'd gotten upstairs.

"Holy shit, look!" Robb was pointing down to a spot about ten feet behind where I had been sitting. There was a snake stretched out on the stone. "It's a rattler."

"Oh my God!" I cried. My head pounded considering all the awful possibilities that could have come to pass moments ago. It seemed that the worries I had about rattlesnakes after finding the snake skin in the barn a few years ago weren't unfounded. Robb paused for a moment than ran off to the garage. He came back with a shovel and a hoe. "What are you doing?"

Robb shushed me, then carefully crept up on the snake and dropped the shovel on top of it to stun it. Curiously the snake didn't move (later I learned it was probably groggy, having just come out of hibernation). Using the hoe, he cut off its head in one clean strike, and then asked me to bring him a jar, which I did without looking at the carnage near him. He placed the head and the rattle inside it and covered them with some powerful alcohol he'd brought back from Brazil. The jar was kept in our freezer and Robb would take great delight pulling it out to shock visitors.

Of course the incident upset me—rattled me, really—but in comparison to other disasters (real and perceived), I remained relatively calm. I had long ago devised a formula for domestic life with Robb. Crises only happened when Robb was out of town, and the farther away he was the worse the crisis. This event seemed to be the exception. In the back of my mind, I kept thinking, At least Robb's here. At least Robb's here.

For these and other reasons, I had resolved that I was going to somehow come up with enough money for a pied-à-terre in Austin. I'd mentioned my idea to Robb and he had wisely not put up a roadblock. I wanted to buy a duplex, keeping one side and renting out the other. I combed the real estate ads in the Austin paper, but I was shocked at how expensive any suitable option was. I was used to Robb financing such major items. Prices seemed different, unattainable, when I was thinking about my own money, of which there wasn't very much. A baby had a way of inhibiting writing output.

When I got pregnant again and was going to have the two kids I felt I needed to be complete as a family, I started fantasizing about getting Robb to move back to Austin. After two-and-a-half years, the Blanco rapport I assumed would come just wasn't materializing. Though I rarely kvetched out loud at this point (I'd made my own bed after all, plus I suspected that in others' eyes, my apparently cushy set-up negated my right to gripe), my stream of consciousness at times had the tenor—if not the humor—of something entitled Woody Allen in the Wilderness. It seemed unnatural, at least for me, and maybe even unhealthy to simmer so long on low disenchantment. After I have this baby, I thought, I could put my foot down. I will insist and Robb won't want to lose the kids and me. At least that's what I told myself to get through the summer.

Fortunately, I did have a more immediate—albeit temporary—escape coming up. We were leaving August 30 for ten days in Portland and Seattle. I'd never been to the Northwest, but I was attracted by their weather reports. I scheduled the trip for Labor Day weekend and beyond because through experience I knew that September was the cruelest month in Texas. A lifetime of programming told me that September should be cool. It was a fall month, for God's sake; temperatures in most of the country started coming off their perch in September. But not in Texas. The expectation that the long journey through June, July, and August should be rewarded with coolness made the heat of September all the more brutal. It was as if someone kept moving the climatic goalpost.

•

Our trip to the Northwest didn't turn out to be the respite I'd hoped for. Working on my sleep piece for *Allure,* I had interviewed a doctor who told me that people develop insomnia when they lose confidence in their ability to sleep. Trying to nod off on the second night at the Columbia Gorge Hotel, I was anxious. This was our first true vacation—no business strings attached—and being genetically careful with money and used to having magazines pay for his hotels, Robb had been making comments about the price of our room.

"This room's not that great, really," he said dismissively. "We could have stayed at a cheaper hotel down the way and come here for the breakfasts." The hotel was known for its glorious morning meals, with waiters standing on chairs to drip honey onto bowls of oatmeal.

He quizzed me about the cost of the hotel we were going to be moving to on the Oregon coast. With his fretting over money and my heightened hormonal sensitivity, I began feeling the need to justify choices I'd made planning the trip—from the kind of car we rented to any pricey restaurant we ate at. Suddenly, the joy I was imagining in our time away evaporated; instead, in the middle of the second night my stomach turned, both with the queasiness of early pregnancy and the fear that a multitude of small money battles lay ahead of us. And thinking of the article I'd just written, I strangely lost confidence in my ability to sleep.

"That means you'll just sleep better tonight," Robb said when I told him of my wakeful hours. "We'll go to bed early."

But the next three nights were almost completely sleep-free. I would be wrung out during the day, but when it was time to put my head on the pillow my eyes would spring open as if I'd been mainlining caffeine. Not being able to use any knock-out drugs, I would lie in bed and listen with envy to Robb's and Gus's lungs as they worked loudly and rhythmically. When I was in junior high, one of my track events was the long jump. I was quite good, but at one meet I scratched three times. After that I could never jump well again. I'd lost my confidence and ultimately gave up the event. I realized now that my brain had taken similar control of my body.

Finally, when I could stand it no more, I told Robb that I had to go home if I was ever going to rest.

"I know it has to be bad if you want to get back to Texas," Robb said with alarm. "Of course, we can go home." When I got to my own bed, away from whatever was plaguing me in Oregon, I slept soundly and long.

"I just think you're not going to be able to take the same kind of trips we took without kids," Robb said. "I think we need to find a cabin, a place where we can cook some meals instead of eating out for every one, and stay put. We can explore from one base."

I wasn't thrilled to have returned five days early. That was five more days of heat I'd have to endure. A week after I came back I had an appointment with my obstetrician, who chalked up the fiasco to pregnancy hormones. "They're very powerful and affect people in different ways," she explained. "You should be better now that you're past your first trimester."

It's true that my equilibrium returned, but in one way I was worse off. Upon our return, I discovered that we had become even more isolated. Because of some technological snafu, our satellite dish wasn't broadcasting many channels, such as PBS, which meant I was missing the *NewsHour* right in the middle of the release of the Starr Report. I also missed the World Series, which I always loved watching. The blackout seemed a metaphor for my life in the country. There were so many amenities I had given up already, I couldn't stand to lose one more.

Yet our satellite shutdown offered a plus: I wrote a piece for the *New York Times* headlined, "Deep in Texas, News Anchors and Teletubbies Are Missing," which included a photo of me reading to seventeen-month-old Gus. The story was about our TV-network-less plight and other challenges of living in the country in the modern age, such as a 1 p.m. FedEx cutoff. "Before the phone company upgraded our lines," I wrote, "we would occasionally think a vacuum cleaner had called when we picked up the receiver."

It was my second *published* piece in my revered paper; after my magazine story missed the light of print because of my trip to Nepal, the Travel section ran an essay of mine about trekking through the Himalayas. Once the current piece ran, I received e-mails and calls from friends and editors, which confirmed in my mind both the power of my favorite paper and the potential lost by not having enough worthy material to write for it regularly.

After two months, I was able to get my TV stations back on. Other patches of brightness included a class I had started taking Gus to called Music and Movement. There I met two moms who became something like friends. One was originally from New Jersey and one from Colorado. They seemed even unhappier in Blanco than I was. But maybe it was because late fall in the Hill Country puts a lot of people in a funk.

During deer season, the first of November to the end of December, the town became a disquieting convergence of camo and ammo. I watched men clad in a khaki approximations of undergrowth loading up on beer at the convenience store (which posted photos of hunters—even kids—with their kills that looked like gruesome versions of prom pictures), driving old pickups with seats mounted on a homemade, six-foot perch in the back bed and strapping their stiff, bloody quarry on the front of their vehicles. I hated the tinge of death that descended on the town. The early morning or twilight stillness was often broken by the *pop-pop-pop* of gunfire. I might as well be in Bed-Stuy, I thought. We didn't dare go out on our evening walks without neon-orange crossing-guard vests, and even then we avoided any routes near the property line. One neighbor across the creek had a deer feeder set near our shared fence, but refused to move it when Robb called to say it was too close to our land. I thought back to the savvy of the neighbors who objected to our "No Hunting" sign and every year prayed that the only victims would be the hoofed kind.

That particular fall, I had something more to set me off—our favorite restaurant, the Chandler Inn, closed. "No more crème brûlée," I said to the other moms in the music class. (I actually used that line in a letter to the local paper lamenting the loss of the restaurant, which surely was fodder for some yuppie jokes around town.)

However, in the closed-door-open-window nature of life, a new restaurant debuted soon after on the Blanco square in the same building that had once housed the old general store. On the Friday after Thanksgiving, the Hardscrabble Café threw a grand opening party—the same day that the town always celebrates the lighting of the white Christmas bulbs that drip from trees around the square and drape over the courthouse. As Robb and I watched Gus convulse happily to the beat of a Zydeco band at the party, I noticed another couple with a boy that looked to be Gus's age. They had a bohemian look that told me we might have something in common. They certainly didn't seem like most other parents I had met in Blanco. Dads wearing Stetsons and with Skoal in their back pockets, the round cans leaving a permanent impression in the denim. Moms with fluffy hair and tight, Rocky Mountain brand jeans. I approached the couple, and hoping that I didn't sound too desperate or too much like a stalker, I said, "Your son looks like he's the same age as mine. Can I meet you?"

Their names were Sally and Alan, and their son was Josh. She had a graduate degree in social work and a job as an assistant to a midwife in Blanco. He
was a brewmaster at a new brewery that was located in the basement of one
of the buildings around the square. In the summer, the whole family left for
Alaska, where Alan's family had been salmon fishing for decades. Leaving the
party, we found that our cars were parked near each other. They had a small
black truck with a bumper sticker I considered very brave in these parts: Texas
Democrat. I had been told that in rural Texas you didn't proclaim yourself as
a Democrat. Instead you used the code word Independent, to preserve the
peace and the integrity of your car and mailbox. Yet here were Alan and Sally
standing up to the right-wing hegemony. I was smitten.

On the drive home from the square that night, I told Robb how happy I
was to meet a mom I thought I could relate to. We saw Sally and Josh often after
that, maybe two or three times a week. I loved being able to meet her at a moment's notice at the Blanco State Park, which hugged the cypress-lined Blanco
River, or at the Pecan Street Café for a cup of tea. I adored my Austin friends,
but I craved moms I could see more spontaneously and more regularly.

On New Year's Day, Alan and Sally were among the twelve couples we
invited for a party we called Game Day. The couples competed against each
other in egg toss, horseshoes, and cards, with the winning twosome taking the
kitty of $360. I had once heard a saying that what you do on New Year's Day is
how you'll spend the rest of the year. We wanted to set the tone by playing on
New Year's Day, hoping that for all of us the coming year would be filled with
fun. However, that was not to be for me.

•

One child was sucking on my breast. The other was pulling off my sock and
putting it in his mouth. The teakettle had been whistling on the stove for five
minutes. The phone was ringing.

Outside, however, on this March morning 1999, all seemed serene. Along
with Robb were my parents—visiting from Tennessee—two neighbors, and
two friends from Austin who supposedly had come out to see one-week-old Jeb
McCoy Kendrick, whose name we had decided upon after I rejected Robb's
first three choices—Geronimo, Rufus, and Atlas. At least I had veto power in
one area and saved my poor child from years of playground hazing.

The seven of them were digging holes in the field in front of our house—

the field that surrounded my gorgeous Thinking Tree—and inserting in them plants the size of large pinecones. Feeling like a penned-up dairy cow, I watched them laughing and chatting as they knelt in the limestone dirt.

After Robb's experiment with plant varieties the previous summer, he found a wholesale nursery that specialized in herbs and asked them to grow two thousand lavender plants of the *lavandula intermedia* variety. The owners of the nursery were accustomed to selling maybe a thousand lavender plants a year to garden stores across the region, but they agreed, making space in their greenhouses for the extra lavender. Because the variety that Robb liked was a hybrid, it couldn't be grown from seeds. They had to find a source for cuttings, which they would grow into four-inch-tall plants ready to go in the ground.

I wasn't happy that Robb was going through with this lavender farm business. First, I didn't think he had done enough research on how to grow lavender or on what he would do with the crop once it reached maturity—which we were told would be in two years. His response was to tell me that the French farmers had assured him that lavender needed very little care. "If you baby it, you'll kill it," was their advice.

Robb had called the Texas Department of Agriculture and Texas A&M University to get information about farming lavender in the state, but he didn't learn much. As far as the ag experts knew, no one was growing it. On his own, though, he learned of other people who had a crop. One was a winery about twenty minutes from us; they had just planted their lavender but were not having luck getting the plants to grow. Toward the town of Fredericksburg was a large farm that grew the Hill Country's famous wildflowers—bluebonnets, poppies—and sold their seeds. Robb had heard that the owner was testing lavender. When Robb approached him with questions, the owner was secretive. He acknowledged that he had planted some varieties but would tell Robb nothing more.

"I guess I'm just going to have to dive in myself," he had said before ordering the two thousand plants from the nursery.

My main objection to the lavender farm was that I felt it was tying us more firmly to the country, interfering with my fantasy that we would one day move back to Austin. What's more, in my mind, it was just one more thing for me to take care of while Robb was racking up frequent flier miles. I imagined myself out in the field, my two babies in tow, weeding plants or laying down drip tape or some other labor that I was entirely unsuited for.

No, I must resist, I told myself. I will not have anything to do with the lavender.

A day earlier, Robb and my father had begun to lay out the field, which Fred no longer leased. Robb consulted his notes from the French farmers. He even asked Ariane—who had come to Texas to go to college after meeting us in Provence—to call Daniel to confirm some information. My dad and Robb were planning to stretch out string in the field every five feet—the row spacing that Daniel suggested. But they had a disagreement over whether the rows should run horizontally or vertically across the field. Robb ended up calling a PhD in botany in Blanco, who with his family had a successful business growing cut flowers, sold mainly to Central Market in Austin. He advised Robb that the rows should follow the slope of the land, which supported Robb's opinion.

When Robb and my dad came in for lunch, they were still tussling over the direction of the rows, politely, of course, since they were in-laws. I decided I didn't want to get in the throes of it and took Jeb downstairs for a nap. As I sang "A Bushel and a Peck" to Jeb (a song from *Guys and Dolls* my mother had sung to all of us), I heard them in an excruciating analysis of erosion potential. In the end, the rows were laid out north to south, with each starting at the top of the field, closest to the house, and running straight toward the road and the Blanco River. Robb must've won, I thought, as I looked out the window before dinner.

On planting day, a Saturday, Robb and my dad were joined by a couple who lived down the road, our friends Roger and Norma Felps. They knew most everything about Blanco and its history, and she was born in a house that had once been on the property, not far from the barn. The house was torn down in the Eighties, with the wood being used to build a new house closer to the Blanco River. They were kind people, who were fascinated by what we'd done to the barn and fond of the boys—she'd babysat for me on several occasions when Juanita couldn't work because of a broken leg. They were especially interested in the lavender project because it was something different, and excitement of the agricultural variety was just their fancy.

"Oh, they've started!" my mother declared that Saturday morning when she entered the kitchen and peered out the window.

"Yes, the great lavender project is under way," I said with a laugh. My mother squinted for a while out the kitchen window, past the fingers of sun poking through the branches of the oak tree next to our house.

"I'm going to see if they need any help," she announced. She'd been gone for about an hour when my friends from Austin arrived. Mary Ellen and Patti had come to bring gifts for Jeb and visit with me, but soon their interest was pulled outside too. Mary Ellen, who had been talking to Robb, brought her gardening gloves. Like most people who heard about Robb's project, she thought it was brilliant.

"I want to get in on this on the ground floor," she said. The thought that maybe I *was* a killjoy, as Robb had charged, entered my mind. How come everyone else was salivating about this new venture except me?

That morning Mary Ellen and Patti also went out—"just for a bit," they told me—to help put some plants in the ground, and they'd been gone a while when my teakettle began whistling. At first I sat calmly, waiting for Jeb to finish nursing, but then Gus began demanding a sippy cup of *leche*.

I jumped up with Jeb, tucked like a football across my chest, still sucking away. I stepped over Gus, playing with a small piano with my sock hanging out of his mouth, and finally turned off the burner. I lifted the kettle, but almost all the water had boiled out. I haven't even gotten a cup of tea this morning, I thought, as I slammed the kettle back on the burner. The jolt made Jeb flinch in my arms and knocked the waiting mug—with the unused tea bag slung expectantly over its side—off the edge of the stove. After releasing a string of fierce curses, I realized it would be impossible to pick up the pieces with Jeb still busy at my breast. I would let someone else clean it up, someone like the father of these boys or my mother who had insisted she would help me with the kids. When they finished playing farmer, I thought, one of them could do it. Trying to keep Jeb comfortable in one arm, I managed to fill up Gus's sippy cup with milk, only spilling a few drops. Screwing on the top was a different matter. I shifted the cup to the hand that was under Jeb's bottom and then carefully, slowly turned the top with my free hand.

For another thirty minutes I sat in the house, cooing to lovely Jeb, who looked so different from Gus. His face was long, his eyes drooped slightly on the outer edges. At times, he reminded me of Robb's father, which was only disconcerting when I was nursing him. As Gus had been as an infant, Jeb was bald. Gus's blond hair had only started to come in when he was one. At two, it was long enough for a first haircut, which he'd gotten right before Jeb's birth. Now as Gus sat in his highchair for an early lunch—throwing his tortellini to Weegee—he had a classic little boy cut, long and straight on top, shaved close on the sides.

"Gus, eat your pasta," I commanded. "Don't throw it."

"Beegee lika da pasta," he answered. I hooted at his words, making a mental note to tell Robb; he sounded as if he'd learned English from Chef Boyardee.

Getting antsy, I decided to take the boys out for some air and—as much as I hated to admit it—to see how the planting was going. I put the boys in a double stroller and pushed them out to the field. Gus, who'd insisted on putting on a blue fleece hat with ear flaps, was kicking his feet in the front perch; Jeb was lying down after I'd folded the backseat flat and was enthralled with the blue-and-white-checked hood overhead.

When I approached, Robb was on his knees in the caliche digging holes along one of the strings he and Daddy had tied up. Mary Ellen and Roger were digging too. Mom and Patti were plopping the plants in the holes and covering up the roots with dirt. My dad and Norma were carrying plastic trays full of plants from the side of the driveway out to the action.

"Come on, Jeannie, plant a few," Mary Ellen called excitedly.

"No way, I just had a baby," I responded as I parked the stroller in the shade and picked up Gus from the front.

"Hey, lots of women around the world work in the fields after having babies," Robb said as I got closer. "They stop working when they go into labor, have the baby on the side of the field, and within a few hours are back at work."

"And this is a good thing?" I asked. I put Gus down and he ran up to Robb, throwing himself flat against his bent back.

"Hey, buddy," he said, stopping to kiss him on the cheek.

"Were these by chance the same women you'd seen in China and Haiti doing squats to help their labor along?" I asked.

"Here." Robb handed me a plant.

I rolled my eyes. "Okay, if it will make you happy to have your wife laboring in the field with you." I bent over slowly, my crotch still swollen from Jeb's fast, train-through-a-tunnel delivery the previous Sunday. The pain made me decide I should just drop to my knees quickly instead. Into the chalky earth. I plopped the plant into a hole Robb had dug and pushed dirt over the roots. Someone handed me another plant and while I was down I installed three more. Then I rocked back onto my feet and slowly rose, brushing the dirt off Robb's jeans, which I'd hijacked since I could fit into nothing else right then.

"Okay, that's enough," I said. "I now feel a sisterhood with all those poor women who are forced right back to work after giving birth. God bless them."

I led Gus up the field, toward the parked stroller. Mary Ellen and Patti joined me for a walk down the county road, which led to a dairy farm and along which we passed newly bloomed bluebonnets huddled in dense bunches, each patch a Manhattan island of indigo-and-white skyscrapers.

•

This summer I'll do it better, I thought. My Texas escape plan would be smarter than the year before. I wasn't going to stay in hotels or move from place to place. I'd seized upon the idea of going to Tennessee to hole up with my parents for a few weeks. The trip would be cheap and I would have plenty of hands to help with the boys. I had enough money to take a luxurious four-month maternity break thanks to *Allure*. The magazine had paid me a lump sum for four stories that according to my contributing editor contract I should have written, but the editors never assigned me, probably because I had lost all beauty credibility (or maybe it was those dirty Cynthia Rowley shoes they saw me in). I was anything but alluring in my present post-baby state and my rural environment. About the only time I saw the working end of a mascara wand was when Gus was using one to write on a wall. I'd given up on manicures because life out here meant my hands were constantly being cut on barbed wire or briars or bitten by exasperatingly ubiquitous fire ants or scraped while cutting baby cedar trees with Robb. If my nails weren't broken to the base, they had thin sickle-moons of dirt under them. The calluses on my heels were as tough as beef jerky, an unfortunate consequence of my newly rediscovered and almost unconscious habit of going barefoot—another sign of my regression. When I was growing up I had gone shoeless so much that my soles were thick enough to run on gravel painlessly.

I was planning to leave for Tennessee right after July Fourth and return at the end of the month. Three weeks out of Texas. It wasn't Provence—poor Jeb was getting a second-class maiden voyage—but it was the best I could do. The month of June was unusually cool and rainy in Texas and once, driving home from Fredericksburg, I rose up over a hill near an unmanned roadside cart of home-grown vegetables for sale under the honor system and was struck by the beauty of the deep green fields, adorned with round hay bales that looked like giant rollers wound with blond hair. I had a passing thought that maybe this year I didn't need to escape.

With the nicely spaced bouts of rain, Robb's lavender plants had almost doubled in size in three months. Neighbors and locals constantly asked us what we were growing in our field. The plants—nubs all in a row—looked lonely in the expanse of brown dirt and couldn't help but attract curiosity.

"It looks like rosemary," several people said to me. Others asked if it was sage and a few guessed, with a wink, that it was pot.

"What in the world do you do with *lavender*?" they would invariably ask when they learned the plants' identity.

"It smells good," I'd tell them, trying to make sure my smile showed patience, not the condescension of a New Yorker who once met regularly with executives at beauty companies. "You use the oil in soaps and perfumes."

At this point, the women would grow more interested. But the men would contort their faces as if I were talking about a crop of skunks stuck tail-up in our field; they seemed to find the idea of a girlie-girl plant in the middle of cattle country offensive. The whole enterprise seemed too *French*. Such attitudes were more reason for me to want to get away.

•

While planning the trip, I worried most about the flight, about getting to Tennessee, though it was actually the *being* there that caused the problem that led to a life-altering turnaround. I kept thinking, How do I manage on my own with two kids, carry-ons, diapers, snacks, runny noses, temper tantrums? I knew mothers did it. I had seen them in the airports. But they always looked as if they'd been dragged behind a truck for a few miles. At least Jeb was nursing and I could just plug him in if he got restless—feeding schedule be damned.

Once we were on our way, Jeb stayed connected at all times in his Snugli. Gus, however, ran amok—throwing potato chips at a man one row back, kicking the seat in front of us, screaming that his ears hurt during takeoff. If that wasn't bad enough, a flight attendant most unhelpfully told me I needed to control my son. "Yeah, I'll do that, if you nurse my baby," I wanted to say.

On the commuter flight from Cincinnati to the Tri-Cities Airport in Tennessee, Gus screamed one line over and over as we taxied to the runway: "I wanna go peepee outside! I wanna go peepee outside." One of Robb's favorite privileges of country life was peeing outside the door. To help get Gus out of diapers, Robb would take him into the front yard to "water the plants," as Gus called it. I was sure we were raising a feral child when one afternoon at a children's festival at the art museum in Austin, I saw Gus pull down his shorts on the patio. As I ran up to him, Gus announced proudly, "I got good p eth i," referring to PSI, which is how Robb complimented a strong and high arc of pee.

When Gus was having his fit on the plane, I was at first appalled, but after his twentieth refrain I began laughing with everyone else—the kind of mad-woman cackle that is known only to mothers who suddenly are blessed with the insight that it couldn't get much worse. When we arrived at the airport, I stood at the top of the stairs down to the tarmac—no jetway for this tiny plane—and saw my parents on the other side of the glass window. I placed my right index finger on my temple and pulled the imaginary trigger.

•

The first week at home was a delight. I loved being in the mountains again. Driving from the airport, we crossed a ridge from which you could see miles to the north, into Virginia. Spread out on the horizon were lines of mountains, each successive range a lighter shade of purple-gray, as if made by a rubber stamp running out of ink. We drove down a winding road that I had once flown down on bikes with my two older brothers, going much too fast for the many curves, but I had squealed the whole way.

I was thrilled to see my parents' mocha-brown split-level with cream-colored shutters that will always be home to me in the purest sense of the word. The house sits on a sloping corner lot under a canopy of trees so thick that my father once cut down twenty-three of them in the front yard and no one could tell the difference. The thick shade overhead meant that while we were growing up we never used air-conditioning. We had simply kept our windows open, letting in cool mountain air and a cacophony of crickets—which I would be reminded of later, strangely enough, by the thumping, rhythmic *cha-chung, cha-chung* of subway wheels passing over seams on the tracks. Even though my parents had gotten central air after I'd gone off to college, it was the climate that allowed us to exist air-conditioning free that I was thinking of when I decided to come here.

Indeed, the temperature was a bit cooler than in Texas, but I had forgotten about the humidity, which unfortunately made up for any savings on the thermometer. During that first week back—when we went joyriding in "my" VW convertible, swam at the country club pool, and visited with my older sister at her house, a mile from my parents—I wondered how we ever survived the summer stickiness growing up.

I'd forgotten something else about being home—how when I was at my parents' house I became the person that my family had already labeled me as. Even though I had an almost embarrassingly normal and happy childhood, I did become known as the black sheep, the one pushing the edges of my parents' patience. I was not an easy child, apparently. While we were growing up, Mom used a pre-Cuisinart contraption to do her chopping that required striking a handle to bring down the blade on the target food. My mother would thump fiercely and say, "This is for Jackie," referring to my eldest brother. She would lighten up for Janyce and Jeffrey, the second and third children. Then she would pound away like a jackhammer. "And this is for Jeannie." My younger siblings, Jimmy and Judi, also got the soft treatment.

I hadn't gotten any gentler on my parents' nerves since leaving home. I hadn't lived like my parents had—or like my older sister, who was married at age twenty-one. I had majored in journalism when my father had hoped for a female engineer in the family; I had moved to Manhattan against my parents' wishes; I had dated too much and too long, and lived with one man, then another. Yes, I was married now and a mother; I had a successful career and had never appeared on *America's Most Wanted,* but your parents' house is invariably a time warp that you step into at your own risk.

During my second week home, my younger sister, who, like my older one, is sweet, came to visit with her two daughters, who are the same ages as my boys. I loved that our children could be together, but I began to sense something disturbing. I had an acute feeling that my children were inheriting my label. Being at home could certainly have been playing tricks with my mind, but I felt that with the arrival of my sister's daughters, my boys couldn't do anything right. They, like I had long been, were now thought of as trouble. Gus was too rowdy, too noisy. He wasn't eating as well as Anna, my sister's eldest. He wasn't sleeping as well, either. Actually neither boy had been sleeping well in the new setting—a problem that took on new urgency when my sister arrived. I didn't want them to wake up her girls, who of course mostly slept through the night.

I became obsessed with their sleeping habits and sleep in general, which I wasn't getting very much of. And one night ten days into my trip, it happened. I was trying to go to sleep but my stomach felt like a chemistry experiment gone bad—I was remembering a tantrum Gus had that day that seemed to disturb my mother. When my heart started thumping like a bongo in my brain, it struck me that this was exactly how I felt when we were in Oregon a year earlier, when I had lost my confidence to sleep. Simply making this connection seemed to doom me. My mind wouldn't let go of it, and the more I worried the more awake I became. After a couple of hours, I bothered my mother for Tylenol PM, but that was like throwing tissue balls at a dragon. I didn't sleep the entire night; I was awake to hear my boys' every grunt and turn, to hear the air conditioner churn on seemingly every five minutes.

The next morning no one could understand why I hadn't slept, but in the afternoon they left me alone in the house so I could nap. Not a moment of sleep fell upon me. The next night was even worse and the next. Three nights without sleep and I thought sanity was slipping from my grasp. Suddenly the idea of surrendering to sleep seemed as arduous and impossible as building a house on top of Everest. During the day, I mainly sat in the house with the boys and tried to figure out what merciless blockade had gone up in my brain to prevent sleep.

On the morning after three wakeful nights, my mother and I went on a walk with the boys in a stroller. As we made our way up the hills and down, she updated me on news of families who lived in various houses we passed, families I knew from my years in high school as a newspaper delivery girl. We got to one pretty brick house with geraniums in the front beds among outcroppings of gray rocks, and my mother shook her head. She told me that the oldest son of that family had had a successful career in Charlotte, North Carolina, but then suddenly suffered a nervous breakdown. He ended up losing his job and his wife and now he lived at home with his mother.

"No one can figure out what happened," she said. The story made me shudder. Maybe this is what happened to him, I thought. Maybe this, what I'm going through, is what a nervous breakdown looks like. I'd always thought nervous breakdown meant crumpling up in a ball, unable to move. But now I began to believe it actually meant that you couldn't sleep, couldn't function, couldn't take care of yourself and your kids.

That afternoon, I called my obstetrician in Austin for some relief. She prescribed Ambien, a powerful sleeping medication that she said wouldn't harm Jeb through my breast milk. My older sister kindly offered to let me stay at her house, away from the crowd at our parents'. With Jeb sleeping in her room, I took half an Ambien in the evening, and Janyce—the professional mother—brought Jeb to me when he woke up for his feeding. Then I took the other half and slept some more. The problem was that the next day I felt like an android; I was groggy, still sluggish from the drugs. The next night, I pumped some milk for Janyce and I took a whole Ambien and slept most of the night—five hours. How I longed for a normal eight-hour sleep.

The curse of Ambien, I discovered, was that it made me more unstable during my waking hours. When I went with Gus and Janyce's son John to a petting zoo, I trembled the whole time like a drying-out druggie. I was a midday zombie who couldn't control my emotions, my thoughts, my body. My mother and Janyce were picking up the slack by taking care of the boys. I had always prided myself on being somewhat levelheaded, but during this period I learned how it felt to be ensnared in a psychotic quicksand.

I wanted to leave immediately but I didn't know if I could do what it took to reschedule my flight home. The task seemed completely beyond my capabilities. The other complication was that I had made a big fuss about a party for my parents' 70th birthdays, which we'd arranged for the third Saturday in July. My two brothers who lived in Virginia—my eldest brother, Jackie, and my younger brother, Jim—were driving down for the event, which meant we'd all be together except for my brother Jeff in Houston. I was determined to hang on for a few more days.

Finally, I found the energy to call the airlines and reschedule my tickets for the day after the party, a Sunday. I told my parents that I simply wasn't well enough to last any longer, that traveling with the boys had proved too much for me. My mother was hurt that I was leaving early, but I couldn't worry. I knew that it was a matter of survival. I was dismally aware that I was fulfilling my destiny, taking my assigned place in the family. The past had recaptured me. I was once again the troublemaker. I just hoped that I could compensate with a nice birthday party.

The Friday night my brothers arrived, I hugged Jackie's neck as if he were a life preserver. I felt safe with him—the two of us having the same agitator label and both, not incidentally I believe, being the only staunch Democrats in the family. I began crying as I clung to him.

"You look awful," he told me.

"I know, I know," I whispered violently. "I don't know what's happened to me. I'm so scared." I told him I was leaving on Sunday, that I had to get home so I could sleep. "Two more nights," I said. "Two more nights." We were standing in my parents' kitchen when I suddenly became dizzy. I was always a little off kilter in their kitchen because the countertops seemed so much lower than they were in memory. But this was something different. "I've got to sit down," I said, and as I lowered myself, it felt as if the floor was rising up faster than I was moving down. The next thing I knew I was lying on the brown-and-gold-flecked linoleum floor weeping. "I can't do it."

"What can't you do?" my brother asked gently.

"I don't think I can make it home." The thought of navigating the Atlanta airport with Gus and Jeb in my present condition was terrifying. I was sure I didn't have the strength or the wits to handle the vagaries of such a trip.

"That's why kids have two parents," my brother said. "Call Robb."

Though Robb knew I was having a hard time, he didn't know the extent of it. I hadn't wanted to sound too fragile; I hadn't wanted him to think that motherhood had blown all my circuits. I reached him in Arizona, where he was shooting a story for a travel magazine.

"Listen, I really need your help with something," I said, fighting back tears. "I can't make it home with the boys on my own."

"What do you mean?"

"I mean that I don't feel strong enough to get them through the airport and get them on a plane and keep it all together during the flight. I absolutely can't manage." I hated to speak those words, to cry uncle. I had always thought motherhood would make me happy. I had pushed for it to fill out my life. In my mind, the children were mostly my responsibility because I had wanted them so badly. Now I couldn't fulfill my part.

"What do you need me to do?"

"You know I would never ask you to interrupt an assignment unless it was an emergency. I've never asked before. But I need you to meet me in Atlanta on Sunday morning and fly with me home." I don't think he heard the last part of the sentence, strangled as it was in tears of desperation.

"Okay, sweetheart. If that's what you need."

Just the thought that I was going home and would be able to hand the boys over to Robb in the airport got me through the next two nights, and my parents' party, which was only a shadow of what I had originally planned. My younger brother, Jim, a chef, made a spectacular cake with ice cream in between the layers, but the rest of the dinner was merely hamburgers and coleslaw. "It's not what we eat, it's having you all together that's important," my father said when I apologized. With his Irish blood, Daddy believed that a good party needed only two ingredients—family and alcohol.

The next morning my mother and Jackie took me to the airport. My mother said she felt terrible that I had had such a rotten time. I insisted that it wasn't her fault, but I couldn't offer any explanation for the events that had left my body so wracked with exhaustion and pharmaceuticals.

Robb was waiting at the gate at the Atlanta airport, and I was never happier to see him. I threw myself into his arms as Gus tugged on his pants and Jeb cried from the commotion. In the airport and then later on the plane, I could feel his eyes on me, as if he were trying to piece together the puzzle of my strange behavior and haggard appearance. Robb held Jeb on his lap the whole way, and Gus sat beside him. I tried to read an article in the Sunday *New York Times Magazine* about couples trying to conceive girls, but I couldn't concentrate nor could I see because of the tears clouding my vision. I cried because I was so happy that I was going home, that I had endured this most awful stretch of my life—truly—and because I felt like an utter failure as a mother. Reading about women worrying about the sex of their child reminded me of when I thought not getting pregnant was the worst thing that could happen. But now with two kids I saw that the worst thing was not being able to take care of them properly. As I put down the magazine and folded up in grief and embarrassment, I felt Robb's hand on my hair, stroking it sweetly, and I thought to myself that everything would be all right once we got home.

Driving up the county road to the house, I was acutely aware of how different I felt now than I had when I returned from France two years earlier. I didn't care that the fields were as brown as expanses of beach, that the creek was dry, that the radio announced that the temperature was 98. I was desperate to see the house; I sat with my face almost pushed against the glass, watching for glimpses of it through the skinny oaks. Then there it was—the mammoth structure in all its splendor. There too was my Thinking Tree and those tufts of lavender strung like lane markers in a swimming pool up and down the field. I turned to Robb and managed something resembling a smile. I realized it was the first time I'd ever been happy to be back at the house.

"We're home," I said with an exhalation that was half laugh, half cry. Now, I thought, I can sleep and return to myself.

CHAPTER SEVEN

Sun

*I too fell in love with lavender after traveling to Provence.
I have vowed to always grow the herb and have purchased many
candles and sachets trying to reproduce the fragrance that
can completely soothe my frazzled nerves.*

— GAIL WILCOX,
June 18, 2003

I thought I knew him. But I had to wonder that early August afternoon, eight days after returning from my Tennessee "vacation." Trying to cheer me up, Robb had taken the boys and me to a swimming hole about forty-five minutes from our house called Krause Springs, which is about as close to Hawaii as it gets in Texas. Water burbles out of a spring behind some reeds and flows into a man-made pool and then over a three-story cliff to a deep, clear pool below. Behind the waterfall is a shallow cave swimmers can duck into after passing through the curtain of cold water. The whole area is shaded by enormous cypress trees—one of which is hollowed out and is about the size of an average bedroom in a Manhattan apartment. Another holds a rope swing that takes those who dare far out over the swimming hole.

The frigid water meant Gus had no interest in using the taxi-cab yellow inner tube we'd brought; instead he was scurrying along a path near the man-made pool, collecting sticks that had fallen from the cypresses.

"Hey," I said to Robb. "Why don't you go off the board. Maybe you can get Gus interested in swimming." I was giving Jeb a bottle of formula since he wasn't getting enough nutrition from my boobs, which were weirdly deflated after my insomnia episode.

"He's having fun. Leave him alone."

"Come on. My dad used to do this dive that got everyone wet."

"I know he won't like that."

"Well, can you at least do a cannonball?"

Robb put down his book, and as he stood up, he hiked up his blue bathing suit. He called to Gus as he walked toward the diving board. When we had arrived earlier Robb had commented that you don't see many diving boards anymore, thanks to lawyers. He ran his palms over his hair as he stepped to the end of the board, where he tested its bounce. I wished Robb would hurry before Gus, who was watching his dad, lost interest.

Robb moved back to the base of the board, paused, then walked purposely forward, bounced hard on the end, and as I waited for the big dive or can opener, for something that propelled him forward, I realized that instead Robb had moved his head and shoulders up and back and his feet were following. His feet were above his head, which looked like it might hit the board. Next his feet were below him, then up again. He stretched out his arms, which pierced the water like a knife into a peach and his body trailed behind.

My first thought was that Robb had a secret stunt double, who had snuck onto the board when I wasn't looking. I was sure the real Robb was hiding in the bushes. It was the same discontinuity you feel in the ice skating scene in *The Bishop's Wife,* when you see Cary Grant close up holding hands with Loretta Young, then the camera pulls back and you see a man with identical clothes and dark hair, but suspiciously shorter and squatter, gracefully leaping around the rink and then spinning on the ice like a whirligig in a hurricane.

"What the—" I exclaimed when Robb surfaced. "Where did you learn that?"

Robb swam toward Gus, who was clapping. "Do it again, Daddy."

"How can I have known you all these years and not know you could do something like that?"

Robb pulled himself out of the water and headed back to the board. "You never asked."

"What else don't I know?" He looked at me saucily and went on that afternoon to do more one-and-a-half gainers like the first, also one-and-a-half front flips, back flips, and precise dives.

As we drove home later that afternoon with both boys asleep in their car seats, I told Robb how his heretofore unknown diving skills had made me forget for a minute that I wasn't feeling well. "How fun to be surprised like that. You know, after you find out there's no Santa, there aren't that many good surprises left. Most surprises as an adult are bad. Like an IRS notice, or something."

Robb shook his head. "You've just got to be open to surprises. Most people are scared of them. They'd rather be safe and comfortable than surprised."

"Well, I don't care how you look at it, what just happened to me was a bad surprise." I was referring to the escape that wasn't, which was still making me feel that the cheese was off my cracker, as a friend used to describe nutcases. That afternoon, I tried to cling to the good feelings of the swimming excursion because night was approaching, as it did every twenty-four hours, and knowing I was supposed to sleep filled me with terror. I was now as afraid of the dark as a six-year-old who had been watching horror movies.

Despite my expectations, I had not recovered just by returning to my own house, with my own bed, with my own Juanita to take care of the kids. I was shocked and panicked the first night I was back in Blanco that I still couldn't sleep. Something deep and inexplicable had taken hold of me and wasn't letting go. More and more, sleep seemed the most mysterious of conditions. How did people accomplish it? How had *I* for all those years? Since there seemed to be no simple fix, I was more distraught than ever the next morning when I called my obstetrician and explained my whole sorry story.

"It sounds like you've got a serious case of postpartum depression," she finally announced. "You need to get on an antidepressant."

I protested. "But I thought that happened right after you had a baby—not *four months* afterward." My obstetrician informed me that at any time in the first year, especially when you're nursing, hormones can hop off the track and take a nosedive into the abyss. She speculated that my lack of sleep and worrying about the boys' sleep were enough to get my hormones cockeyed and then it was a downward spiral after that. It sounded plausible to me, and so much better than a diagnosis of, Basically, you're a crackpot.

"I'll call in a prescription for Zoloft. It's safe to take while you're nursing," she said. "It'll take a while to get in your system, but then it should snap you out of this."

Snap me out of this. Was there really something that could do it? Would there really be an end to what I was feeling? I eagerly agreed to the Zoloft, even though I had in the past scoffed at antidepressants. I remember at a book club meeting back when I was living in Austin the subject of antidepressants came up and I called them a cop-out—only later to discover that half the women present were on them. Now, I was fully prepared to wolf down my words and, as Robb drove me to the pharmacy in Blanco, I realized that I would happily drag myself over broken glass to get them. Anything to give me peace.

While in Blanco picking up my prescription, I got a massage from a woman who owned a natural food store; she advised me to take borage oil and something called Bach's Rescue Remedy—a combination of calming herbs—to help with the depression. To restore my breast milk, she recommended an herb called fenugreek. I had lost so much weight and was so frayed that my boobs were as full and useful as pita bread. It's a wonder that Jeb didn't starve. A midwife I knew suggested I drink a live beer—one with active hops and yeast—to help with my milk supply. Luckily, the brewery that our new friend Alan worked for made a live beer. I was only too happy to buy a six-pack. I also loaded up on a homeopathic sleep aid a friend recommended called Calms Forte.

On the second night home, with my first dose—50 milligrams—of Zoloft starting its guerrilla war against my demons, I set up my bed on the foldout sofa in the office. Robb said he would handle the boys in the night so I could try to get a solid block of sleep. The Zoloft wouldn't be battling alone. I took my Rescue Remedy, my borage oil, and my Calms Forte. I had already drunk a beer and was sipping on a cup of Calm tea as I arranged my herbs and elixirs near the sofa bed in case I needed reinforcements in the middle of the night.

"You know lavender is good for sleeping," Robb said.

I smiled at his endearing attempt to help me and to promote the lavender at the same time. "That's right. But didn't we use up all our lavender stuff from France?" I slipped under the covers. "I hope this will have passed by the time those plants bloom. Maybe then the whole place will smell like lavender and we'll all be sleeping perfectly."

Having my sleep altar near my pillow, I felt more confident about getting through the night. It took a couple of hours, but sleep did finally come over me.

Though I only lasted three hours, I was ecstatic when I woke up at 3:30. It was the first stretch of Ambien-free sleep I'd had in about two weeks. I was so proud to have accomplished it without that drug. I thought that this must be how an impotent man feels when he finally achieves an erection without Viagra.

Each night, I slept a little longer, though I was still far from a full eight hours. My muscles ached deep within as if they'd extracted every drop of spare energy my sleep-deprived body could wring out. I was grateful for Robb's help—dealing with the kids every night, his sensitivity, his concern, which weren't always a given. Taking him away from work was, I knew, asking the ultimate, so mixed in with gratitude was guilt for making him endure this with me. I knew he wouldn't have limitless patience, which brought up a new worry. What if I didn't recover fully? What if I remained in this hobbled state? I thought ahead and pictured him divorcing me because he couldn't handle me any longer. I imagined him having grounds for taking the children because I was mentally impaired. I thought I might have to slink home like the neighbor's son in Tennessee, but how would I ever face my family? I was humiliated enough that they had witnessed my meltdown. This new concern spun out to the worst possible ending—living at home like a flunkee—left me sweaty and sleepless after five nights of progress.

When Robb first mentioned that he needed to get back to his assignment, I put on a brave act. "Sure, sure," I said. "I'll be okay." Fifteen minutes later he found me facedown on our bed in tears. I was sure the impatience that would lead to our divorce had begun. He sat down beside me quietly for a while as I wet the pillow that I was cognizant enough to notice smelled like grass and sun. For an instant, I was comforted to know that it had dried out on the clothes line. But only an instant.

Great, he gets to see me crying again, I thought, as the tears continued. I was tired of hearing myself cry, so I was sure he was doubly so. It occurred to me that I probably had cried more since having kids, or wanting to have kids, than I had in all my previous years combined. I thought back to the days when I refused to cry; I went my whole first year of college without crying because I was determined to be strong though I was staggering with homesickness. Now a veritable weeping machine, I was making up for those days.

"What's wrong?" Robb finally asked.

"I just don't know if I'm ready to be alone in this house, alone with the kids. I'm too scared that I can't handle it." God, I was such a hopeless case. Robb scooped me up into his arms and held me.

"You can do anything. Remember you had two babies without drugs."

"I can have a baby without drugs. But I can't fucking get through a day without them now," I said. "I'm pathetic."

"Shhhh!" he insisted.

"Physical pain isn't anything compared to mental pain."

Robb wondered if one of my girlfriends wouldn't be a better help to me than even he could be. As soon as he said it, I thought of Ellesor, my best friend from college, who was an antidepressant in human form. I knew she'd make me laugh again and the guilt of keeping Robb from his work would be gone. When I asked Ellesor to come babysit me, she immediately said yes, even though it meant leaving her husband for a week.

"Bo," she said, using the nickname for friend we always called each other. "I'm there. I'm your PPD EMT." PPD was her shorthand for postpartum depression. "You got PPD? You got OCD? You got ADD? You got FBI?" she said in her singsongy southern accent. "You got some other jumbly, bumbly bunch of letters? Just give me a call and I'll hop on a plane anywhere."

•

Ellesor flew in a couple of days after our trip to Krause Springs using Robb's frequent-flier miles. That evening I saw them in his office talking seriously, surely about me and what I'd become. When Robb left the next day, he hugged me hard. "Get better, okay?"

With Ellesor there and with the Zoloft slowly taking effect, the shackles began to loosen. My milk was coming back. I was sleeping longer stretches. At night, Ellesor would prepare me for sleep by soothingly reciting a relaxation drill she used at the end of the yoga classes she taught in South Carolina.

In the mornings, before it got hot, Ellesor and I went on walks around the property—sometimes with the boys and sometimes alone—trying to mow through my problem with talk. I called them my Walks with Ellesor. I told her she had a new career awaiting her. Combine her personal training with therapy. "Get your counseling degree and you'd have a goldmine," I told her. "Everybody is pressed for time. They could kill two birds with one stone."

One morning as we walked on the back of the property by the old stone chimney—the last remnants of a late-1800s homestead—I heard a rustle in the tall dry grass that had grown up around the chimney's base. It was followed by a canine outburst. Katy and Weegee shot off from my side, issuing high-pitched yelps that sounded as if they were coming from a record player stuck on the first syllable of "Yippee." The noise made Diego—our black and white cat who, like a dog, went on walks with us—wail and start up a tree. I immediately ran after the dogs, knowing what they were capable of.

"It's an armadillo," I shouted back when I saw their prey. The dogs were nipping at the armadillo as it ran into a grove of trees and flung itself into a depression in the ground under some tree roots. Emitting grunts of fear and exertion, the armadillo used its sharp claws to fling dirt behind it as it tried to dig itself deeper into the soil. The dogs were scratching at its back, but its bony, jointed armor protected it. I knew if the dogs continued they would flip it over and attack its white unprotected belly. I yanked the dogs away by their collars. Katy tugged ferociously, raising up on her back legs trying to escape my grasp.

"Eeew! That's an armadillo?" shouted Ellesor as she peered at the flailing animal. "It looks like a baby dinosaur. Eeew. It's got little hairs poking out of its back." After the armadillo ran off, I released the dogs, who immediately went back to sniff the site of their near-kill.

"Most people don't see armadillos alive, you know," I said to Ellesor as we continued our walk to the creek, past some long grass that had been tamped down, a sign that deer had been sleeping in that grove the night before. "You normally only see them squashed on the side of the road." For the remainder of our walk, I told her of other armadillo experiences—such as the time Juanita found one near the house and, wanting to get it away from Gus, picked it up by its tail and flung it over the fence like a frisbee. When we were almost back to the house, I stopped suddenly.

"Ellesor, oh my God. I went about thirty minutes without thinking about my stupid PPD." It was the longest stretch in weeks that my brain hadn't resorted to its angst-ridden default track.

"It means you're getting better, Bo."

·

By the time Ellesor handed me back to Robb, I was mostly restored. I wanted nothing more than to hole up with him and the kids on the property. I felt like a wildflower the boys loved called sensitive briar; it grew low to the ground and had a pink puff for a flower. When the delicate leaves were touched, they folded up like a fan, retreating from contact, going into themselves. Retreating into myself, that's what I needed to do.

Being at home—no matter if it wasn't the home I would have picked for myself—was calming, recuperative. I could have felt defeated. After all, the place I had been trying to escape had reached out halfway across the country and brought me back whimpering. But I didn't feel that way, maybe because of the Zoloft, which I'd been on for more than two weeks. Or maybe in some version of the Stockholm Syndrome, I was starting to see the world from my captor's point of view. But if I was a psychological prisoner of the place, I didn't mind.

I spent hours with the boys on the property, looking for the heart-shaped fossils Gus collected and occasionally finding a fossil conch shell—both kinds left millions of years ago when this part of Texas was underwater. One day when we ambled along the creek bed, I listened to the breeze through the far reaches of the cottonwood trees. It was as if a microphone had been put to the treetops and I wondered how I hadn't noticed the soothing swishing before. On many nights after Jeb was in his crib, we sat outside with Gus admiring the thickness of the stars, which looked as if glitter had been spilled across the sky.

On my daily walks—I would have preferred to run but I still didn't feel strong enough—I would stop at the Campsite and marvel at the view over the undulations of treetops as if I were seeing it for the first time. When fall came, the reds and golds of the Spanish oaks seemed more vibrant than usual, billows of color among the green clusters of live oaks, which didn't lose their leaves in winter. Though Texas isn't known for its fall colors, especially compared to the vivid spice-rack tones I grew up with in Tennessee, either my eye or the weather had changed that year.

Every other Friday, the Zydeco Blanco band—which we had first heard at Thanksgiving the year before—played on the patio of the Hardscrabble Café. Gus loved the jaunty music and every night they performed we went for dinner so that Gus could stand in front of the band and jiggle and shudder. The band members—made up entirely of guys living in Blanco—soon began referring to Gus as their biggest fan. We invited different friends out from Austin for every performance and I looked around at our table each time, laden with dishes of pork tenderloin and grilled tilapia and glasses of good wine, and thought that all was well. As long as I was sleeping, all was well.

•

That fall, a college friend of Robb's came to visit from Dallas with his girl-friend. We took them out to the Pecan Street Café for lunch, but it soon became clear they weren't enjoying themselves. Karen wanted a grilled cheese sandwich, but the waitress had explained that they didn't have a griddle. Karen snapped the menu out of her boyfriend's hand to take another look.

"I guess I'll have the chicken salad sandwich," she said with a pointed sigh.

"You know, this really is a nice place," I told her after the waitress left. "It's the only place for miles that serves cappuccino."

"No, it's not, Jeannie," she barked. "What kind of place can't make a grilled cheese sandwich?"

I could feel my face go hot and red like a stoked-up ember. I instinctively pushed my shoulders back, my chest up. How dare she be so unkind about one of the only tolerable prospects in Blanco's meager restaurant offerings? Later at home, I fumed to Robb about her stinging judgment. Robb agreed with me, but something about my rant made him laugh.

"Look at you, defending Blanco," he said. "Normally, you'd be right with her talking about how rinky-dink the town was."

I hated it when he was right, but I had to admit that that day he was. Something had shifted in me over the months since I returned from Tennessee, something I hadn't fully recognized until that moment. Could I be feeling some affection for Blanco? Was that why I was defending the town as if someone had insulted my family? It was a gasping revelation, like in *Gigi* when Louis Jourdan realizes that what he really feels for Gigi is love. At least I didn't break into song.

The truth was that even the part of living in the country I hated the most—the scorpions—no longer traumatized me. I had become so used to killing them that one day while talking on the phone with my friend Mary El-len I saw one scurry across the polished cement floor in the hall. While calmly continuing our dialogue about her rotten boyfriend, I stepped on it with my running shoe, got a piece of toilet paper, scooped up the squashed remains, and dumped them in the toilet. "Guess what I just did?" I said after I'd flushed. "I killed a scorpion without a droplet of sweat."

"Go girl," Mary Ellen responded.

Actually, I wasn't even scared of their sting any longer. I had been bitten three times and discovered it was a fleeting pain—more like a fire ant bite squared. Twice while walking to the bathroom barefoot in the middle of the night, I'd stepped on one and contrary to prior beliefs, my foot did not end up looking remotely like something fished out of a Chernobyl lake. One night while lying in bed talking to Robb I felt something fall from the ceiling above and hit my shoulder. The lights were out, so I rolled over to reach the switch. As I turned, I felt the sting on my upper back. Robb clicked on the light and there was the creature—looking as heinous as the one I spotted in the same bed after I'd brought Gus home from the hospital—but his ugliness had no effect on me. I brushed him off the bed then grabbed a shoe to end his three-dimensional days. After each attack, I had used an antidote suggested by a neighbor—a dab of Clorox or meat tenderizer, either of which neutralizes venom by breaking down its proteins, I was told. At least I now had advanced weaponry.

I no longer thought about convincing Robb to move back to Austin. I decided to save that battle till the boys were school age. Static was the last thing I needed at the moment. I was happy to be in my house, surrounded by my support network, and in any case, I couldn't conceive of leaving Juanita at that point. As much as anyone, she nursed me through my recovery, even though I was never able to explain in my minimal Spanish what had happened to me. She cooked for us—chicken mole, soups, pico de gallo—loved our boys as her own, and taught them Spanish, which thrilled Robb and me since we both wanted them to be bilingual. I also had Sally nearby to help me and take the boys at times to give me some relief on weekends when Robb was traveling. Over a four-day stretch when her husband was redoing their wood floors and Robb was out of town, I was grateful that she and Josh stayed with us.

I was so happy to be well and so terrified to go beyond my safety zone that I didn't dare spend the night anywhere else. When I had to go to Phoenix to write a story about a middle-class family living without health insurance, I made the trip in one day—thanks to felicitous flight schedules and time zone differences. The insane dash, which included pumping my breasts with a handheld motorized device while driving from the Phoenix airport to the family's house, left me exhausted, but at least I didn't have to sleep away.

The irony of feeling like I couldn't leave our place thanks to my efforts to escape it in July was not lost on me. But since I couldn't go away, I must have realized on some level that I had no choice but to learn to like it. "Holy Silver

Lining," I wanted to shout, like Batman's young ward, when I realized it was my g.d. PPD that provided the jolt I needed to feel the love.

Instead of venturing too far, I began throwing big parties to keep friends coming to me. On the Y2K New Year's, thirty people came to celebrate, including my parents, Robb's parents, my brother Jim from Virginia, and dear Ellesor, who returned with her husband. My pitch line to friends considering other events was that if the terrorists struck or Armageddon descended, we were where you wanted to be. We now had 55,000 gallons of rainwater storage capacity, we had a windmill we could hook up for electricity if necessary; we had space to grow our own vegetables and could hunt for meat. Other enticements were Juanita's homemade tamales and a T-shirt I had made that read, Y2K at BDR (for Bad Dog Ranch), next to an image of a lampshade-wearing dog. On the back we printed up guests' hopes or resolutions for the new millennium. My favorite was from a reggae-playing friend from East Texas, who called for "Less biscuits, more gravy."

All the guests except those who lived in Blanco spent the night with us. I loved house parties and with sofa sleepers and the boys' extra beds, we managed to fit ten adults besides ourselves in the house comfortably. That night, we had mattresses on the floor as well, and some people slept in tents on the property.

For Jeb's first birthday and Gus's third, I went as unabashedly country as *Hee Haw*. The theme was tractors. A grove of trees back near the creek was decorated entirely in green and yellow streamers and John Deere paraphernalia—tablecloths, plates, napkins. Robb hooked up a trailer to the back of his own John Deere and kids and their parents, who'd come from Austin and Blanco, were driven to the party site sitting in the trailer on bales of hay.

When the party was finished, all the guests stopped by the house to see the latest addition to our compound—our pool. The water was in but a crew was still putting in a deck around it, using stones dug from the bed of the large stock tank on our property. We had installed the pool up near our old metal windmill, next to the stone cistern where Gus and Jeb had been baptized. Robb had been reluctant to put in the pool because it was such an extravagance—financially and water-wise. "We didn't put in a whole rainwater collection system just to turn around and use thousands of gallons of water on a pool," he said. I had never wanted a pool before but I was insistent. I doubted I could leave Texas in the summer again, but I knew I couldn't endure the heat without help. Finally Robb gave in, not wanting a repeat of the previous summer's fiasco. To fill the pool, however, he was determined to use rainwater. He designed what he called a "rain barn," a low structure with a big expanse of roofing hidden behind trees uphill from the pool. When it rained, the water collected would be piped to a holding tank he had dug so that we could keep the pool topped off with that instead of well water. We also added an arbor near the pool—the top made from hog panel, a simple kind of fencing—so that we could have a shady place for a picnic.

The pool was lovely; we painted the walls a light gray instead of white, which meant that once the water was inside it appeared more like a natural blue-green pond, rather than a shocking turquoise (white pool walls intensify the blue). Tumbling out of the rocks to one side was a waterfall meant to echo the look of the cascade at the swimming hole at the back of our creek. The editors of *This Old House* magazine were so impressed by photos they assigned me a piece on the pool's creation. Much to Robb's annoyance, it was one of the few stories I had written since returning from Tennessee. Robb was anxious for me to get back at the computer and start earning some money. My only other articles since the previous summer were for either *Parents* or *Parenting*, both of which during the fall had asked me to be a contributing editor, with *Parenting* ultimately making the best offer.

"Oh God, now people will expect me to really know something about parenting," I said, feeling anything but an expert.

•

From the kitchen window I saw fifty people scuttling through the field near the year-old lavender plants. A friend with a nine-hundred-acre ranch had brought two ATVs, which his children were using to deliver full flats of lavender to the designated planters. We were in the midst of a planting party and Robb had called in every favor, hit up every friend to get the labor force needed to put in ten thousand plants—five times the number he'd installed the year before. His total crop would be twelve thousand plants spread over eight acres—fifteen hundred plants per acre, we had figured—and two fields (the one in front of our house and a side field near the pool). His first two thousand plants were thriving—they'd survived a summer drought, even after his irrigation system broke and a herd of Fred's angora goats jumped the fence.

The goats sampled the lavender then spit it out, like kids who had broken into their parents' caviar.

"No, deer don't like lavender. Even goats don't like it!" Robb exclaimed whenever curious friends or neighbors asked how the plants stood up to the deer—deer being the most common assassins of Hill Country gardens.

While planning his new field, Robb jokingly declared that he was going to be the largest lavender grower in the state, which shouldn't be hard, I pointed out, since there were only two other growers in Texas, as far as we could tell— the winery and also a retired couple near Fredericksburg, whom Robb had learned of only a few months earlier. (The owner of the wildflower farm apparently had decided not to pursue lavender.)

I knew that Robb was competitive, but I thought he was getting ahead of himself; I hated to see him spend $10,000 on this round of plants when he still didn't have a plan for the crop once it bloomed. But I didn't say anything. I wasn't going to battle over lavender. I was going to stay in the kitchen that day, making lunch. Food and beer were the only compensation Robb offered his crew.

I set up two long tables on our screened-in porch—covering one with the lavender tablecloth I'd bought in Provence—and filled them both with sandwiches, coleslaw, potato salad, chips, and Juanita's pico de gallo. I made chocolate chip cookies and my very own apple pie. I felt so domestic that I thought next I might cross-stitch a little saying about a happy home to hang in the bathroom. The workers who swarmed in for lunch included people I'd never seen before—high school students from Arlington who studied photography with one of Robb's best friends. Robb had also hired four Mexican guys, just in case his free work crew didn't progress quickly enough.

Our neighbors Norma and Roger, the veterans, were there again. "Back for more punishment?" I said to Norma that morning. We'd just been to their house a few weeks earlier so the boys could watch their forty-five baby goats gambol around the pasture, playing king of the hill on the rocks and butting their heads on their mothers' utters when they needed to nurse.

"How are those darling baby goats," I asked Roger, when he came in for lunch on planting day.

"Uh, well," he said, smiling nervously.

"Oh no. Not already?" Roger had told me when we visited that the babies would soon be sold off for *cabrito,* roasted goat, but I didn't think it would have happened yet. The baby goats Gus and Jeb romped with were likely hanging up skinned and naked in the window of some Mexican restaurant in San Antonio. We would not be telling the boys that story.

As the other workers came in for lunch, they talked animatedly about their day in the dirt; they seemed to view the event as the cousin of a barn raising.

"Do we get a share of the profits?" someone asked Robb, as he pushed a sandwich in his mouth with dirty hands.

"No, but all of you get as much lavender as you want once it blooms," he announced. He tilted his baseball cap back on his head, stuffed some chocolate chip cookies in the pocket of his jeans, which were stained with splotches of dirt at the knees, and headed back out.

I was still washing dishes when Robb ran up at about 3:15. "We're done," he shouted. I looked out the window and saw that most of the workers were heading toward the house; a few remained in the field picking up empty flat trays and plastic pots. The Mexican guys were riding on the two ATVs, two on each one, spraying each new lavender plant with water from a plastic cylinder. Soon, most of our guests were scrounging in the kitchen for more food or doing cannonballs in the pool.

When almost everyone had left that afternoon, Robb and I picked up stray pots and litter. "How does it feel to be the lavender king?" I asked.

Robb didn't answer. He bent down to inspect a plant; its leaves were tinged gray. "Hmm," he said. "I've seen a few of them like this. I hope they didn't sit out in the sun too long before we got them in the ground."

"I'm sure they'll perk up with some water."

But they didn't. In fact, they started looking worse. The next morning, I saw Robb pacing through the field hunched over, stopping every once in a while to stoop closer to a plant. "It looks like more are gray today," he reported. Making his rounds that afternoon and the next morning, he found that the grayness had spread like a San Francisco fog. Some were undeniably dead. He walked through the field tossing lifeless plants into a pile. Three days after the planting, 95 percent were gone. That was too many for Robb to remove himself. He hired the Mexican workers to return to clean up the carcasses.

"I don't know what was different this time," Robb wondered out loud after the extent of the devastation became clear. He asked this of me and others—the nursery owner who had provided the plants, Roger Felps, and the Blanco PhD with the cut flower farm. "Welcome to farming," the PhD snorted. "Don't quit your day job."

Robb talked to the agricultural extension agent in the area, who suggested he send some samples of the dead plants to Texas A&M for testing. The tests revealed that the plants had died from something called Rhizoctonia, a root fungus that develops in overly damp conditions, often in greenhouses. With this information, Robb called the nursery that had provided the plants and worked out a deal for compensation. The nursery owner couldn't absorb the whole cost, but would split it. Robb could either choose to get ten thousand replacement plants for $5,000 or five thousand free plants. Aware that we were out of favors to call in for another mass planting, Robb decided to take the five thousand plants, to be delivered in the fall for filling out the field in front of our house.

Frustrated enough at the monetary loss, Robb had to endure more discomfort every time he spoke with someone who had helped with the planting.

"How's our lavender doing?" they would invariably ask.

"Uh, not too well," Robb would respond. "We've had a little problem." He'd go on to explain about the fungus. Then he'd end with borrowed wisdom. "Hey, it's farming."

•

As summer approached, I tried to prepare myself psychologically for the heat, four whole months of it, since I wouldn't be escaping anywhere this year. To tolerate that which I'd normally run from, I camped out at our pool, spending huge chunks of the day there. We'd often cook out on the grill underneath the arbor, which was shady now that grapevines were growing over the top. I arranged for an instructor to come to our house to give swimming lessons to Gus and his friends.

With Robb's encouragement I did flips off the board—something I hadn't done since I was a kid. He also pushed me to try a back flip.

"A back flip is actually easier than a front flip," he called from the shallow end as I stood backward on the end of the board, looking out over the stone wall, down the slope toward the Blanco River.

"No it's not."

"Come on, Mommy," Gus yelled. He was playing on the stairs near Robb. Jeb was wrapped up in a towel on a lounge chair.

"You just jump up and kick your legs over your head then tuck into a ball," Robb added.

"Oh, is that all?"

With my arms out in front of me, I jumped up and, feeling as graceful as a Hell's Angel, tried to swing my legs over my head, tried to tuck, and only made it three-fourths around, landing on the water like a pancake on a griddle.

"Oooooh," Robb cried.

"Mommy, are you okay?" Gus asked.

"Just because it's easy for you doesn't mean it's easy," I said as I swam to the shallow end, my front side feeling like I'd sunbathed with a mixture of baby oil and iodine—something I stupidly did in high school. I tried a back flip many more times that summer; the best I ever managed was a 90 percent rotation. It wasn't pretty, I knew, but at least my feet were going in first.

Since I wasn't going to Austin as much, I was determined to find, or make, ways to engage the boys in Blanco. I was disappointed to learn that the local library—which was quite comprehensive considering the size of the town—didn't have a story hour. But when I met a former teacher and story-teller from Santa Fe, Lily, I asked her if she would lead one, and we began a regular Wednesday morning event. With my new link to the library, I was soon asked to be on the board of the Friends of the Library, and when I immediately found myself planning a program, I called the editor of *Texas Monthly*, a friend, who agreed to speak.

That fall Gus was three and a half and it was time I thought about his pre-school. Six months earlier, I had tried out a day care in town, hoping to send him two days a week so that Juanita could focus on Jeb. I left Gus there for an hour to see how he fared and when I returned, I found him in a supply room where glass jars and cleaning compounds were kept. No one had even noticed that he slipped into the room. Sally was sending Josh to a preschool affiliated with the Blanco Public School but wasn't happy with its don't-color-outside-the-lines mentality. In general, I was against public school, imagining it to be a mindless place more focused on testing, rules, and conformity than real learning. But what could we do out here, away from any real options?

Dissatisfied, Sally and I began talking about starting a Montessori pre-school, and soon our discussions included Lily, since she had a teaching back-ground and a daughter the same age. Through the fall, the idea of our own school remained a fantasy; we didn't quite seem qualified for such an adult task. But I had started to form the opinion that if you wanted something in a small town, you couldn't wait for it to appear. You had to do it yourself. I hated complainers and I had grown to hate hearing myself complain about what Blanco didn't have. My new philosophy was: Work with what you've got.

Replacing my condescension with a journalist's curiosity, I visited events in the area where I would never have ventured before. We took the boys to the Blanco Rodeo, which was to the Fort Worth Rodeo (the only other rodeo I'd seen) what a dugout canoe is to a cigarette boat. The participants were from small towns and the clowns' outfits were hopelessly frayed, but it was authentic and endearingly silly and earnest. We also attended a hog auction with new friends who had moved from L.A. and were thinking of buying some of the beasts for their ranch. As the auctioneer rattled away unintelligibly in what seemed like an Arabic dialect, Gus climbed into a pen and chased a couple babies, matching his squeal to theirs. That fall, we made an appearance at a Blanco High School football game and saw that the whole town had turned out to watch the boys in blue and yellow scramble under the lights and to hear the eight band members scratch their way through what sounded like "Smoke on the Water."

With my new interest in the community—the schools, the library, plus any new shops or restaurants that might be opening to add to the scant selection—I began to pay more attention to the weekly Blanco paper. I kept up with the high school's winning football season and the police blotter, which once told of the police's efforts to round up two escaped goats named Spike and Eddie. One Thursday, the day the paper landed in our mailbox, I was especially interested in a story about the construction of a new bridge across the Blanco River. Walking back from the mailbox, I unfolded the paper to read it. By the time I reached the house, I had a revelation. In my bundle of mail was also the day's *New York Times*. I was flabbergasted to realize that I had opened the Blanco paper before my beloved *Times*.

·

Though I had new appreciation for the country, at times I still itched for a different life—usually during rural-specific crises. Such as the night the dogs came home reeking of the head-knocking smell of skunk, a smell that made me think Robb's running shoes had been marinated in garlic and cooked in an old tire. Because Robb was gone, it was my job to yank the dogs down to the hose bib and wash them with a compound—a sure skunk de-stinker, we were told—of hydrogen peroxide, baking soda, and dish soap. In the tussling with the dogs, the stench was transferred to me and wouldn't come off completely in the shower. That night, I felt like I was napping in an ogre's armpit. At least in the city, even in the worst of August, you can escape the smells.

Soon after the skunking, the sky broke open, sending thirteen inches of rain down in one day. The clouds will do that in the Hill Country—be stingy for months then make up for all they've held back in one dumping. The day of our storm, the water began seeping into Gus's bedroom, something that had never happened before, and spread into Jeb's room next door, swamping rugs and a rubber mat made up of alphabet letters hooked together.

The water also gushed into the guest bedroom we'd created a year earlier by closing in a porch off the garage. Juanita couldn't get to the house because the creeks were too high to cross. I was left alone with two toddlers who thought their indoor ponds were a new form of entertainment. I was running from one room to the other, throwing towels on the floor and trying to mop up the water as fast as possible. When Robb called from Iceland, I was working the mop in Gus's room and the boys were jumping on the beds with wet socks and pants.

"How's it going?" Robb asked innocently.

"How's it going?" I barked back into the receiver cradled between chin and shoulder. "Well except for the fact that the house is floating away, and the boys are on speed, and Juanita's not here and I have a deadline today, and you are off in some nice hotel with dry feet and no need for a mop? Besides that it's fine."

"Jeannie," Robb yelled back. "Chill, will you?"

"Damn it!" I screamed. Gus had just thrown his pillow in the water and of course Jeb had to follow suit. "I've got to go." I hung up the phone and retrieved the pillows. A high-rise apartment, I thought. This never happens in a high-rise.

Of course, I called Robb back later and apologized, after the last of the rainwater—and the shrew that had been possessing me—dried up. I still had to work for weeks, though, to remove the moldy smell that clung to the soaked rugs.

The lowest point of country living that year had to be the 2000 election. I longed to be out with my people, raising hell, getting comfort. Instead I was surrounded by the opposition, the reddest part of this red state. One night, I cursed and threw a stuffed bear Gus called Osito at the *NewsHour* when some Republicans were justifying a win for Bush. "You know, I just can't see the other side on this," I said to Robb as I turned off the TV. "Normally I can get a glimpse into their minds, no matter how skewed. This time I just don't get how they can say a recount is bad. Or that Gore's trying to steal the election."

After the program we left the boys with Nene so we could try out a new restaurant in a country inn called Rose Hill Manor, only twelve minutes from us in the opposite direction from Blanco. (It was still important to us to keep track to the minute of the drive times to any notable place in the vicinity.) At the restaurant we ran into a retired couple from my church who were eating with another couple who'd just moved to the area. After we finished dinner, they invited us to join them for dessert. As we waited for our order, my church lady asked if Robb and I were interested in joining the Blanco County Dinner Club, which held monthly gatherings at different homes. "It's a real nice group," she told me. "Good solid Republicans."

I tried to suppress my fangs and amiably offered an excuse—too busy with the kids. "Plus," I added. "I'm an Independent." I was taking the cowardly way out instead of confronting them head-on with the big "L" word. Though my friend insisted that Independents were welcome too, I was able to exit the exchange when dessert arrived.

As I ate my chocolate truffle cake, talk turned to the election. "That Gore is such a crybaby," the husband of my church friend said. "Get over it already."

I felt my cheeks flush, but it was a formal restaurant and I knew to rebut would risk a brawl. "I heard a comedian say that Gore is running out of ways to lose," someone said. The woman sitting next to the window tossed her head back in laughter. The next thing I knew, I was having a *Carrie* moment. It was as if my thoughts had become manifest. A candle was sitting on the windowsill and when the woman's teased-up, hairsprayed hair came close enough, it caught fire.

I pointed and opened my mouth to say something but no noise came forth, like a ventriloquist's dummy with a laryngitic operator. "You-your hair," I finally managed.

The woman reached up, felt the flames, and began to scream. Her husband dipped his napkin in his water and patted the fire out. Oh, what I would have given to be able to release all the mirth inside. I knew if I looked at Robb the dam would break. Instead, amid the scent of burned hair, I concentrated on getting every dollop of chocolate on my plate.

The election debacle often made me wish I could repeat this little fire trick. I felt surrounded by enemy combatants and had an almost irresistible urge to go knocking down Bush-Cheney signs, of which there were many. I would have been singularly possessed by politics if not for my fortieth birthday party, which fell toward the end of the five-week election standoff.

•

The two singers wore gingham blouses and short denim jumpers and their hair was in pigtails beneath their white cowboy hats. On stage with them were a guitarist, a fiddler, and a drummer. They were a country swing band playing jaunty tunes that I never would have listened to growing up. Living five hours from Nashville, the radio stations and local concert halls had been filled with the twangy music and kitschy lyrics of country music. I couldn't stand it. But here I was on my fortieth birthday celebrating this very same music, showcasing it. It was partly an ironic bit of camp. But there was a certain if-you-can't-beat-'em-join-'em element to my choice of band and venue. We were in my favorite of the many Texas dance halls I'd seen—in Fischer, twenty minutes from Blanco. It was a near shanty, with walls that seemed as substantial as melba toast and slits between wood planks that let in the frigid December air. The rafters were skeletal, but their thinness was disguised by coils of white Christmas lights—a permanent fixture of the hall. The lights gave the space a dreamy, wonderland feel and added extra dazzle to my outfit. I was wearing my Nudie jacket again, only its third outing. I couldn't wear something like that too often.

Surrounded by one hundred friends and family members—including Ellesor and another college friend, Barbie, who surprised me by flying in earlier that day from South Carolina—I spun around the dance floor with my father. Both my parents were such good dancers that they often won dance contests against people much younger. Gus and Jeb also danced with me, each clopping on the floor in their tiny cowboy boots. Often, I would pick one up in my arms and twirl until we both were dizzy. I was determined to instill in them a love of dancing, even if their father never got on the floor.

The music was perfect for clogging—a dance common in the mountains of Appalachia. I purposely never learned it growing up, but it was close enough to another form of dance I knew something about—tap—that I had no problem executing it that night. I had taken tap lessons all my childhood and while in high school I was part of a Radio-City-Rockette-like kickline, taking great pride in my high kicks, fan kicks, and hitch kicks. My dance instructor, a crusty old woman with Broadway experience, used to say, "Jeannie may not be the best dancer out here, but she sure knows how to sell it." It was the highest compliment from the instructor, who would walk around with forehead furrowed, barking to her company: "Smile. Smile."

When the swing band took its first break, Robb stepped up on stage and grabbed a microphone. "We're all here because we love Jeannie, who is a great mother and a great wife and the most giving person I know." As he led everyone in "Happy Birthday," my eyes and heart filled up. I knew Robb wasn't much for public displays of any kind, but especially not sentiment or praise. He had once told me that he didn't go overboard with compliments because he didn't want me to take such niceties for granted. But the softness the boys had brought out in him had led him lately to collecting quotes, taping them to the side of his computer—as close to introspection as I could expect from him. "Life is ten percent what happens to you and ninety percent how you react to it," was one of his favorites. Another was, "A loving atmosphere in your home is the foundation for your life." I always wondered if he could truly fold such wisdom into his persona. He's making progress, I thought as he stepped down from the stage.

Once the band began playing again, he presented what was in my mind better than any gift—himself. I had long ago accepted that Robb wasn't a dancer, but while I was talking to my brother Jeff and my little sister, visiting with her daughters, Robb tapped me on the shoulder. I noticed my mother flitting around, looking on eagerly.

"Wanna dance?" Robb asked with a stupid grin.

I stared at him dumbfounded. "With *you*?"

"Sure, why not?" I noticed that other people had gathered around us. He grabbed my hand and I felt as giddy as an eighth-grader who'd been asked onto the floor by her longtime crush. We began to circle the floor, cautiously, gingerly at first, doing a simple Texas two-step, which gets its name because the dance is a series of two quick steps then two slow steps. As Robb moved forward, steering me by his touch, I stepped backward.

"Where'd you learn this?" I asked.

Robb beamed. "I've been going down to Jan and Jon's shop for a month for lessons," he said, referring to our friends, the Briegers, who had a pottery store on the square in Blanco. "I knew you'd want to dance."

I couldn't think of anything that would adequately express my gratitude and love at that moment. I just leaned in slowly and put my head on his shoulder. After a few passes around the floor, we fumbled our feet.

"Hey," Robb said, pushing hard on my waist. "Stop trying to lead."

"Why?" I said laughing. "Don't you think I've followed you enough?"

"Come on, I haven't done too badly by you."

"Hmmph," I snorted quietly.

"Well, I—"

"Shhh."

I didn't want him to ruin my good feelings. Yes, I had made a kind of peace with Blanco—for now—but was feeling that I'd lived on Robb's terms too long. I doubted I could keep my feminist credentials if I continued to allow him to set the parameters of my life. Now that the kids were getting older and I felt more confident about motherhood, now that I'd come back to myself—even without the Zoloft, which I had recently given up—I was freer to charge ahead with what I wanted to do. I'd taken five years off from serious writing. Not that I didn't work or was forgotten by editors, but I hadn't been writing the kind of articles I knew I was capable of, but instead a lot of articles that paid the bills, like "How to Build Intimacy with Your Husband." While in New York in September, I had met with an editor at *Vanity Fair*—someone I knew from his days at *Life*. I was determined to find a good story for him before too much time passed. One of the quotes Robb had tacked to his computer was, "No regret is more painful than not pursuing your goals."

I was thinking of my fortieth birthday as a new start. First we'd have a ski trip to Park City, Utah, where Robb would begin a *Geographic* assignment previewing the Winter Olympics and I would finally be able to ski again—a true passion that I hadn't had time for over the past eight years. I'd help get this Montessori school off the ground and then I'd concentrate on becoming the serious journalist I knew I could be, that I had been.

But I wasn't done with surprises.

Part Three

THE BLOOM

Prized down the centuries for its perfume, medicinal properties, and rich violet hues, lavender has been the darling of all herbs since time began. Among its many qualities, it is thought to calm irritable children and relieve insomnia, anxiety, and depression—in other words, to create a wonderful sense of well-being.

•

—TESSA EVELEGH,
Lavender

CHAPTER EIGHT

Buds

Before the car had even stopped, the woman was opening the door and putting her foot out. She had blond upswept hair, white bauble earrings, and a bold black-and-white print blouse over white pants. Raising her oversized sunglasses onto her head, she screeched at the sight of lavender bushes growing on both sides of our driveway. "Oh my God! Oh my God!" she said as she stopped at the closest plant and stroked the lavender blooms, as if they were a favorite cat. She then brought her hand to her nose and inhaled deeply. "I can't believe this. I'm just *beside* myself. Lavender! *Lavender!*"

Having spotted her jumping from the car, I was on my way down the driveway to talk to her. Like a bee, she was flitting from one bush to the next.

"Hi," I said. "Welcome to Hill Country Lavender."

"Oh, darling. Is this your farm?" She grabbed my forearm with both hands. "Bless you. This is just so fabulous. I can't find the words. Lavender *here*. I saw your sign up at the Natural Gardener shop, but I didn't think it would be like *this*. I've been to Provence twice, but I've always missed the lavender bloom."

A young man in jeans and a teal polo shirt walked up behind her. "Oh, Harrison. Look, darling! Look! *Lavender!*" The young man peered at the plant she was pointing at and nodded his head, unimpressed. We both walked with her as she made her way to the field, the scene of more ecstasy. "Oh my! Oh my!" She stepped into the field and let her fingertips brush against a whole row of blooms. She brought her hand to her nose again. Giggling, she jumped over the row and ran her fingers along the top of the next bushes.

"Would you like to cut some flowers to take with you?" I asked.

"I can cut the lavender? Are you *sure?*"

"Absolutely. I've got some scissors over there," I said pointing to a table under an oak on the upper left corner of the field. I'd set up the table and brought down a couple of pairs of scissors earlier that morning.

"Harrison, Harrison," she called. "Go get some scissors and help me cut some flowers. Oh Lord; I can't believe there's a place like this." She clapped her hands together, and seeing her hands must have reminded her that they had been busy collecting aroma. She thrust her face into them.

"Yes, Mother," the young man said as he followed me to the table.

For about forty-five minutes, I watched the woman gamboling through the field and her son trying to keep up, like someone after a butterfly with a net. I was surprised that she could maintain her enthusiasm this long. But after she'd collected an armful of blooms and checked out the canopy under our Thinking Tree, she came to pay for the flowers, her emotional state as hyped up as that of a girl who'd just made cheerleader. "I'll be back. I'll bring my friends. They're just gonna D-I-E!"

"Uh, do you think she liked the lavender?" Tasha, my tall young employee, deadpanned after the woman almost skipped down the driveway.

It was the first day our lavender farm was open to the public—Memorial Day weekend 2001. Robb was coming home the following week from his *Geographic* assignment in Utah, and I could have just done my duty—delivered flowers to Central Market, the grocery store in Austin, and the florists—and been finished with it. Harvesting and delivery days had gotten easier since the first day when I did it mostly by myself. Tasha, sixteen, who was originally supposed to be working for Robb in his office, was now coming to help me bundle flowers. My ranch helper, Antonio, was arriving earlier, at 6:30, to cut flowers with me. But I was still angry at Robb for dragging me into his project, which I was never supposed to be a part of, and for further delaying me from getting back to the kind of writing I had planned to be doing at this point.

But as I'd worked myself up into my huff, a conflicting emotion started tugging at me. Looking at the field, as gorgeous as anything I'd seen in France even if the flowers were a paler purple, I saw possibilities. This was truly miraculous, this field, and as much as I wanted to—as much as I knew I had story proposals to work on—something wouldn't let me leave the flowers alone. Maybe it was weakness, not being able to stand up to Robb. But I like to consider a more positive possibility—the intoxicating effect of the lavender.

Although we thought that selling flowers wholesale to florists was going to be the big moneymaker, I knew after a few days of cutting that we could never sell all the flowers we had in the field. I would cut and cut in the mornings. Antonio would snip away for hours, and when we finished I couldn't even tell that we'd been there. It was as if flower fairies followed behind us and made more blooms. There had to be something more we could do with the lavender.

The first idea I had was for Antonio to harvest on nondelivery days and dry those flowers. With Robb's advice over the phone, we managed to make an apparatus for drying bouquets in our garage. I bought some bicycle hooks and Antonio screwed them into the wood ceiling. Then he took hog panels—the same kind of fencing we used to create a roof over the arbor by our pool—and hung them on the well-spaced hooks. Antonio wrapped a rubber band around each bundle and, using Christmas ornament hangers, he attached the bunches, upside-down, to the hog panel. Soon I realized I didn't even need ornament hangers. Partially unfurled paper clips did just as well.

"Very low tech," I explained to Sally when she came to look. The scent of the drying lavender that wafted upstairs into our office was at first almost unbearably thick. But soon, I became used to it. Nearly immune.

I wanted the dried lavender ready for my next inspiration—opening up the field to the public. I remembered all too well how perfectly enamored I was with the fields in Provence. It seemed a shame not to show ours off.

"It's just too gorgeous to keep to ourselves," I told Robb when we were discussing the idea. Robb was concerned about having so many people crawling around our property. We did, after all, live in a sue-happy world.

My friend Lori thought I should ban kids in the field because they might trample the plants. But I felt sure the lavender was resilient enough to take some traffic. I wanted to give it a try, put the word out and see what happened. Robb finally agreed.

To bring customers to us, I was hoping to get some newspaper or TV coverage. With Robb's *National Geographic* connection, I knew the lavender farm made a good story, so I wrote up a press kit very hurriedly late in May and delivered it to Austin TV stations and the *Austin American Statesman*. When I dropped off the package for the garden editor at the *Statesman,* I included a bouquet of lavender. I got a call back nearly immediately.

Disappointingly, the local media didn't move fast enough to do any stories before we opened. Instead I made up flyers on my simple Hill Country Lavender letterhead. "Mornings in the Hill Country are enchanting enough: scarlet sky, cool breezes, rolling landscape, groves of shady live oaks," I wrote on the flyers. "Now imagine a field of purple lavender in this setting. On the next four Saturday mornings, you can do more than imagine it. You can experience it." I set the Saturday of Memorial Day weekend as our first open date, and posted the flyers in Blanco and at a few garden shops in Austin.

At seven on the first morning, I spread out the tablecloth I bought in Provence on a card table near our driveway. I smiled to think that I could have written it off as a business expense on our tax return. Had I known.

On one side of the driveway, near the entrance, I put out a hand-lettered sign that said Parking with an arrow to direct cars over into the empty field near our pool. I opened the front gate, which I always closed at night when Robb was traveling. Tasha arrived at eight, as unhappy as any teenager would be at having to get up so early on a Saturday. She was the daughter of friends of ours, the Briegers, the potters who had taught Robb how to two-step at their store. We had known Tasha since she was twelve, when she was working as a hostess at our old haunt, the Chandler Inn. Even then, she had a preternaturally mature bearing and sense of responsibility. I always attributed it to her being an only child, spending so much time among grown-ups and artists. When Tasha's father, Jon, told Robb she was interested in photography, he took her on two afternoons a week to help him organize photos and files. Lavender was never part of her bargain either.

After Tasha showed up that morning, I took some bunches of dried lavender down from the hog panels in the garage, and as the boys, now four and two, played in the field, Tasha and I sat under the tree talking about what it was like growing up in Blanco and rolling bunches of dried lavender stalks in our palms, as if we were trying to warm up our hands. The Provence variety of lavender is especially brittle when dried, so the buds fell off easily into buckets we each kept at our feet. Any stubborn buds we removed by running our index finger and thumb over the stalk several times, as if we were stroking a feather.

At about 9 a.m., the first car slowly approached our driveway. I had put specific directions on the flyers and was happy to know that they had been understood. By 9:30 three cars were parked in the field across the driveway from the lavender. At about 10:15, the excitable lavender junkie and her son arrived.

Each person who turned up at our field made some swooning comment, and almost everyone said they were suprised that lavender could grow in Texas. I could honestly answer, "So am I."

I thought that the cutting would be easy for people, but most wanted instructions. I went out with almost every group and showed them how to pick out the choicest flowers, then follow each stem down to the woody growth. "Cut right above this bushy part," I would tell them, as I snipped their first flower for them and placed it in their bucket or basket—whatever container they'd brought.

Our visitors wanted to know how many lavender stems were in a bunch, which we were selling for $3.50 (far below the $8 retail price Central Market was asking). I told them forty to forty-five, about the number I put in each bundle for the florists. But in practice, it didn't make sense to count out every bloom. I ended up grabbing a handful and declaring it a bunch, always leaning toward the generous side. Probably each bunch I sold that day had sixty or sixty-five stems, but it seemed only fair since the customers had done the work, saving me from further aggravating the blisters on my hands.

As I was putting her three bouquets of lavender in a Super S plastic shopping bag, a woman in a yellow plaid shirt and yellow pants stood on her toes to peer inside the metal bucket on the card table. When I noticed what she was looking at, I cupped a mound of dried lavender buds in my hands and lifted them toward her. "This is lavender we've dried ourselves," I told her. "We harvested it from the field a week ago."

She gave the handful a quick inspection. "How much are you selling it for?"

I looked at Tasha. I shrugged. She shrugged. I laughed at my naïveté. Maybe I should have come up with a price beforehand.

"Um . . . I don't know," I said thrusting my cupped hands closer so she could get a better look and a real whiff of it. "How much would you pay for it?"

She agreed to give us $3 for a handful and I sent Tasha up to the house for a ziplock bag.

As an entrepreneur, I had a lot of room for improvement, but I reminded myself pricing comparisons were the kinds of research Robb should have done before we'd ever gotten to this point.

During the four hours we were open that first day, we had about fifty-five visitors and made roughly $150 from the sales of the bunches, the dried lavender, and some vegetables from the garden we'd put in earlier in the spring not far from the pool. I had brought out the vegetables because I was eager for more products to sell and I was practically drowning in zucchini, yellow squash, and tomatoes.

Like so much on our property, the vegetable garden had been Robb's idea. Around a one-third-acre plot, he installed deer fencing—high enough to thwart the hoofed invaders. Inside, we had a crew of stone workers build a chicken house that looked as if it had been there for decades. After Antonio had prepared the soil and heaped up dirt in rows, Robb had a shopping spree at the garden store. He bought sixty tomato plants, ten cauliflower plants, ten broccoli plants, ten cabbage plants, and packs of seeds—zucchini, squash, cucumbers, beets, okra, several varieties of beans. From our neighbor Roger, he got advice on growing asparagus and blackberries—two crops Roger and Norma had shared with us in the past. Antonio then laid down drip tape to keep the plants watered, though he hardly needed to. It was a magical spring, with ideally spaced bouts of rain and not too hot, not too cool. Just right. Even Fred couldn't seem to think of a weather worry that year.

"Nice weather, huh?" Robb had said to him in late April, when we saw him in the field across the road tending to his sheep.

Fred stammered a bit, then replied, "Yeah. Yeah. I think we're doing okay."

"How much rain did you get yesterday at your place?" Robb continued. This had become a habit with him after a rainfall, to check how our rain-gauge showing compared to everyone else's.

" 'Bout an inch."

"Yeah, us too."

After Robb rolled up the window, I said, "Incredible! He didn't complain."

"Yeah, but did you hear him: okay. Not great, not wonderful. Just okay, and I bet it took everything out of him just to say that!"

Soon I was absorbed in the vegetable garden although I'd never been interested in gardening before. In Austin, Robb often planted flowers in the beds, but when he was gone I'd forget to water them. Invariably they'd all be withered, looking like clumps of black yarn, by the time Robb returned. I thought I simply had the Typhoid Mary of thumbs. But the vegetable garden struck me on a different level. These were plants with a purpose: to feed us. My desire to nourish my family probably stemmed from the same Italian gene that made me want to stuff food down the throat of any friend who came by the house.

I began reading a book on organic farming to learn what I needed to do to keep the plants thriving till they were able to fill our dinner table. Every evening when I went to close the hens up in the chicken house and every morning when I let them out, I strolled through the vegetable garden clearing away weeds and watching each of my fledglings progress.

I couldn't have been more proud of myself for nixing an infestation of cabbage loopers, a kind of caterpillar that dines on broccoli, cabbage, and cauliflower. As the book instructed, I sprayed the plants with a coating of a natural substance called BT, which paralyzes the loopers' digestive system. To get rid of aphids, I ordered ladybugs from an organic farming website and the boys and I danced around the garden releasing them from a small burlap sack. They landed on our heads, our arms, our noses. "They're going to eat the bad bugs," I told the boys, which made them love them even more. When a friend from DC visited and saw the garden, she was impressed—unduly so, I thought at first. "I don't think I've ever been this close to my food source before," she said, and in her, I saw my own naive, concrete-centric mind-set of my city years.

By early May I was picking vegetables for dinner, eliminating the need to buy organic products from Central Market. By the end of May, I had so many tomatoes, so much squash that I would send visiting friends away with bagfuls. Norma Felps told me that the only time people lock their cars when they park on the Blanco square is during zucchini season. "If you don't someone's liable to leave a whole box full of the stuff in your backseat," she told me. I understood. If I missed a couple days picking squash—the rabbits of the vegetable world—I would need a wheelbarrow to bring in my haul the next day. One solution to world hunger, I thought: a squash plant for every family.

On the first day our farm was open to the public, I was mightily proud of the kudos my well-formed vegetables attracted. But everyone has seen an eggplant. The compliments I received over the lavender were more effusive, more emotional, more tinged with awe. Even though Robb got the credit when I told the story of how we got started, I felt the sun shine on me too. It was nice to be fussed over.

•

Robb, I think the clippers work best," I suggested gently at six the following Friday morning. Robb had just come home from Utah and was determined to help me harvest the lavender blooms that day for our delivery to four different stores in Austin. Robb was cutting the flowers in one whack with a small sickle.

"This is how they do it in France," he responded.

"I know, but they were doing oil production, not selling them as cut flowers. The florists like that we cut each flower individually, and they love the long stems." I showed him how using the clippers allowed you to go to the very bottom of the eighteen-inch stems. Robb took a pair of garden clippers from me and I went back to my own bush. A few minutes later, I saw him cutting flowers again in one whack—only this time with the clippers. I sighed and kept working. I'll make sure he picks out the short, immature ones when he is bundling, I thought.

When Tasha arrived to help tie the flowers into bunches, I thought I would let her show Robb how to do it. I planned to write up the invoices so Robb would be fully prepared to take the deliveries into Austin. But Robb, who would leave again in a week for *Geographic* headquarters to lay out his Salt Lake City story, kept getting calls from editors. He'd retreat into his office to talk, and after a while it became clear that to make our deadline I would have to help.

Besides thinking his way of harvesting was better, he didn't see why I stripped off some of the green leaves at the bottom of the stems when I made the bundles. "The bunches look fatter if you keep the leaves on," he said.

"But it's so much cleaner looking to have them stripped a bit, and one florist told me flowers keep longer without all that crap at the bottom," I told him. He also had a problem with the sugar-pack-sized hangtags I had started adding on the lavender bundles. For each bunch, we had to thread a piece of raffia through a hole in the tag. Not used to such fine work, Robb got easily frustrated. "Are you sure we need these?" he asked.

"No, we don't need them," I said. "We don't need all the thousands of people who shop at Central Market to know about us, or that this is Texas lavender, not California."

After we finished bundling, we loaded up my Trooper and I handed Robb the invoices. I gave him instructions on the delivery process for the two Central Markets and the florists—all of which had specific requirements. By the time I made notes for each store and he drove off, Tasha and I fell back in our chairs exhausted.

"Maybe it would have been easier to do it ourselves," I said. Tasha nodded her head quickly and laughed.

I realized that this was a tactic some men employed to get out of housework. Be so thick about it, make supervision such a problem that the wife decides it's less trouble to do it herself. But I knew Robb was not that type. He was the one usually supervising *my* housework, and I couldn't imagine Robb Kendrick being intentionally thick about anything.

Robb and I both began to realize that I simply was more suited to the sales and marketing end of this venture. Maybe it took a woman to know what other women—our main customers—were interested in. As Robb later joked, "Real men don't market lavender." I knew best how to meet expectations and create an image, possibly because of my years as a beauty writer—and of course the beauty business is about nothing if not packaging—and from the many travel stories I'd written for which I paid close attention to details of service and presentation.

At each of the three other Saturdays we were open that season, we had increasingly more visitors. A friend in Blanco called on the second Saturday to say she had heard a local gardening expert talk about our lavender farm on the radio. It seemed that news was getting out in the most old-fashioned ways—radio, homemade flyers, word of mouth. Robb's role on the two open days he made an appearance, was to put out directional signs—hand-lettered with a fat Sharpie—along the main highway and smaller roads and to answer questions about the actual farming, mostly from men who were waiting for their wives to finish cutting bouquets.

We both fielded queries about our house, which most people were eager to know more about. They could see enough of it from the edge of the field to know it was big and unusual. The fascination with our house made me realize that people were interested in our so-called "lifestyle" almost as much as the lavender. The house, the kids, the romantic notions of a *National Geographic* photographer were icing on the lavender cake.

On our third open Saturday, I decided to close the second of the two gates on our driveway, the gate nearest to our house. The week before we had found several women wandering into our screened porch. They giggled when Tasha spotted them and told her they were looking for the bathroom. When Robb heard about this, he wanted me to make sure no one came into the fenced area around our house, even if they did need the pottie. Tasha was tougher about enforcing this edict. I found it hard to turn away women who had to pee, especially if they were very old or if they'd already turned blue from the strain of holding it. For some reason, I trusted these lavender people. I didn't feel love of lavender dovetailed with criminal behavior. I snuck them into the downstairs bathroom and told them not to tell anyone.

"My husband would kill me if we had a big run on the bathroom," I said.

Inside the house, most of them looked up and around in wonder as if they were New York tourists. They commented on the rich, red shiplap walls against the stone ones, the doors of different sizes and with various degrees of peeling paint. One stout woman pulled out a camera and took photos. "You are living my dream," she said earnestly as she shut the bathroom door.

Reflexively, I wanted to say, "If you only knew." But I simply smiled. Though it was true I'd never had such a dream, I was beginning to see why others might.

•

By the end of the season, our deliveries into Austin had grown substantially. We'd also send flowers once a week to the Central Market in Houston on a van driven by our friends, the cut flower farmers. One day, I prepared 215 bunches for various stores—about 9,675 flowers. For these big orders, I cut and bundled at least half the flowers the night before and put them in a preservative in an old refrigerator in the garage—even though I initially wanted them in the stores only hours after harvest. I often lured friends from Austin out to help the night before a delivery, enticing them with food and wine and all the lavender they could bring home—which I would have given them anyway. On those nights, we'd bundle up flowers as we drank wine.

"Oh, great," my friend Cathy, a transplanted Aussie, said when she came out to tie up flowers. She held up her wineglass and giggled. "My wine is filled with lavender buds. Lavender wine. There's a product for you."

"Wait. Let me see something," I said staring at her teeth, which looked as if she'd been eating poppy-seed bagels. "Oh God, you've got lavender buds stuck in your front teeth!"

"Okay, that's going too far," she cried, as she picked at her teeth. "It's lavender mania here."

By the end of June, the flowers in the field were still in good shape. We could have been open the last weekend of the month, but we had to make Saturday, June 23, our last cutting day. We were about to leave for Isle of Palms, South Carolina, where my parents were celebrating their fiftieth anniversary. They had rented a ten-bedroom house on the beach to hold all twenty-nine of us—the six kids, plus spouses and children. I had taken on the jobs of planning the party (hoping to make up for the seventieth birthday party I'd muddled in Tennessee) and making a video on my Mac—composed of old photos set to Barbra Streisand's "Memories" (a requisite) and Natalie Merchant's "These Are the Days." I knew that my mom would cry when we showed it because I wailed myself while making it—reliving wonderful childhood memories and feeling the painfully quick passage of time.

Before I left I also needed to finish up a quirky story for *Conde Nast Traveler* about celebrities who wreck hotel rooms. Though I loved working for a travel magazine again, it wasn't the kind of writing I had hoped I'd be doing at this point. Despite my big plans for 2001, I hadn't gotten a chance to pursue more serious reporting.

Prior to May and June, when the lavender was sucking up all my time, the Montessori school had. With so many sidetracks, I was beginning to feel like Jimmy Stewart's George Bailey in *It's a Wonderful Life,* who is continually thwarted in his efforts to escape Bedford Falls.

I had delved into the start-up of the school more deeply than I expected. Sally, Lily, and I met constantly during the spring, trying to put all the pieces into place—interested parents, finances, a building to house the school, teachers, our application for nonprofit status. By June, a teacher had signed on and we had commitments for eleven students. We'd also found a space—the former home of our local health food store, which was moving to a bigger location on the Blanco square. I had spent the spring writing articles for the local paper and the text for a website—which a graphic-designer friend of ours, Trish, put together for free—and arranging fund raising. We determined we needed to come up with about $13,000 to purchase Montessori equipment, furniture, and other supplies. To get us near our goal, Robb volunteered to sell prints of some of his best photos at a special price of $165 and donate all the proceeds to the school. We posted this offer on the school's website, publicized it through the local paper and contacted friends, editors, and photo associates urging them to buy one for a good cause. As we were leaving for the anniversary party, orders had started coming in, which I would have to fill when we returned (we ended up raising $9,000 through the photo sale).

The day before our flight to South Carolina, an older man named Bert stopped by to talk to us about the lavender. It was drizzling out, and Bert—an attorney from Midland who had retired in Blanco—was wearing a khaki trench coat and a houndstooth fedora, like the kind Coach Bear Bryant famously wore. He had just heard about the lavender and wanted to find out how we got started, where we got our plants, how we laid out the field. I handed him off to Robb while I packed our bags, but soon grew irritated at the amount of time Robb was spending with him when we had so much work to do. Before Bert left, he paid $20 for a bucketful of lavender that Antonio had just harvested.

"He sure had a lot of questions," Robb said after he left. "We need to figure out how to handle people who want information. It's not good to be giving away all that for free."

I agreed, but Bert seemed harmless enough, and since he lived only a couple miles away, I thought—unwisely—that providing some help was only the neighborly thing to do.

•

Kendrick, a photographer, and Ralston, a writer, met on an assignment for *Life* magazine 11 years ago and married. Now, with their sons, Gus, 4, and Jeb, 2, they are reinventing life in the Hill Country. On a 200-acre farm west of Blanco, they're figuring out how to combine big-time free-lance journalism with parenthood and another very different enterprise, niche farming. Kids in tow, fax on line, tractor in gear, they are Blanco County's new FedEx agrarians."

"FedEx agrarians?" Robb shouted as he sat on the sofa with Jeb, reading the *Austin American Statesman* article on the lavender. "What does *that* mean?"

The story, on the front page of the feature section with a photo of me silhouetted in the lavender field, appeared on July 19, too late to have any immediate impact on our cut-your-own business since the season was already over.

The article recounted the Provence trip that sparked Robb's idea. It also included confirmation from our agricultural extension agent, Jim Kamas— who didn't have any specific knowledge of lavender, but had offered us some general farming advice—that lavender seemed to be suited to the rocky, alkaline soil of the Hill Country. The writer even included a few quotes from Robb. She had timed her visit—as had the paper's photographer—to coincide with one of Robb's visits home during the blooming season. In response to a question about why he had started the lavender when he already had a full schedule, Robb said, "I've always thrown myself in deep water and tried to swim my way out."

When I read the article, I couldn't help but shout out, "Yeah, but you don't have to drag me out there with you." Robb shrugged and went on filling his coffee cup in the kitchen. I was sitting at the dining room table, which had a view of a ridge and some live oak groves on the north side of the barn, away from the lavender field. What does it mean, I thought, when you have to learn about your husband through the newspaper? It couldn't be good. Even though I already knew he liked to challenge himself, I'd never heard him explain himself so succinctly. Reading about this quality through the author's eyes, it didn't seem so bad. It was almost attractive. And I considered that, as exhausting and exasperating as his need to mix things up in our lives could be, the alternative would be worse. I couldn't imagine being married to a complacent, lazy man—though someone in between the extremes might be nice.

The article ended with a quote from famed Texas historian Walter Prescott Webb. He said that the region's history is one "of adjustments and modifications, of giving up old things that would no longer function for new things that would, of giving up an old way of life for a new way."

I read the article wondering if the writer could have really met me. The way she wrote about me I didn't recognize myself. I seemed almost interesting, on the leading edge of something new and exciting. I didn't come off the way I had been feeling about myself since I'd moved out here: dull, out-of-touch, isolated. How strange to be the subject of a story, not the writer; to be the one lauded, not the invisible person behind the byline doing the lauding. And how especially odd and ironic to be cast as the very thing that Robb always promised we would be when pitching a move to the country—pioneers.

The way the writer had encapsulated our experience and the response we got—calls about the lavender started coming in almost immediately—made me think I should write a story myself for a different publication. I found out that an editor I had once worked with at *McCall's* was now the features editor at *O, The Oprah Magazine,* so I shot off an e-mail, hoping she would remember me. She quickly assigned me an essay about my change-of-life-at-forty experience. I was relieved that at least all the time I'd put into the lavender wouldn't be wasted. I would get an article out of it and some money, which would be nice since the $10,000 we grossed over the first season all went to reimburse Robb for the cost of putting in the field.

Most people who contacted us after the *Statesman* article wanted to come pick lavender and were disappointed when we told them to wait till next spring. Many others wanted to get started in the business, and we soon realized we'd never be able to spend time individually with every person who wanted to grow lavender. That's when Robb decided we should conduct a seminar, gathering all would-be farmers together and going over the information one time. We started taking names and told people we would contact them in the spring.

I didn't know it at the time but I could have invited people back to cut lavender that fall. In mid-October, I was shocked to discover a new, lighter flush of purple over the plants. The lavender was blooming again—second blooms, I read, are common but only about one-third as prolific as the main show. I wanted to shield my eyes when I passed by, so I wouldn't be tempted to do something with the flowers.

I was too busy, mostly with the Montessori school, to be diverted again. We had opened in August with thirteen students—the bare minimum, in our minds—but that wasn't the end of my job. We needed more kids and more money. While Sally worked as the administrator of the school, overseeing the teacher and the teacher's aide, I was absorbed with fund-raising ideas, as well as the school's image. Many people in town called us the "monastery" school and thought we were associated with one of the churches. Others thought worse of us. In early August, we had hosted our first open house in our newly spiffed up classroom, and just before the first parents arrived we found a stack of flyers on our front doorstep. "Thinking About Montessori? Consider This!" were the words on the front. Five pages of small type followed, describing the Montessori method as part of a New Age scheme to brainwash children.

I was appalled. For a moment, with the group of like-minded parents working so hard on the school, I had forgotten what a small town we actually lived in. I heard reports of flyers at different stores and went to each to collect them. At the Super S grocery store, several flyers were posted on the public bulletin board. I took them down and asked the manager to please notify me if anyone tried to put up more.

"I don't think this is the kind of thing you want your store to be associated with," I said to the woman, who had brittle blond hair. "Montessori is a very respected education philosophy."

She studied the flyer for a moment and agreed that they shouldn't be posted. "But I have some advice for you," she said. "You might want to change your name. That word, Mon-sen-tori, it's really hard to pronounce."

Eventually, one of the parents learned from a friend the identity of the

Montessori mudslinger—a couple who were deeply involved in an evangelical church in town. The husband had once called the owner of the health food store a witch because she sold herbal remedies. I had seen the guy around town—his father had even done some painting at our house—but I had always steered clear, knowing his reputation for intolerance.

Another reason that I didn't even consider making anything of the fall bloom was that I was still shattered by September 11. Like most people, especially those who lived in New York or had at one time, I was distraught and, for over a month, my energy was depleted. I was relieved, however, to be in the country far from threats, or so I assumed. I resorted to my Y2K thinking: At least we had plenty of water, and now we had chickens and our vegetable garden, which was at the time producing fall lettuce.

"I think we need a cow," I announced to Robb one night while lying in bed.

"What?"

I had been thinking of what we would need to be truly self-sufficient and it seemed that our own milk was the major piece we lacked. "A cow. If there were a dirty bomb or something and nothing could work. We couldn't get groceries. The boys would still need milk."

Robb split into laughter. "But you'd have to learn to milk it."

"I could do it if I had to," I said, smacking the back of my hand on his chest. "I did a story once on a dairy farm in North Dakota and they let me do it. It's kind of like pumping breast milk."

"That I would love to see. Jeannie Ralston milking a cow," Robb said.

"What? I thought you *wanted* me to be some tough homesteading kind of woman." Maybe, I thought, Robb's insistence that we move to the country would end up serving a real purpose. Maybe we'd survive some apocalypse that felt as if it was coming. I took consolation in this.

•

The way we see it, the Texas lavender industry could be like the Texas wine industry. I bet twenty years ago people scoffed at the idea of Texas wine, but now Texas vineyards finally are getting recognized. Lavender is so suited to Texas that I think it will be only a matter of time before people begin to think of Texas Lavender as an industry, its own brand. And I think your support of

Hill Country Lavender would be the first step in getting lavender truly established here."

I was sitting at the end of a long bare conference table in a fluorescent-lit room in some state office building in Austin. I was making a pitch to a committee of the Department of Agriculture for a matching grant that would allow us to establish a website, logo, signs, a marketing campaign. The men and women sitting at the other end of the table were looking over the grant application I had written up weeks earlier.

"What type of soil do you need for lavender?" one of the men asked.

"It does best in alkaline soil, between seven and eight pH," I answered. "And it needs to be well drained. Basically, it likes all that caliche in the Hill Country that everyone thought was good for nothing."

A vote was taken right then, with everyone on the committee agreeing to give us the grant.

"That was pretty easy," I said to Robb when I called afterward to tell him we would be getting $6,250 from the state. We had to put in $6,250 ourselves to meet the $12,500 budget we'd planned for marketing.

With the grant money, we concentrated on taking the lavender to the next level, which would be to look like a real business. The first thing we needed was a logo, which our friend Trish designed for us. It was a highly stylized sprig of lavender in the foreground with striped hills in back. Trish also produced a lush website, using photos mainly from France since, ironically enough, Robb had not taken many photos of our field that first season. "It's because he was hardly around," I told Trish.

The website was in place soon after the *Oprah Magazine* story came out, which led to a torrent of e-mails, phone calls, and letters. *National Geographic* also ran a short piece that spring about the venture that had sprung from one of Robb's assignments.

"We've really got to roll now with all this momentum," I said to Robb. This time my use of the *we* actually referred to me since Robb was shooting for five weeks that spring in Qatar for *Geographic,* an assignment that started out as a fairly mundane story when he got it the previous August, but had become dangerous and intense after September 11 and the U.S. invasion of Afghanistan.

My favorite part of ramping up for the next season was product research. I ordered lavender products from various farms and companies in Northern

California, Oregon, and Washington, where lavender was mainly concentrated in the United States—until now. I would show the products to Tasha for her feedback. Young and uncensored, she was always good for an honest opinion about which seemed promising. I bought various kinds of sachets, including ones specifically designed to fit in the toes of shoes—which Tasha thought were silly. I tried lavender-infused honey, which meant that some lavender oil had been injected into the honey, but it was a blander version of the true lavender honey I'd tasted in Provence.

When Robb returned home, he found a beekeeper in Blanco to put a hive next to our field, so we could have our own, true lavender honey. I bought fabrics for our own sachets, including—my favorite—a cotton voile with lavender flowers embroidered on it. I hired a Blanco seamstress to begin making sachets from my various fabrics.

"I think we're really going to make money this year," I told Robb.

•

My wife and I have tried growing lavender at our ranch, and it always dies. What could we be doing wrong?" asked an engineer type with three pens in the front pocket of his denim shirt.

"Probably watering it too much. Lavender doesn't like its feet wet," I answered, putting on an authoritative, anchorwoman tone and face. I'd heard Jim, our extension agent, use that line once before and it was so good, I couldn't help but borrow it. "The surest way to kill a lavender plant," I went on, "is give it too much water."

Behind my words, I was laughing, knowing how ridiculous it was that I was dispensing advice on plants. Robb and I were sitting under the Thinking Tree at a foldout table borrowed from our church facing eighteen eager people, most of whom were taking notes. It was our first lavender-growing seminar, and most of the participants were gardeners or retirees looking to turn their Hill Country land into a moneymaking hobby. There was one conspicuously young woman, an employee of the nearby vineyard that was trying to grow lavender. She was sent to find out why they weren't having much luck.

Even though it was a nasty March morning with the wind driving right through us, I rejected Robb's advice of moving the seminar inside. Sitting under the Thinking Tree should be part of the whole experience, I maintained, since the people were paying so much money to attend.

When we had first decided to hold the seminar, Robb insisted we charge $200 a person, though I was embarrassed to tell people that price. If you charge more, I reasoned, people expect more. I wasn't sure we could deliver the goods for that amount of money.

"The great thing about lavender," I said later to the group, as they pulled up collars and rubbed arms against the cold, "is that it's not hard to take care of." I told them that Robb hardly knew anything about lavender before we started.

"That's not true, Jeannie," he interjected, glaring at me. "I did a lot of research with the French farmers."

"Okay, whatever," I said. "Well, I can tell you that *I* didn't know anything about lavender—or gardening either."

A blonde who had been well coiffed until she had gotten out in the wind raised her hand. "So are you saying if you can do it anyone can?"

Robb and I looked at each other and joined in the laughter around us. "Basically, yes," I said.

When we were about an hour into the seminar, a special guest, Don Roberts, joined us under the tree. He had grown lavender in Oregon for more than twenty years and was also a broker for lavender oil. His brother had sent him the *Statesman* article about us, and he had called to tell us he was interested in buying any lavender oil we might produce later. Because we were nervous about being able to pass on accurate information at the seminar, we had given Roberts a ticket to come to Texas and fill in our knowledge gaps.

With Roberts in the audience, both Robb and I grew nervous. I felt we might get blasted out of our erroneous ideas, like the scene in *Annie Hall* when Woody Allen produces Marshall McLuhan to refute the pompous notions of the man in a movie theater line. When Robb talked about the farming, his eyes were constantly darting over to Roberts to see if he seemed to be agreeing.

"Lavender is a perennial," Robb said, "and you should be able to harvest off the plants for ten to twelve years." Robb glanced over at Roberts and cringed a bit. "Is that right?"

"Actually, we've found it's closer to eighteen to twenty years," Roberts said.

"Whew," Robb responded. "Well, at least if I'm wrong it's good to be *under*estimating."

When it was time to break for our catered lunch, so many people were feeling pummeled by the wind that I relented. We moved the seminar into our garage, which still retained a faint scent of lavender from its days as our drying room. After lunch, Roberts spoke about marketing and lavender oil, passing around samples of different varieties of oil he'd distilled. He emphasized that the most prized lavender oil was from a family of lavenders called "true" or "English" lavenders. The oil from our hybrid *lavandin* variety wasn't as high quality as the true lavenders, though each plant produced more oil. He pointed out that in any case—either with the true lavenders or the *lavandins*—organic oil was far more valuable than nonorganic. After the seminar, we filled out the paperwork to become certified organic before the upcoming lavender season.

"What do you think the market is for lavender here in Texas?" asked one of our seminar participants.

Robb began to respond then stopped himself and looked at me. "Jeannie should really answer that," he said with a wink. "She's the Lavender Queen."

"Ha, ha," I said. "Honey, that's the nicest thing you've ever called me." I in turn lobbed the question over to Roberts. He told us the story of a well-known lavender-growing region in Sequim, Washington, sixty miles west of Seattle. Because it is located in what's known as a blue hole, an area that rain clouds seem to skirt around, Sequim receives relatively little rain, making it ideal for lavender growing. Years ago, he told us, there was nothing much happening in Sequim, but now with lavender farms popping up all over, the area has a lucrative tourism industry.

"The thing you really have going for you here," said Roberts, who grew up north of Austin, "is that the Hill Country is already a big tourist destination. You get people from all over the state, so you're ideally set up for agritourism."

The eighteen attendees left that day telling us they'd learned more than they had hoped for, which made me feel more justified in the $3,600 we'd collected for our five hours of work.

Before Roberts took off, he inspected our plants and told us they looked to be in good shape. "They're just emerging from their winter dormancy, which is just about right as far as timing."

But a few days later, we had a late freeze, with the temperature dipping down below 20 degrees. Four days later we had another below-freezing night. We had no idea what this meant for the plants, but we heard the freezes had ruined the peach crop in the Hill Country, killing the flowers as they were just beginning to bud. This did not bode well.

CHAPTER NINE

Fragrance

I *visited your farm a week ago and was delighted by the
lavender products you offer. In fact, I arrived with a list of
"requests" from friends and ended up spending $168.00!
I have to say, nobody has been disappointed.*

—Meko Kofahl,
June 15, 2003

The cruelty of Texas rain clouds is their fickleness. They are not egalitarian, sweeping across a region bestowing their bounty equally on thirsty patches in their paths. They are hopelessly broken, like Yugoslavia, with each fragment deciding for itself how much to dispense. This reality led to, in spring 2002,what I can only call "rain envy." From my days in Manhattan I was well acquainted with apartment envy. In the auto-centric world of Austin, I would occasionally have pangs of car envy, especially if I spied a sporty BMW convertible tooling down the freeway on a cool spring afternoon. But out in Blanco, with a crop at risk, I found that instead of being jealous over material objects, I was coveting my neighbor's precipitation.

Through the early part of the year Robb, being the weather junkie, had noticed we were low on rainfall. He had gotten especially fussy about the lengths of our showers. And so had Gus. During one of my friend Mary Ellen's visits, five-year-old Gus began knocking furiously on the bathroom door while she was showering.

"Hey, Miss Ma-wy Ellen, you're taking too long. Hey, you're using up all our water. Miss Ma-wy Ellen, turn the water off," he was shouting before I could quiet him down.

But it wasn't until Easter that I really took notice of the sky's pathetic performance. Normally we had an Easter egg hunt for the boys and their friends in the thick swath of bluebonnets up the hill from the house. That year, most of the bluebonnets stayed in hiding. By mid-April the lavender, which had recently endured two late freezes, was gasping for water out in temperatures that were already in the nineties.

One evening, Robb and I watched a spectacular thunderhead the color of steel wool march in from the north. It was an angry cumulonimbus column that slowly obliterated the setting sun. Purple blooms on the sage bushes were open, which Roger had told us was the old-timers' way of predicting rain. Weegee even started to shiver and drool—another sure sign that rain was imminent. The wind picked up. I was certain we were in for a drenching. We braced ourselves and waited for it to hit. And waited. And waited.

Though the sky above us was nearly dark, it became obvious after about an hour that the real business of this storm was occurring just to the north. I looked at the lavender in the field and out toward the vegetable garden, which this year was struggling severely. I imagined all those plants to the north bobbing joyously as each drop hit them. I imagined puddles forming, stock tanks filling. I thought of northern neighbors smugly watching the sky empty itself on their stretch of dirt and feeling like the chosen ones. In my mind I saw them running out to their rain gauges afterward so they could rub their accumulation totals in everyone's faces in town the next morning. As I stood in the middle of impending brown, I knew that I was in the grips of a bad case of rain envy.

"It's just not fair," I whined to Robb after the storm cloud had skirted us. When I lived in New York, I only saw rain as a nuisance—slowing me down on my walk to work or tarnishing new shoes. But here I was desperately craving rain, as if it would relieve my own thirst. In other environments, I thought unhappily, the metaphor for bad luck is a gray cloud over your head. Here, it seemed to be the opposite; it was the cursed sun constantly on your back that made you wonder if you were born under the wrong sign.

"We'll get our rain eventually," Robb said confidently.

But after another waterless week, Robb agreed that we needed to irrigate the lavender. By then it was late April. When the irrigation lines on the first two thousand plants had broken a year earlier, we hadn't bothered to fix them, nor did we install any for the newer five thousand. We believed that since the lavender had survived this long without water from us, it didn't really need supplements. But with the season fast approaching, we had to take action to ensure good flowers. At this point, the plants should have been sending up scores of small tender shoots that would lengthen and mature into blooms, but the plants were looking alarmingly sparse, like birthday cakes with only enough candles for a teenager, rather than a centenarian. Robb found enough drip tape—plastic tubing with holes spaced at every thirty-six inches—for barely four rows.

"Four rows of blooms are better than nothing," I said. I helped him lay out the drip tape and several times a week we irrigated, using a pump to send water from the holding pond near the pool through the tubes.

On May 1, when twenty florists and retailers came out for a "lavender lunch" under the canopy of the Thinking Tree, I had hoped to show off the ready-to-burst field. Instead, they got to see desperate, balding bushes. I tried to compensate for the lack of progress in the field with lavendery center-pieces—dried lavender buds and rose blossoms sprinkled on small bowls of water.

The following week, I was encouraged that the lavender plants around our pool were dense with mature blooms and there were even enough to make a nice bouquet. Somewhat maliciously, I took the bouquet to a meeting of the four lavender growers in the region—the vineyard owners, the couple north of Fredericksburg, ourselves, and now Bert, the old man who, with advice and contacts from us, had put in a couple acres of lavender in March. I knew that the vineyard owners and the couple north of Fredericksburg were having problems with their crop—the fungus Rhizoctonia—and I, unattractively I admit, wanted to show off our blooms. I thought that the field was simply a few weeks behind the pool area, which I was told by Jim, our extension agent, had its own microclimate because of the body of water.

Our first public event of the season was Sunday, May 11. I had advertised a Mother's Day picnic under the Thinking Tree, and set the price at a whopping $33. I thought the experience of eating under that spectacular canopy in the midst of the lavender field was more than worth that price, plus I didn't want to go to the trouble of feeding people if we didn't make a decent profit. I bought the box lunches from a restaurant in town for $9. I also had a friend make lavender tea cookies and served my own lavender lemonade, which I made according to a recipe provided by the caterer who served lunch for the florists (first make a tea from the dried lavender, then add it to a pitcher of lemonade).

Though we got compliments from moms, I considered the event a disaster. The field wasn't pretty, plus the restaurant had skimped on the box lunches. Instead of a full chicken salad sandwich, it had only included a half. With a salad, chips and salsa, the cookie and lemonade, it didn't seem quite like $33 worth and I ended up giving most guests a bar of soap to compensate.

"Next year we're going to call this a 'Lavender Preview' to cover our butts," I said to Tasha.

"You really want to do this next year?" she grumbled.

When Jim came out to look at our field, his diagnosis was that the two freezes had nipped the plants. He pointed at one of our painfully few sprigs; it was coiled on top like a spring and its small green bud was bent on the end. "See this one. The stem is wacky and the bud is not the right shape. That's probably the effects of the cold." He explained that because the plants had already sent out new growth (something he called "bud primordia") when the late freezes hit, the plants had used most of their energy keeping this greenery alive instead of pushing out stems. We were told to expect shorter and fewer shoots, and some deformed buds. It was a bitter assessment on the eve of the season. I had wanted to open the third weekend in May; now we would have to wait to see if the field filled out more.

"But last year at this time—" I began.

"Don't base anything on last year," Jim said with a laugh. "Last year was God's gift to farmers. The perfect season. Those don't come along too often."

"Does that mean it's all downhill from here?" I asked, prompting a shrug of his shoulders.

I had already placed an ad in *Texas Monthly*, which would be coming out the end of May and had planned on running ads in the Austin and San Antonio papers. Now with the bad crop news, I decided to hold back. I didn't want to encourage people to come only to disappoint them. "Last year we had the blooms but no marketing; this year we have the marketing but no blooms," I said to Robb. I hadn't even contacted my buyer at Central Market, the grocery store in Austin, because I didn't think we'd have enough tall, pretty blooms to sell to her.

As we waited to see if the flowers would make a respectable showing, more trouble descended. Grasshoppers. Normally the Hill Country has a slew of grasshoppers in spring—with windshields and radiator grills being the final resting places of many. But this year, in place of water, it rained grasshoppers the size of shotgun shells. There were swarms of them, flying through the sky like an invasion of small Apache helicopters, crawling all over the grass and eating the vegetables in my garden, the sage bushes, even the yucca—a tough, spiky succulent. I watched them bounce through the lavender field. "Okay, this is getting biblical," I said to Robb.

After much study, we determined that the grasshoppers weren't actually eating the lavender, thankfully. Instead they would chew on the stems, decide they didn't like them, and go find a zucchini plant to munch on. These tastings would leave the stems broken and flopped over like downed telephone poles. The main problem was that there were so many grasshoppers having so many tastings that a huge portion of our viable lavender stems was mowed down.

"Couldn't they just get the word out that the lavender sucks instead of everyone sampling for themselves?" I asked, as I kicked at a bush, which sent a whole pack of grasshoppers buzzing into the air.

We couldn't use conventional bug spray on the plants because we'd just gone organic, and the organic product for grasshopper management—Nolo Bait—took three weeks to work. Someone suggested that guinea hens would take care of the overpopulation, but with two killer dogs we knew who'd be taking care of the guinea hens. "I guess we're screwed," I said, more depressed over the lackluster lavender than I expected.

"How do real farmers do this?" I asked our neighbor Roger when I took the boys down to his woodworking shop to watch him make a toy top on his lathe. "I can't imagine if your whole livelihood depended on a crop."

Roger lifted his shoulders. "I guess you just know you're not the one in charge."

My friend Judith said she thought I had ended up in agriculture to learn these life lessons: the need for patience and letting go.

I never before considered the Zen of farming.

·

Even without the flashy field, without the tinge of purple over the plants, we opened to the public. The pressure was too great. The *Texas Monthly* ad had come out; people who had read the stories earlier in the *Austin American States-man, Oprah,* and *Geographic* were calling. An article in *Southern Living* about both our house and the lavender had just been published, as had a story in the Houston paper. The San Antonio paper was coming out with a story in early June. I quickly had posters printed up with our open dates—Memorial Day weekend and the four weekends in June, both Saturdays and Sundays, 9 a.m. till 1 p.m.—and held my breath.

Feeling bad about what wasn't in the field the first weekend, I let some people cut at the lavender bushes around our pool. I couldn't resist the sob stories. "I'm visiting from Germany and I won't be able to come back next weekend," one woman told me. "I've driven five hours to get here," another visitor lamented. Since Robb wasn't home—he was back in Nepal shooting a follow-up to his Sherpa story of eleven years earlier—he didn't see me escort people up to the pool; he would not have approved.

After the pool lavender was gone, I expected to have to battle off complainers, but most visitors that season were surprisingly content. Having never seen a field before, they didn't know exactly what one was supposed to look like. I saw it as horribly barren, but they seemed satisfied with the aroma, however faint, from the lavender leaves, the neat rows, the Thinking Tree, and the view across the Blanco River valley. Gus and Jeb, now five and three, made an adorable addition to the staff. I set up a stand near me where they could sell lavender lemonade for one dollar a glass. Gus made his own sign, and being older, was the more devoted of the two to the project.

"Want some lavender lemonade?" he'd ask in his husky voice to visitors walking up the driveway. "It's for my college fund." Not many could resist such a sales pitch.

Even though customers weren't cutting lavender in the field, they were buying our lavender products, which I had set out on two tables. We offered organic goat milk lavender soap I bought from a woman in South Texas, lavender seedlings that people could plant in their own gardens, dried lavender— properly priced at $2 an ounce after I'd done my research—and various types of sachets that Tasha and I had filled, even though we had learned that Tasha was allergic to lavender. We had standard sachet bags and also a "baby sachet," which had a strip of Velcro on the back so that it could be attached to a diaper pail. One of our bestsellers was lavender essential oil. I had bought the lavender oil in bulk from Don Roberts in Oregon and poured it into one-ounce bottles, which we sold for $18. So powerful was the scent that when it was bottling day, I had to be sure Tasha and I had nothing else scheduled. Invariably, we'd become groggy and silly and need a nap.

Before he left for Nepal, Robb came up with several products himself—some more successful than others. One he called a car sachet. Two small bags filled with lavender attached by a pretty ribbon to hang over the rearview mirror fuzzy-dice style. I counted that among the flops, though he always argued I never gave it a chance. Later, a car rental company ran a commercial showing what would happen if they added aromatherapy to their rental cars; drivers became so relaxed they fell asleep at the wheel. "That's why the car sachets weren't a good idea," I told Robb.

But Robb did come up with a winner we called Scorpo-Shoo. I had read that scorpions don't like lavender or citrus—and actually we had noticed that we saw many fewer scorpions than before we had our lavender crop—so Robb thought we should combine lavender and dried lemon or orange peels. I bought small muslin bags and gave them a droll, retro look by adding two rubber stamps—one of a scorpion, the other the red international No sign (circle with a slash through it). We also made Moth-Away bags with just lavender inside and a rubber-stamped moth getting the same No treatment. (Eventually we replaced the lavender buds in the two products with lavender refuse—parts of leaves or buds sifted out from the dried lavender that smelled just as good.)

Ever efficient, Robb also thought of a brilliant way to transform waste products into something salable. After Tasha and I stripped the lavender buds off the stems for our dried lavender, we were left with what I considered ugly stalks. Robb reminded me that there was still lavender oil in the stems and he thought we should gather them in bunches and tie them up in a ribbon. Lavender Smokes was the name he suggested. The idea was to put them on fires in winter to scent the room, or in summer, add some to charcoal to flavor grilled chicken or fish. The lavender smokes ended up being a good money-maker since they cost us nothing. Robb also wanted to use the dried leaves for lavender kitty litter, though somehow I never got around to that. "Where's my kitty litter," he often asked with a laugh.

Tasha and I would groan. "Honey," I'd say. "You are more than welcome to start a cat poop division. That would certainly be a new level for the business."

·

The lavender was first an invitation to a truce with the country and now it's become a love affair," I told the interviewer, as I sat on the screened-in porch, wrapping up bundles of lavender with Tasha and my two nieces, visiting from Houston. The interviewer from a television show called *Central Texas Gardener* had caught us during one of only three deliveries we made to Central Market that season. Somehow we scrounged up enough decent blossoms. I was waxing poetic about the lavender for the camera because I had begun to appreciate the richness it had added to my life. I had stopped worrying so much about the articles I wasn't writing. I'd get twinges now and then, but I had accepted that it was all right for now just to maintain, tread water career-wise, rather than break new ground. And I saw that instead of being busy as a bystander, as a witness to life through journalism, I was busy living life.

The boys made me happier than I could have imagined after my rough start. I would have pressed for more kids if I hadn't fallen into the horrifying postpartum sinkhole. I couldn't risk a repeat. I felt by working at home—either on my writing or the lavender—I got the best of both worlds as a mom. I was still engaged in the world, yet at the same time plugged into the boys, avoiding much of the angst working mothers usually wrestle with. Robb's caution with money had given us flexibility and little financial stress.

At the moment, I couldn't think of anything to whine about, which was more true to my nature. I was part of a community of parents that had grown up around the Montessori school; a yoga studio had opened in Blanco and I'd found a Suzuki piano teacher for Gus. Our house felt completely and finally done. The landscaping was in and grown up, and Robb had cut all the cedar on the property. We'd planted wildflowers and native grasses—Lindheimer's Muhly, little bluestem, sideoats grama—on the property, which was now a designated wildlife habitat. We also put the land under a conservation easement, so that it could never be divided for a development, even if we were to sell it. With no more projects left, I felt liberated, but I should have seen that task-oriented Robb would soon grow antsy.

Feeling settled and secure—or maybe it was from inhaling too many lavender fumes—I surprised myself and said in some wildly exuberant or desperately weak moment on camera, recorded for posterity, so that Robb and all my Austin friends could later faint over the statement: "I can't imagine living anywhere else but Blanco."

That evening, alone in the house with the boys, I marveled that I'd actually uttered those words. What a leap I'd made. What territory I'd covered crossing over to the other side. What Kool-Aid I'd imbibed. But I didn't feel the urge to ask the producer to erase my quote. I tucked the boys in bed, their heads on pillowcases made from a vintage fabric I'd found with drawings of different cowboys, one of whom amazingly enough was named Gus and another Jeb. Then I got into my own bed. I was alone but I wasn't scared. I had become so comfortable in the house that recently I had stopped setting the alarm at night.

I had achieved something remarkable, I felt. I had endured, toughed out the isolation, the demands of a perfectionist husband and had found real peace. I felt that, like the lavender, I was a nonnative transplant that had somehow thrived. I never knew it would take so long, but the move, the kids had proved to be worth it. I could see that Robb may have been right about the country being the place to raise kids—though I wasn't ready to let him know that yet.

I loved watching the boys run free on the property—not hemmed in, not hovered over by me or any other adult. They rode their training-wheeled bikes on the dirt roads, "drove" the tractor with Robb, picked blackberries in our patch, camped out in a real tepee we'd put up at the Campsite and had stick races down the waterfall at the swimming hole. Not a bad childhood, I realized. Even before Gus was born, we had joked that not many kids would be able to say, when scolded, "Why, yes, I *was* raised in a barn." I had started to appreciate how being brought up in the country might impact their worldview; I thought it would make them more independent, more confident, more attuned to nature. The same way the country had begun to affect me.

On the wall in our bedroom hung the cursive words *Bad Dog Ranch* that our onetime housemate Beverly had twisted from a single piece of baling wire she'd found on the place. My bad dogs, sleeping on beds beside mine, were older and stinkier now. Their rhythmic breathing soothed me as I did my *Times* crossword puzzle. It was the only sound I could hear and I liked it that way.

·

Despite our host of horrors that season—freezes, drought, grasshopper plague—we still had a good year financially. Enough people came out and bought products that we grossed $30,000. I realized that the secret to making this business a respectable moneymaker was having enough lavender products to sell. The lavender in the field was the draw, but while people were out, they wanted other mementos of their day in the country, their agricultural experience. They were a captive market, in many ways. My friend Judith, who had a store in Austin, told me they kept a statistic on the percentage of people in the store who actually bought something. She said 50 percent was considered high. I realized that our conversion rate, as it's called in the retail industry, must be 98 percent. Very few people left without buying *something.* At the end of the season, I determined that my job before next spring was to come up with more and better products.

But first we had to get to the next season intact. I naively thought our agricultural tragedies were over just because that season was done. At the end of July, the Hill Country was hit with a ferociously prolific storm. Fred and Roger, who'd lived in Blanco for much of their lives, couldn't remember a sky-opening quite as intense. Though the Hill Country rarely gets rain in July, a low-pressure system camped out over the state for a whole week, with water rushing from the heavens as if Texas had been moved under the Niagara River. We could hardly venture from the house because of the swollen creeks, but the blessing was that Robb was home, so he could help mop up flooded rooms, clean muddy shoes and paws, and unclog gutters. On the Weather Channel, which seemed to be on nonstop that week, we learned that a dam overflowed in a city only forty minutes from us and saw footage of a house being swept away in the current. Our rain gauge registered more than thirty inches that week, but some places in the Hill Country got as much as forty-two.

"A bona fide turd floater," exclaimed Robb, who was thrilled he had made it back from Nepal just in time to witness weather history in the making.

When the rain finally quit we fully expected to find a beached ark up at the Campsite. With the boys, we walked out in the lavender field in rubber boots, which quickly grew grizzly-paw-size from the accumulation of mud. Many places that had once been level dirt were now gullies. At the bottom of the field, where the land flattened slightly, small ponds had formed. Any plant that had spent more than a moment in the standing water was either dead or on its last gasp.

"Shit," I said, "I hope this doesn't wipe us out."

"I think the stuff up higher will be okay; the water just raced right past those plants," Robb reassured me.

In the end, we lost six hundred plants, about 10 percent of our crop. It could have been worse. One grower we'd helped get started lost almost all his plants.

We had Antonio comb through the rows and remove dead plants for burning. Our mangy, spotty field made me sad. It was once so handsome with its plump, straight rows.

"Don't worry, we can fill in the bare spots," Robb said, when I fussed over the irregularity of the rows.

"What are the chances," I said, "of having a drought and a flood in the same year?"

"It's the Hill Country," said Robb. "Feast or famine. Or I guess feast *and* famine."

·

When we first launched our website, our system for buying products was as antiquated as making a phone call through an operator. We only sent out products after customers had mailed in checks. That fall, we decided to catch up to the century; we started accepting Paypal, which immediately boosted our sales, especially for Christmas. The extra Internet sales meant that Tasha, now a college freshman majoring in photography and graphic design, needed to come in once a week through the year to fill and ship orders.

"Hey, Miss Jeannie," Tasha said one Friday, using the ironically formal name she had for me, as I walked into the office. "I'm done with the orders. What else do you need?"

"Will you *please* do something about her mess?" Robb said from his side of the office. "I think any time you're not working on lavender you should help organize her." Poor Tasha. With the lavender workload, she had been diverted almost entirely from photo projects with Robb. Now this.

"Sure. I keep my mom organized too," Tasha said cheerfully as she looked toward my desk, which seemed about normal for me. There were stacks of files in three piles—one for each story I was working on. Several prototypes of lavender products I was considering sat to one side; an application for an art class for the kids was flung on my computer keyboard.

"Honey," I protested. "I've got a lot going on right now. I need to—"

"And I don't?" He spread his hand out toward his maddeningly orderly space.

"Well, you don't count. You're anal." I should have known that Robb's competitive spirit would hear a challenge in my statement. This who's-busier contest was nothing new, and it was not anything I could win, even though that year Robb had consciously cut down on the amount of work he was taking. He had decided two major international stories in a row—Qatar and Nepal—was too much time away from the boys. Robb Kendrick turning down work was like a starlet shying away from a flashbulb. But the boys were at an age when Robb couldn't stand to miss a day with them if he didn't need to.

He also had personal work he wanted to concentrate on, a type of historic photography called tintypes. It was a photo process used in the mid 1800s, in which the image was made directly on a piece of tin. After studying with an eccentric hermit who had resurrected the art form, Robb had special cameras made and found antique lenses from the time period. He designed a portable dark room so that he could develop images anywhere he went—not too different from the way Mathew Brady shot the Civil War. The handmade, one-of-a-kind images were an antidote to the speed and perfection of the digital photography he did for paying work. In a serendipitous and ironic dovetailing of interests, the substance used to varnish the plates after they were exposed was lavender oil.

But no matter if his schedule was excruciating, or light enough to allow him to experiment with his new passion, Robb always had the trump card in the busy sweepstakes. He was hectic in a way that made the major chunk of the money for the family. He had the weight of responsibility. What I had was the frenzy of juggling too many worlds at once—kids, writing, lavender, house. I always thought I should get extra slack for keeping them all in the air at once, but really no one but me was keeping track. On top of everything I still had the Montessori school pulling at me, long after I thought it would be sailing along mostly on its own.

As much as I adored Sally, I began to sense over that fall that the job of school administrator was too much for her, especially when she was running the classroom at the same time, which she had to do after our third teacher quit. As a board member, I was worried about the school's cash flow. When I tried to get involved in the day-to-day finances of the school, Sally accused me of micromanaging. Though I was no fiscal genius, I knew we needed strict guidelines if we wanted to stay afloat.

Our *High Noon* came at the end of 2002 when I learned that Sally—without notifying the board—had been giving tuition discounts to parents in exchange for help at the school. I was livid. Parents should help at the school without any compensation, I argued, especially since we were still a shaky start-up. Why was I trying so hard to bring in money—I had organized every school fund-raising effort, including Halloween Festivals the past two years—if it was being given away so easily. Slacker parents, always irritating, became my pet peeve.

As the battle became vicious, I couldn't help but analyze and overanalyze my role in the falling-out. I came to believe I was too heavily invested personally in the success of the school.

"Will you please quit the board," Robb said. "You don't need this." But I couldn't let go that easily. I was despondent over the loss of my first real friend in Blanco, who had made such a difference in my attitude toward living here. I was not in the habit of losing friends, especially in such a dramatic upheaval. In the end, I waited for my term on the board to expire in February, so that I could exit more gracefully, and before I left I made sure that other board members would more carefully monitor budgets and tuition breaks.

"I swear, Jeannie, after this, if you join another board, it's grounds for divorce," Robb said, standing over my desk. "If you'd put this much time into paying jobs, you'd be hauling in some real cash." He cited all my affiliations and the events I was responsible for, such as library programs. The latest one, a talk by Shelley Duvall, a neighbor I'd recently befriended, was standing-room-only, drawing people from Austin to hear the reclusive actor who moved to the Hill Country after her house was destroyed in the 1994 Los Angeles earthquake.

"Yeah, yeah." I fluttered a hand to shoo him from my desk. "I'm embracing, I'm embracing. You wanted me to embrace living here. You got it."

My embrace soon got even bigger. After leaving the Montessori board, I transferred Gus to a private school that was just getting started. Run by a woman known as Miss P, who had taught Tasha for several years, the school emphasized the classics and experiential learning. Miss P had to be good, I thought, to turn out such a self-possessed young woman as Tasha. Classes didn't meet on Mondays so that families could take field trips together. I used the time to take Gus (and Jeb, though he remained at the Montessori school) to museums or the zoo in San Antonio. I loved the time together regardless that I was losing one-fifth of my workweek. Immediately, I began helping Miss P organize into a real school and get more students, writing a story for the Blanco paper and getting her website under way.

"Here we go again," Robb said with a sigh.

"Come on, it's for the boys' education," I maintained. "What's more important than that?"

Hoping the adage "the busier you are the more you get done" held true, I couldn't resist adding one more project. I happened to be on an advisory board to the Blanco Community Center, which was affiliated with the local public schools. At one of the board meetings, I noticed that the center's auditorium had been renovated—cushioned seats, a new sound system, a large pull-down screen. "I want to show old movies here," I told the director of the center. "People are always complaining there's nothing to do here. I'm sick of it." I knew that instead of grumbling, I needed to make Blanco the kind of place I wanted to live in. With the director's blessings, I found a way to screen movies without violating copyright laws, and the Blanco Film Society was born.

When Robb heard about my plan for the weekly movies, he smiled and put his arm around me as I made scrambled eggs on our old Chambers stove. "You know, I'm going to go apply for a grant from the state. They ought to pay for you to go live in small towns across Texas." I turned to him with a screwed-up face, trying to figure out where he was going with this. "Jeannie Ralston. Improving Texas, one town at a time."

I wasn't sure if he was complimenting or teasing me, but I laughed and waved the spatula in his face. "No, no, no," I said. "That will *not* be happening. I will *not* be moving. I'm not going through *this* again."

The movies were an immediate hit, especially with retirees who didn't want to drive to Austin or San Antonio for a film. My goal was to show movies that couldn't be rented in town, which basically left me wide open. Mostly we stuck to classic films, but we also ran foreign and art house films, such as *The Umbrellas of Cherbourg* and *Babette's Feast.* The most fun for me was choosing the monthly theme and introducing the film every week. Among my favorite lineups were "numbered" movies—including *Five Easy Pieces, The 39 Steps,* and *The Third Man,* the best movie ever made in my book.

Our first season, the alternative paper in Austin wrote about the film society and our slate of movies for May, which I was billing as a Texas Film Festival. I'd scheduled *Red River, Raggedy Man,* and *The Last Picture Show.* I'd forgotten how much sex there was in *Last Picture Show* and cringed through most of it wondering if I'd gone too racy for rural Texas. But no one objected, maybe because the territory was not unfamiliar. Blanco had recently seen its own sex scandal, with the vet's wife taking up with his business partner.

I also invited a filmmaker from Austin to come out to screen his quasi-documentary about Shamrock, Texas, which sponsors a beard-growing competition every St. Patrick's Day. He was the first of many filmmakers I would have out to Blanco. The last movie on our Texas slate was *Giant,* which I felt a new connection to on this viewing—a cosmopolitan woman from back East finding her place in the wilds of Texas. Okay, I was no Elizabeth Taylor, but I thought Robb—with his piercing blue eyes and delicate features—bore a certain resemblance to James Dean. I don't know where the Rock Hudson character fit in, but identifying with a piece of fiction is always a stretch anyway.

Soon, I became known to Blanco in one of two ways. Either the Movie Lady or the Lavender Lady. Most people had no idea that I was also a writer. At least locally, Robb began to exist in my shadow.

One day, when we ran into an older woman, a regular at the film society screenings, outside the Blanco post office she was happy to finally meet my husband. "I heard you work for the *National Geographic*. When should I look for one of your stories?"

"I have one out on Elko, Nevada, this September," he said.

"Oh good," she said. "I'll look for Robb Ralston."

"No, actually it's Robb *Kendrick*," he corrected kindly.

"Oh, I'm so sorry," she said, patting at the tight curls around her ears.

"It's okay," Robb said, laughing. "I'm a progressive guy. I kept my own name when we got married." The old woman nodded her head wearily, realizing there was a joke in there she couldn't quite grasp.

"That line still works, huh?" I said as we walked to the car.

"I guess I'll need it more now that I'm only known as Mr. Ralston."

•

When I heard the message on our answering machine, I gasped. It was Gus's new little league coach telling us the first practice date, and I knew his name too well. It was the same man who, with his wife, had led the anti-Montessori campaign eighteen months earlier. "What are we going to do?" I asked Robb, not wanting to expose Gus to his influence.

"We can't pull him out. That would be dumb."

"Yeah, but we've got to be careful. We can't have Gus go evangelical on us." I decided I would watch the coach vigilantly, listening for any hint of proselytizing, bias, or plain stupidity. But what I heard instead surprised me: lots of tenderness and encouragement. "Hey, it's no big deal," he'd tell kids who got upset about missing a ball. "It's all about having fun. Are you having fun? Are you having fun?" Gus grew to love him and his son. By the end of the season, Gus pushed to have his son over for a playdate, which I agreed to, and I'd arrived at a shocking new assessment, despite every instinct to the contrary. His dad was a lovely man. Misguided, to my mind, but lovely all the same.

It was then that a thoroughly counterintuitive thought occurred to me: To be part of a small town, or at least my small town, I had to be more broad-minded than I had been living in New York. My years in New York never taught me the kind of openness and tolerance that allowed me to befriend—I had to gulp when I said it—a Christian fundamentalist. The truth was that living in Blanco had forced me to socialize with people I would have never associated with before. Narrow-minded, right-wing hypocrites. That's what I might have called them if I didn't have to get to know them. And in a big city, I wouldn't have *had* to get to know them.

The more involved I got in the community, the fonder I grew of it. With kids, the time warp that had once irked me felt like a miracle. There was no McDonald's or Burger King to tempt the boys. The Fourth of July parade was only five blocks, but it was long on charm—horses, carriages, antique cars, farming-themed floats, and miniature donkeys in sombreros. We never locked the doors to our house, even when we left on a trip. Amazingly, Robb and I didn't know where our house keys were.

One afternoon while the boys were eating ice cream cones in town, I recognized that Norman Rockwell could have painted the scene. Two tow-heads with chocolate ice cream dripping from their faces, sitting on a porch in front of a window that bore the store's name in hand lettering. On that day, I sensed that I had in my little town something many people are searching for. Maybe it was more *Cheers*ian than Rockwellian. But nevertheless, as corny as it sounded, I belonged somewhere; everybody knew my name. I had a real community.

•

Isn't it like, 'plant it and they will come'?" the interviewer pressed me as we sat under the Thinking Tree. It was May 2003 and he was at the lavender farm putting together a segment for a statewide TV show that was like Charles Kuralt's *On the Road,* but within the Lone Star borders. The producer was blatantly leading the subject, and as an interviewer myself I resisted such heavy-handed tactics. He wanted me to make a *Field of Dreams* comparison, but it seemed such a facile and overused metaphor, one that I would never employ on my own.

"Well, it would seem so," I said, motioning out beyond the gnarled branches to the lavender field that surrounded us. In the near distance, about two hundred people were bent over cutting flowers from rows of puffy purple bushes. I was ecstatic that we had a good bloom again. This was our third weekend open to the public, and the publicity, groundwork, and notes to our e-mail list were paying off. "They certainly do come, don't they?"

He wouldn't be deterred. "Isn't it like, uh, a *Field of Dreams* for women?" I wanted to roll my eyes, but the camera was right in my face, too close actually. I had been so busy that morning, making lemonade, putting out signs and tables and products—we now had about thirty—I hadn't even had a chance to put on makeup. My hair—which I'd recently cut short because I thought it would be easier than keeping it tied back—was sticking out in places, like Christmas tree branches (but at least I was getting regular highlights again). Oh well, I thought, at forty-two the camera's not exactly going to be my friend in any situation. I remembered how I used to fuss about my photos for the contributors' pages of various magazines. These days, vanity seemed like a quaint hobby of my youth.

"You know, I've never thought of it that way." I could feel his irritation. Beyond his camera, I saw Tasha walking down one of the rows toward me holding the telephone. I saw lines of people up at the top of the field, looking at products and waiting to pay our two new workers—two fourteen-year-old cousins who Tasha and I affectionately called the Little Girls. I'd better get this interview over with, I thought.

"It's almost like a field of dreams for women," I said, looking directly into the camera, giving the producer the sound bite he sought but at the same time noting the absurdity of this coming from me since it was never my own dream.

After the interview, I walked up to the tables where customers were clustered. We had three tables now, and I'd added so many products to our line over the past year that the display of lavender soy candles (made by a woman in San Antonio) was almost spilling off the edge. As I greeted our visitors, I straightened the stacks of brownie-sized soaps in the two baskets.

"Tasha, could you get some more lavender chamomile," I said, prompting her to duck under the table for refills. The other variety we were selling was plain lavender, and I noted how much faster these bars were going than those made by the two other soapmakers I'd tried last season. Through Tasha's mom, who sold soaps at her pottery store, I'd hooked up with an exceptional soapmaker, whose purple bars had a creamy consistency and an aroma so tantalizing some people stuck them in their drawers in place of sachets. Even my store-owning friend Judith, an exacting critic, thought they were among the most sumptuous soaps she'd used. The new soapmaker also concocted bubble bath, lotion, shower gel, and bath bombs for us. One woman—from Beverly Hills of all places—couldn't seem to get enough of the lavender shampoo and conditioner the soapmaker produced for us. I laughed at the idea that this customer, living at ground zero of conspicuous grooming, chose to order her beauty products from middle-of-cowpatch Texas.

"Can I set these here?" a customer asked, placing a pile of purchases on the only spare space on the table. After adding her total, I wrapped the items in purple tissue paper and slipped them in a brown kraft paper bag with handles, which I'd started using instead of my hideous leftover plastic grocery bags.

"You know how to use this?" I asked before I put the blue, beehive-shaped oil warmer in the bag. She shook her head. "Put a bit of water in this bowl up here with a couple drops of oil. When you light the candle below it'll scent a whole room. It's wonderful." She smiled and thanked me. I had begun offering oil warmers, also called diffusers, in response to a common question: What do you do with the oil? Earlier I would tell people where to buy a diffuser, then I realized with a duh! that I should be selling them myself instead.

"Oh no, I forgot to bring scissors," a woman said meekly. She had just arrived with a group that was reading a sign I'd posted telling guests to cut first and pay afterward and how many flowers were considered a bunch.

"We've got some loaner scissors right here," Tasha said pointing to a tub labeled just that, Loaner Scissors. I noticed the woman was entirely empty-handed, even though on our website we told people to bring, along with scissors, a basket or bucket for flowers. "And over here, we've got some buckets that are just right for lavender," I added as I picked up a long, thin galvanized tin bucket. "You can borrow it while you're cutting in the field and return it when you're finished. Or if you want to take it home, it's only five dollars." I had begun selling the buckets because so many customers like this woman came without any container for their blooms and most who borrowed the buckets for the field ended up buying them once they saw how striking the lavender looked in them.

"God, these tables are full, Jeannie," Robb said as he walked up after finishing his interview with the producer. "It's a good thing you didn't do all that food stuff." I sighed quietly and began calculating the total for another customer. That spring I had been determined to develop a line of lavender food products since I'd been reading that lavender had become popular in cooking. I bought large bags of ingredients to make lavender Earl Grey tea, Herbes de Provence, and lavender sugar, but Robb worried about the liability of selling anything edible. All we needed was for someone to plump up like a saguaro cactus at teatime, he said. Reluctantly, I put away the bulk ingredients—for the time being, I told myself.

I couldn't even sell our gorgeous lavender honey, which was sitting in our pantry right then in pretty jars. Juan, a new worker from Mexico who'd started the previous February, had bravely and remarkably extracted the honey without a smoker or a bee suit, but I'd learned that there were strict controls on honey making. We would need a license and a certified "honey room"—the name made Robb think of special quarters at a brothel. Instead we kept the honey for ourselves, which wasn't a bad fate by any means, and later gave jars as gifts to friends and editors at Christmas, who were generally astounded that it had come from our very own farm.

"Hey, you're at $79," Tasha said to the customer she was helping. "If you get to $90, you get a T-shirt." She motioned to a sign tacked to the tree that said, "Free T-shirt with $90 purchase or more." The Estée Lauder–like gimmick had been Robb's idea, and in the first two weeks of the season it had worked well, prodding many customers to buy just that much more to get our good-looking T-shirt, which normally sold for $13. It had a small logo on the front left pocket and a bigger version on the back that also gave our website address, of course. All of the staff, including the boys, were wearing one. The woman handed Tasha three more soaps, for a $15 boost. "All right!" I exclaimed, thrilled that Tasha had remembered to make the push. Sometimes she and the other staff forgot. "Thank you, thank you."

As I helped Tasha fill the woman's bag, another customer accidentally knocked a stack of straw hats to the ground. "It's okay, it's okay," I said, as I swooped them up. These hats—hand-painted with lavender flowers on front—were undoubtedly my favorite new item. I had gotten the idea because many people, obviously lacking sun sense, arrived at our place without any shelter for their scalp. On the Internet I tracked down an artist in Haiti who painted garden scenes on hats. I e-mailed him a photo of lavender blossoms and he sent me a photo of a prototype back within days. This is just too fun, I thought. Think of it and it is done.

The only hitch was that the artist asked me to wire $500 in advance to

Haiti to cover the hats and shipping. Robb had been to Haiti many times and knew how unhinged the country was. "Don't you dare send the whole amount," he warned, "and don't wire it to Haiti of all places."

I blithely ignored his warning. I felt good about the guy, merely based on the cheery tone of his e-mails and how quickly he got back to me with photos of the prototype. I nervously sent the money without telling Robb, and after six weeks I began to suspect that Robb had been right. I e-mailed the guy, asking how he was coming along. He wrote back with a photo of dozens of the hats stacked up on a table. Two weeks later, two large boxes arrived for me.

"My hats! *Mis sombreros!*" I exclaimed to Juanita when I saw the return address. I tore into the box, which attracted the attention of the boys, who were only too happy to rip cardboard. Inside were stacks of hats—each with a tall crown and narrow brim. I picked up a whole column and placed it on my head.

"Who do I look like?" I asked the boys as I paraded around with my wobbly load.

"The Caps for Sale guy," Gus said, referring to a character from one of our favorite books. I put a short stack on both Gus and Jeb and we all walked into the office giggling. Gus's pile was set on his head like the Leaning Tower. Jeb's made a slow-motion tumble to the floor, as he desperately tried to grab it with his little hands.

"Caps fwo thale," Jeb announced.

"What's this?" Robb asked, looking up from his computer.

"It's our hats. From Haiti!" I said smugly. "He was honest after all."

Robb shook his head. "You sent the money anyway, didn't you?" I raised my chin and nodded my head. "I'm glad it worked out for you," he said, with his eyebrows raised and a scold obviously congealing in his head. "But I still say you need to be more careful. Not quite so trusting."

"But you always say I don't trust you enough. I was just practicing."

"No, the problem is you trust everyone *but* me."

"Okay, okay," I said as the boys and I—all the stacks now intact—turned and sauntered out of the office.

Out at the field, the woman who had knocked over the hats later bought one. "How do I look?" she asked as she modeled it.

"Lavendery," I answered. "Lusciously lavendery."

She smiled and handed me her other purchases—soaps, lip balm, candles. "Do you make all this here?" she wanted to know, looking behind me I suppose to see if we had a factory. Many visitors assumed we manufactured our products ourselves, and I wished I could have; it would have meant a much higher profit margin. But I didn't have the time, or the talent, for that feat.

"We make some things here, but mostly we find really great people to make them for us," I answered. "To make everything ourselves, we'd have to quit our day jobs, and we both like our day jobs too much."

I knew even as I said it that in any case, it would never be a matter of Robb quitting his photography—he earned too much. Plus, it was completely obvious that he had no desire to manage the business. He still ran his tractor through the field to clean up weeds and oversaw the pruning in November, when we cut the plants back so that they could have a better bloom in the spring. As he so graphically put it at our second seminar earlier that spring, "Jeannie is the neck up of the business; I'm the neck down." I couldn't help but conjure up a Franken-farmer—part man, part woman, a head for PR and a body for BO. But I began to sense he was losing interest in the lavender in general. "I just wanted to see if I could grow it," he said more than once. "Now that I've done that . . ."

Not for the first time, I was moving in the opposite direction, and that third season, when every weekend we were inundated with visitors—six thousand in total, fueled partly by a flattering story in the Fort Worth paper—I figured out why the lavender had become so fulfilling, so important to me. Each day we were open, cars streamed down our small county road. Some neighbors had complained about the lavender rush hours—especially when tour buses would unload a garden or church club at our front gate, blocking our narrow road. Others put the traffic to good use, scheduling open houses or garage sales on lavender days. I met people from all over the state—people I'd known in Austin, friends of my brother's from Houston, a woman I'd gone to high school with who happened to live in the area. I told our story so often that I had to work to make it sound unpracticed. Mary Ellen often came out for the hoo-ha with her boyfriend, and later began selling her own lavender vanilla ice cream, which normally was gone in a couple of hours. People had questions for me; they sought me out to drool over the products, the lavender, the whole setting. I had once worried about feeling isolated in Blanco, but through lavender that problem had been solved and then some. Now every weekend of blooming season, I was the hostess of an enormous party, surrounded by grinning, happy flower people.

Our visitors were so numerous and enthusiastic that before the third season even started we realized we needed an automatic security fence across the front of our driveway. We had learned from the past two seasons that if the gate was open—and we often didn't close it since it had to be shut by hand—people would drive up snooping around for lavender. We were once grilling burgers at the pool with some friends when, like hand puppets, four heads popped up over the stone wall. "Can we cut some lavender?" they asked. Back then, even when we did shut the gate after the field closed, the determined ones pushed it open.

"The gate was the best investment," I told Robb at the end of one lavender day. "No stragglers or stalkers." One weekend evening, however, I noticed a car parked on the road next to the lavender field. I saw two women climb over the fence where a strand of barbed wire was broken, snip some lavender, then jump back. It might as well be crack, I thought to myself.

Crowd control was a particular problem the last weekend we were open, the date of the vineyard's lavender celebration—which they held despite never having had a full bloom. For the past couple of years they had invited craftspeople to sell their wares in booths, while chefs demonstrated lavender cooking or gardeners talked about lavender growing. The first year they held the event in July, since that was when the lavender bloomed in France. Using the experience of others, they switched their festival to the last weekend in June, which still seemed too late since our flowers were on their very last breath by then. This year, all the lavender growers in the area—five in all now—came together loosely for a lavender driving trail through the Hill Country the same weekend as the vineyard's celebration.

I was happy that we all found a way to cooperate, but I was more than a little disturbed to discover the name that Bert, the retired attorney, had chosen for his lavender operation: Lavender Country. It was awfully close to ours, but I didn't say anything, fearing I would seem too niggling. I let it pass, which was a mistake, as I was to later learn.

On the weekend of the lavender trail, Mary Ellen's boyfriend remained all day at the bottom of our driveway, directing cars in and out of the empty field we were using as a parking lot. At one point, while he was sorting out a traffic jam, someone honked his horn.

"Oh no, no, no," I shouted from behind our product tables, a football field away. "It is so completely *wrong* to get upset at a lavender field."

We had never seen our home so overrun. After four hours, Gus said he was closing his lemonade stand. When I protested, he became annoyed. "Mom, we've already made $112. I'm going to watch some cartoons."

I let him go, but whispered to Tasha, "He's definitely not his father's son if he thinks he's made enough money."

I hadn't needed to whisper since Robb was nowhere near. He was traveling that day, but I heard from him often. He called several times to find out how much money we were pulling in. Tasha would often disappear during the day with stacks of bills and checks to count the take and hide it in our office.

Twelve hundred dollars, I told him at eleven o'clock, $2,300 at one, $3,500 for the day at closing time. "And that doesn't count our lunch sales," I told him.

For this season, I had revised our under-the-tree dining experience—which I was now billing as a box lunch to keep expectations in the proper place. I kept the same chicken salad sandwich—a whole one instead of the half, and lowered the price to $19. People could make reservations online, paying in advance. We offered the lunch every day that the field was open, and sometimes we had no diners, but during the driving trail weekend, the tables were packed.

"You and your lunches," Tasha would grouse every time she passed me that weekend carrying boxes of food or bags of trash. Once she stuck her tongue out at me playfully.

That season many visitors came wearing lavender-colored shirts and sometimes a whole group would be in purple—even the men. I started giving a 10 percent discount to anyone dressed in lavender, and on the Saturday of the driving trail I gave the same discount to the owner of an apricot poodle named Lavender. The man lifted the small dog in his arms to show me her collar tag.

Customers came that weekend from all over Texas and beyond. On Sunday, two wild-eyed women made piles on the table—two or more of everything we sold. "We drove down from Oklahoma!" they announced. "Just to see the lavender." They had barely slept the previous night, having driven the ten hours after they left work on Saturday evening. Together they spent more than $800—our largest single sale to date. I cleared my throat and announced, "The winners of the Biggest Lavender Fan award are . . ." I stopped to find out their names. I presented them each with two bars of soap and a T-shirt. "Wear them with pride and wear them often," I told them. "We need more Oklahomans like you down here!" Though I was exhausted, or probably because I was exhausted, I was giddy. I knew the day, the weekend, the season were almost over. We'd had our best weekend ever, and later I would receive calls from businesses in town, such as Hardscrabble Café, telling me that with so many lavender people streaming through Blanco, they'd also had their best weekends. "We love lavender," the owner of the restaurant told me. I did too.

CHAPTER TEN

Essential Oil

*I read about your lavender farm all the time and drool like a
Labrador with envy—although it's quite clear how much hard
work you and Robb have done.*

—BELINDA HARE,
June 5, 2003

I didn't see any of it coming.

Just as Katy didn't see the trailer coming.

On a brilliant October morning, when we were almost to Sea World in
San Antonio, which was an hour from our house, Robb received a cell phone
call. "What? Who? What color?" Robb was saying urgently into the phone,
as he slowed the car and found a place to make a U-turn. "We're on our way,
right now."

After mouthing the words "What? What happened?" I finally got to ask
out loud when Robb hung up the phone, looking distraught.

"That was Wallace, the welder. He said when he was leaving our house, he
backed up his trailer and hit Weegee. But he's not dead, just hurt." As his eyes

narrowed in pain, he stepped on the gas. Wallace had been at our place working on the lavender distillation equipment my dad and brother, both chemical engineers, had designed so that we could start making our own lavender oil.

"Weegee? Is he sure it's Weegee?" Weegee was lithe and skittish and generally stayed away from strangers and strangers' cars.

"Well, he said it was our white dog. He said, 'I'm so sorry. I hit your white dog.'" Panic clenched my throat. I put my hands on my face, then realized I needed to tell the boys what had happened, as gently as possible.

The boys began bouncing in their booster seats. "Daddy, Daddy, hurry! We've got to save Weegee." Robb shushed them so he could call our new neighbors—an Austin advertising executive and his family who came out on the weekends—to ask them to meet us at the vet's with Weegee.

On our rush back to Blanco, I couldn't imagine what Weegee was feeling, alone and hurt. He was so sensitive at times he seemed psychic. His name really did suit him—it came from a 1940s New York photographer, who so regularly made it to crime scenes before the police that they gave him his nickname—a bastardization of Ouija as in Ouija board. On the morning of September 11, while I sat outside obliviously reading newspapers, Weegee began trembling and drooling, just as he did when a thunderstorm was approaching. But the sky was perfectly clear. I pulled him onto my lap and held him close, before going inside and getting a call from a manic friend instructing me to turn on my TV.

When we got to the vet, our neighbors were waiting with Weegee wrapped in a sheet. He had thrown up on their front seat—a little gift for their trouble. He looked fine to me, and to the vet too. "There's nothing wrong with him," she announced after her exam. "Nothing seems broken. There's no internal organ damage from what I can tell."

Robb and I were elated and we loaded Weegee back in the car. "You know, I'm going to call Wallace just to make sure there's not a mistake," Robb said. After he dialed the phone, I watched Robb nod his head then widen his eyes. "The fat one? With the two black circles around her eyes? Oh shit." He moved the phone away from his mouth. "It was Katy, not Weegee!" The feelings of relief dissolved into anguish at the thought of Katy—who was blond, not white—lying alone, possibly dying, possibly dead, in our driveway. Never had hair color been so critical.

Our neighbors, who said they had seen Katy lying on the driveway wagging her tail when they picked up Weegee, took Gus and Jeb to their house so we could speed the eight minutes to our place to get Katy, who at twelve was suffering from arthritis in her bad knees and was partially blind and deaf. As we drove to the house we reconstructed what must have happened. Katy had been lying in the driveway and probably didn't see or hear Wallace as he was backing up and then when she did, she probably couldn't move fast enough. We knew that Katy was in a far worse state to manage an injury and as we neared the house, we were both in tears, knowing this might be her last day. There she was, still on the side of the driveway, looking weary but still managing to wag her tail. We didn't see any blood, but she couldn't walk.

The diagnosis by the vet was as bad as we'd feared. Her spinal column was broken. She was in shock. There was nothing she could do for her. Robb and I took some time alone to caress her and remember all the way back to the days when she was so small she would ride on the back of Robb's motorcycle in Austin tucked in my leather jacket. Robb was weeping as fiercely as he had the two other times I'd seen him turn on the full waterworks—when the boys were born. Just before the vet put the needle in, I swear Katy looked both of us in the eyes, as if to say it was okay, or maybe thank you, or maybe I'll see you later.

We buried her body by our pool so she could be with us in a place we were sure to be having fun. The boys made a cross for her grave, for our darling pet, our first child in so many ways. One of our beautiful bad dogs.

I cried for two days over Katy and thought that was the end of my grief. I told myself she was old and I had known she didn't have much more time. The next four weeks were unusually busy, and even though I caught my breath every time I looked at the place where she slept and kept expecting her to hobble up and nuzzle my leg, I ordered myself to move on. I was writing a story for *Parenting* on worrying. We had a fall growing seminar for forty-five people coming up—our biggest ever. Plus, we were going to use the people from the seminar to help us plant a new field—just for lavender that would be distilled into oil—an hour and a half away near a town called Mason on some new property Robb had bought. The weekend after the planting we were opening up the field at our house, and I had invited Miss P's school to sell food and drinks to visitors to earn some money. But it wasn't looking good for a fall bloom. Then the following weekend, we would be testing the lavender distillation unit that my father and brother had put together.

A few days after we buried Katy, right before my period when I was always most wacky and weepy anyhow, it hit. I didn't know what to call "it," really—

maybe depression, but prolonged anxiety attack seemed more accurate. All of a sudden I couldn't sleep again. It was more than the garden variety of sleepless night, with some tossing and turning as global warming ramifications are considered. It was the bullfrog-in-my-chest kind of insomnia, exactly what had descended on me at my parents' house four years earlier. For three nights, I couldn't sleep at all, feeling that the growing seminar, the weekend opening for the public, the test of the distillation equipment were all too much for me. I couldn't imagine making my way through it all. Even figuring out how to get the boys to school suddenly seemed too taxing. Those first three nights, I tried to stay calm and watched my favorite videos—one night I watched the whole five hours of the BBC's *Pride and Prejudice* just to see the spectacular Colin Firth as Mr. Darcy emerge from the water to encounter Elizabeth at Pemberley.

But even a wet Colin Firth wasn't enough to free me from the dreadful choke hold. Feeling like the biggest loser known to mankind, I went back on the Zoloft. What a cop-out, I thought to myself. Before, I could justify my crack-up because I was nursing and coursing with strange hormones. Now, what was my excuse? I had never had problems with depression before my postpartum bout; now I had to consider I might have real psychological problems. I had associated my insomnia and panic with traveling, but now they had found me in my own house. I felt like someone whose safe room had been invaded by burglars.

I would have liked to cancel the growing seminar the next Saturday, but knew that we'd be making $9,000 more or less in one day, plus we were getting all the free labor to plant the field in Mason.

"You're going to have to do all the talking. I don't know if I can even pretend to be cheery," I said to Robb as I sat in my office assembling small books. We had decided to "publish" our lavender growing advice in book format. Previously, we had put all the information from our seminars in a purple pocket folder and offered it on the website for $35. Amazingly this homemade job had quickly become our top seller, which to me indicated how scarce good information on lavender was. Even though people were truly paying for our expertise, we decided to upgrade the book so buyers would feel they were getting more of their money's worth. With a cover designed by our friend Trish, the forty-page book (later to grow to sixty-four) looked quite professional.

"At least you won't be contradicting me," Robb said with a laugh.

"Don't worry, I'll save enough energy to correct you if you say something goofy," I added, as I stapled a book together.

●

It's showtime," I said to Robb the following Saturday morning as we stood at our bathroom window, watching cars arrive for the seminar. Tasha was there to greet the forty-five participants, handing out packages to each that included a book, two plants, and a sachet. I had slept maybe two hours the night before, even though I kept a tissue dabbed with lavender oil next to my nose hoping the scent would calm me, but it only made me think of everything I needed to do over the next two days.

"Remind me to never do this again," I said as we walked out to the Thinking Tree.

"Come on, it's the easiest money we can make with the lavender."

"It doesn't seem easy right now."

"Just sit and smile," Robb said, as he ducked below some branches to enter under the canopy. That's exactly what I did, occasionally nodding my head at one of his statements.

At this seminar were two middle-aged couples who were real farmers. One man grew grapes in the Panhandle, which he sold to different Texas vineyards. The other farmed sorghum in East Texas.

"You may know more than I do," Robb said to them. "You're welcome to jump in if I say something wrong or if you have better advice."

During lunch, which Tasha and another worker brought out to the tables, someone asked why so many of our plants looked gray. It was a good question. Many rows—especially those at the far end of the field, where we'd lost a lot of plants to the flood—were tinged gray. I had told people that the rains had hurt those plants too, even though I knew they were high on the slope, far from any standing water. Robb offered his own explanation.

"Well, I think when I was driving the tractor through the rows, I got the sweep too close to some of the plants," he said. It was the first I'd heard of this. "The plants are so much bigger now and I didn't adjust the tines on the sweep. I think I severed some roots."

The farmer from the Panhandle raised his hand. "That's what we call cultivator blight."

"Cultivator blight," Robb repeated laughing. "Yeah, that's about right."

At the planting in Mason that weekend, the euphemism of the day was "installer error." We had thought that we were so Tom-Sawyer crafty, offering participants the chance to plant a field "at no extra expense." However, it turned out we would have been better off hiring a crew for the job.

A day earlier, Juan, our worker, had laid out strings for the rows across the field, which had already been plowed up by a neighbor. The only tasks for our free labor force were digging holes and plopping in plants. The problem was many participants—once they got a taste for how it was done—got tired quickly and left. I spent much of the 90-degree November day crawling along the lines of string on my knees, like some sort of penitent. Progress was horrifically slow.

"I was about to say that I forgot how hard the planting was," I told Robb when we took a break for water, "then I realized I'd never actually done a planting before."

"Well, this will really let people see a lavender farm isn't all glamour. I'll bet a lower percentage of this group starts a farm than any other seminar."

After his rest, Robb walked the field where a few dedicated participants were still working along with Juan. "Shit," he exclaimed as he passed by a plant that hadn't been covered with dirt properly. He packed down some dirt lightly on the roots. Then he saw another misplaced plant and another. "Well, looks like we've got a high installer error rate. I hope this field makes it."

By about 4 p.m., we were still three hundred plants short of finishing, but I felt like I'd been marathon dancing in the desert. I decided to sell the remaining plants for only a tiny profit to one of the women who had stuck it out till the end. The demand for lavender in Texas had grown so much that our nursery, which we recommended to all our seminar participants and in our book, was taking six months to fill orders. The woman was thrilled to get these three hundred; now she could start her own lavender patch immediately.

The sun had already gone down by the time all the plants were in the ground and Robb had fixed all the installer errors. The boys were exhausted from the day climbing on the red granite outcroppings on the Mason land. I had hoped that the physical exertion would allow me to sleep better that night, but I still only managed three and a half hours. The Zoloft hadn't fully kicked in yet, and I was tired of waiting for it. The next morning, I started running again—something I hadn't done faithfully since before I got pregnant with Gus. I was trying to run the anxiety out of my body, the anxiety that really hadn't lessened even though the seminar and planting were done. There was still the coming weekend when we'd be open to the public, and my major concern was that I had told Miss P that the school could make lots of money off all the visitors who would come. Why had I spoken so boldly? Why had I even tried to help?

The following weekend was frigid—a dreary contrast to the excruciating heat the weekend of the planting. Miss P and her crew set up to sell soft drinks and tacos, but the weather and the lack of a good fall bloom kept people away. I didn't worry that Hill Country Lavender only made $1,000 for the two days—our final gross for 2003 would be close to $100,000. I was most upset that the school only brought in $100 on Saturday and less on Sunday, which seemed hardly worth the trouble. At the end of the day Sunday, I secretly snuck $80 into a donation jar. Miss P was almost in tears when she found the money. "I wonder who that nice person was? I would have liked to say thank you," she said. Knowing that she was somewhat satisfied with the event eased my mind.

The last hurdle—the test of the distillation equipment—was not as crunching as I'd expected when I looked at the month ahead during my earlier panicked state. By then the antidepressant was working its spell and the test had an unforeseen benefit: We came up with a new product. My father and brother intended to distill only one batch of lavender leaves that we had cut back from the plants for the winter to see if the complex machine worked well enough for our real target—the lavender flowers we planned to distill in the spring. The oil from that first batch was much more camphory than true lavender oil, and after taking in a few breaths I realized that my sinuses—clogged from a bad cold—had cleared up. We decided to distill more leaves and sell it for use in steam baths or instead of Vick's. "We could call it something like Therapeutic Lavender Oil," I said, as I stood in a fog of the pungent steam billowing from the rumbling machinery.

"That's it. It's all in how you market it," declared my father, an entrepreneur who had set up his own consulting firm after taking early retirement from Eastman Kodak. The weekend ended with lots of clinking of glasses as we celebrated a successful test and our new product. I sat back contentedly during dinner that night and thought how lucky I was that I had the chance to work with three such wonderful men—my father, my brother, and my husband.

•

The first time Robb mentioned the idea, it was as if a penumbra had appeared out of nowhere on my sunny day. It was like swimming underwater, surrounded by turquoise and sun sparkles, then sensing a shadow falling from a figure beside the pool. Having come through another bout of panic, depression, or whatever had set upon me, I was content again. Then in early 2004 Robb dropped the idea casually—though knowing Robb, I was sure there was nothing casual about it.

"You know that ranch down McKinney Loop, past the creek. It sold for $6,500 an acre. That's $5,000 more an acre than we paid for this."

I nodded my head and let out a wan "Wow." I was sitting on an old metal glider beside the boys' playscape, watching them swing. Jeb was just learning how to pump his legs.

"If we got a price like that . . . it sure would be a nice profit."

If we got a price like that? I wondered if I could have heard Robb correctly. I turned my head from the boys. "What did you say?"

"Oh, I'm just thinking." Robb sat down beside me.

"Mommy, watch this," Gus yelled as he leapt from the swing at the top of its arc.

"Oh, nice, but be careful, honey. . . . Thinking of what?"

Robb explained that he thought if we sold part of our place, maybe just the barn and seventy acres, he would be freer financially. He could turn down more of what he considered stupid assignments—commercial jobs that paid well but required him to photograph an endless number of executives or employees in front of computers.

For a minute I stared down at the peeling teal and yellow paint on the glider, not seeing any color but white. I barely managed a breath. I shouldn't have gotten off the Zoloft yet, I thought. My barn? Sold? Our home?

"Mommy. Can you push me?" Jeb said as he stood up on the fort—pointing to the zip line that ran from the playscape to a tree across the yard.

"I'll do it," Robb said rising.

He couldn't be serious, I thought. We couldn't leave this place. It was part of us now. And what about the lavender? We couldn't sell our lavender field.

When I brought up his bomb of a suggestion later that evening as we walked to the chicken house to put them up for the night, he told me not to worry.

"I'm just thinking, okay?"

"That's what scares me. That's how all your other ideas have started. With thinking." The boys opened the screen door of the chicken house. "Gus, Jeb, be careful of the rooster. Go slowly." The boys loved to find the eggs in the nests, but we'd recently inherited a misanthrope rooster from a neighbor. He had long fighting spurs and would come after Robb and do battle with his legs. He once cornered me when I was in the closet of the chicken house getting feed. I had to fend him off with a garbage pail lid and the scoop from the feed bucket. The only reason he hadn't ended up in the stew pot was that he kept away poultry executioners—owls, foxes, raccoons. I was relieved to see that he was in the yard, far away from the boys.

"Look," the boys yelled as they ran from the chicken house holding in each hand eggs the same color as their skin. Gingerly they placed them at the bottom of the plastic bucket we'd brought along.

"I just need to find a way to spend more time with you and the kids," Robb continued when the boys went back for more eggs. To stave off a hasty sale, I proposed that I try to make more money with the lavender that year—enough that he could take a couple of months off to work on his tintypes.

"I don't know," he said of my idea. "Let's see."

But I *did* know. I knew there was a real threat that Robb would start pushing to sell the house, which was unthinkable to me. It was a betrayal, really. He'd wanted me to love the house, and the country, and once I did, finally, after so much time and all that angst, he was thinking of taking it away from me. I was determined to make extra lavender sales so we could quash any talk of selling. I lay in bed that night, with my tissue blotted with lavender oil, and looked at the rich red long-leaf pine shiplap on the wall beside my pillow. I knew every inch of this house; I had seen it put together. After giving up the idea and more importantly the desire to move back to Austin one day, I felt that Blanco would be our long-term home. I marveled at the turn of events that had me conspiring to keep hold of the house when for so many years I had wanted anything but.

·

Until that year, when people had asked how I fit the lavender in with the kids and writing, I had told them that since lavender had a limited seven-week season, it wasn't a year-round drain on my time. However, this year, 2004, there seemed to be no end to the lavender. Not only did we have the Internet sales, but in February, we began building a store on our property—part of my plan to wring more money out of the lavender. We needed an inviting retail space that matched the image we had created. We needed to grow up and be a real business. Piling products on a table, as we had done for the past three seasons, was quaint and people liked our no-frills authenticity, but it wasn't going to work any longer. We would create a store by closing in a shed on the side of the building that housed Robb's tractor and the five rainwater storage tanks.

"I knew when we got to three tables of products we were in trouble," Robb said, referring to the expansion of our lavender line that had partly made the store necessary. But soon we would add even more products. I had to fill a gorgeous store—stone on the outside and stained concrete floors and warm shiplap inside—and to do so, I happily went on buying trips to trade shows in L.A. and New York, my first visit to the city in almost two years. While in Manhattan, I fit in meetings with editors and was struck by how different I felt compared to my trip right after moving to the barn, when I seemed to have nothing to offer but severe blandness. Most of my editors had received lavender gifts from me and they couldn't ask enough questions about the farm and the products. Was I really making money at it? How'd I come up with the lavender tea cookies I'd sent the Christmas before? How do you make lavender oil?

"I always thought I'd do something entrepreneurial one day," one editor said. "But here I am." She swept a hand around her office, which reminded me of the tiny office I'd had at *McCall's* years ago.

At the trade shows, I ordered quantities of neck and body pillows filled with lavender, lavender detergent and air freshener, and an aromatherapy line that included a natural bug spray as well as treatments for migraines, car sickness, and insect bites, all made from lavender.

Assisting me in my shopping spree that spring was Judith, who as a buyer for her own store scouted other lavender items for me at the many trade shows she attended. She introduced me to a line of sheets, pillowcases, guest towels, napkins, and curtains, all embroidered with lavender. Through her I found an exceptional lavender incense and the most over-the-top lavender product I'd encountered—lavender-scented colored pencils.

"Oh no! Jeannie!" Robb exclaimed when I showed him the pencils. "That's just too much." Robb couldn't even mention the pencils without folding into laughter. Once when a local TV station was interviewing us, Robb wasn't able to answer the question "What types of products do you sell?" He kept snickering when he started to utter the words "Lavender pencils."

After several takes, the interviewer finally said, "Maybe you could just forget the pencils, okay?"

We also added note cards to our line, which we made ourselves. One group of cards was of Robb's photos of the lavender field. The other was of oil pastels that an artist had created the year before at our field. She had come out many times during the season to set up her easel. We liked her work so much we bought three of the paintings and the rights to reproduce them. One in particular touched a sentimental spot. It showed people bent over cutting flowers among the rows with their pastel flush. She had painted it one morning when a garden club from Seguin was in the field. Part of the Thinking Tree is on the right side of the picture and in the background is the view of the pasture across our county road and some distant, blurry gray-blue hills.

"When I think of our lavender field," I told the artist when I first saw the painting, "this is exactly the picture I have in my mind. People in the field enjoying it, this vista. My tree." In addition to using the image on note cards, I also had it made into a poster to sell at the store.

"We'd better make some good money this year. We've spent enough already," Robb said over dinner one evening after we'd been buying antique furnishings for the store—counters, tables, and cases, all of which were piled in the back of Robb's truck that day in the restaurant's parking lot. We were eating at one of my favorite restaurants, the Welfare Café. In the center of a great stretch of nowhere, housed in the former post office for the town of Welfare, population thirty-six, it served sophisticated food—a roasted poblano and goat cheese au gratin appetizer, coffee-encrusted angus beef, pistachio shrimp—plus a clever twist on German cooking. While the boys looked at the goats on the edge of a nearby field, we sat outside sipping wine under a trestle of wisteria that hung over us like our own private rainbow. The early May air was so crisp I thought the sky might crack.

"I don't want to talk about money. Hush," I said, and to my surprise he did. I was feeling too good just then. He hadn't said more about selling the house probably because he had gotten a grant from a Texas bank to shoot tintypes of working cowboys across the state. He was going to get to do his tintypes without using his own money. "I'm having a moment." I raised my glass of wine and closed my eyes in ecstasy. "A perfect moment. Everything feels just right. I swear I could be in Provence right now."

•

Perfection didn't last long. One morning the next week Robb was waiting for me in the office after I'd dropped off the kids—both were now going to Miss P's school, Gus in first grade, Jeb in pre-K. He had a cup of tea waiting for me, which should have alerted me. He told me that he'd asked Skip, the realtor who had sold us the property ten years earlier, to do an appraisal on the barn and seventy acres.

I let myself down, hard, in my office chair. "What? You're not really serious about this," I said.

"Jeannie, we're sitting on a gold mine. I think we should get our money out of this place before the market turns." He sat down on a long cabinet—an old counter from a general store that we used for files—that divided his part of the office from mine.

"But, but . . ." I didn't know where to begin there were so many buts. But we have a lavender field. But we just put in this store. But I love it here. But this is the boys' home. But you brought me here. But I don't want to sell it. I managed to get most of my buts out before the inevitable onset of tears.

Robb tried to calm me, insisting that putting the house on the market didn't mean it would sell right away. "It could take years," he offered. He had an answer for every objection I could think of. We could plant lavender in another location near Blanco, he insisted.

"But it's our home. I can't imagine anyone else living in it."

"Jeannie, it's an investment. Things like this are investments. I've got so much money tied up in this and I need to see a return."

"Oh, it's about money. Fucking money. This is our house—there are some things that you can't put a price on, Robb. You know that commercial: 'Priceless.'" We had reached one of our major fault lines—his tendency to see the world through a financial prism (how much something will cost him, how much does he stand to earn) versus my certainty that quality of life trumps money matters almost every time.

"Hey, it's not like I'm going to blow the money," he said. "I'm just thinking of the future, the kids."

"Yeah well, don't forget to think of them now, in the present."

"Jeannie, this is sticks and stones," he said, jerking his hand toward the screened-in porch and the barn on the other side. "We can build another house up on the Campsite, with that great view." Selling the house and seventy acres would leave us 155 acres in the back, including the Campsite and the swimming hole on the creek. He enumerated ideas he had for a new house— solar panels, a one-floor design with a courtyard, screened sleeping porches, energy-efficient walls.

The thought of building another house was like a hot brand touching my backside. "Build another house? Uh-uh. Not me. I will *not* go through that again." Robb started to object. "You weren't there last time. I was here for every fucking drain pipe and light socket. I know how hard it is. And I'm not doing it again. Don't even think about it. I'm not selling."

Robb's eyes narrowed, as cold as I'd ever seen them. "*You're* not selling? *You're* not selling? Jeannie, it's not *your* decision." He started toward the door.

"It's not my decision, huh? Oh, it's just *your* decision then. You're going to force this on me," I shouted as he walked into the screened porch. "You're going to *make* me and the kids leave the house." He'd just made the ultimate marital power play. The I-make-more-fucking-money-than-you move. He'd paid for the house. His money made our comfortable life possible. Normally that fact drifted behind us like background noise. Now it had reared up as a shout, a detonation.

The tension between us was so intense that we merely huffed at each other for days, sometimes speaking through the kids. "Tell your dad . . ."

I did speak to my friends, however. "He's not serious," Mary Ellen said.

"Maybe he's going through a phase, and he'll drop it," suggested Lori.

"Doesn't he consider the emotional costs on you and the boys of going through construction? You have kids this time; last time you didn't," said Judith.

"Jeannie, put your foot down," my mother prodded. So it had come to this: getting lectured about being strong by my mom, who would never identify herself as a feminist.

"Does Robb need a Walk with Ellesor?" Ellesor asked. "Bo, would he go to counseling with you?"

This seemed like an answer, and I was relieved when he agreed to see a therapist we'd visited before. As we arrived at her Austin office, I felt confident. Surely, Rachel would agree that he was pulling the rug out from under me. That he already had plenty of money. I was so sure I was right that I was taken aback when after we'd both aired our sides, Rachel said, "Well, Jeannie, it seems as if he wants to do this so he can spend more time with you, so he doesn't have to travel as much."

"Yeah, he says that, but I think he just wants to do it for himself, because he's a squirrel and wants to have more money in his savings account. But he'll still not be able to say no to work. He'll still travel because he can't just sit and he needs to have a certain amount of money coming in or he goes crazy."

"Jeannie, you have to admit that I've been turning down more work ever since we've had the boys." This was the first complete sentence Robb had said to me in days. "I'm gone only half the time I was before Gus was born."

Rachel asked me to think about how hard it was for him to be gone from the boys. My counter was that all he had to do was adjust his notion of how much money he needed in the bank.

"Well, people have different comfort levels on how much money is enough. I know I need a lot more in my savings account than my husband does," Rachel said.

I couldn't believe this. She was siding with him. My crazy, restless husband, who had never learned how to be still and happy. Where I saw a perfectly finished house and yard, he saw a place utterly lacking in projects or challenges. He was the one who needed help. He was the one who needed to be searching his inner soul. How did we end up with a therapist who couldn't see that? I'd trusted her. I slumped in my chair like a popped balloon.

"Jeannie, what's your worst fear about leaving the house?"

I didn't know where to begin. I could imagine moving if we could blink a new building into existence, but I was sure I couldn't endure another construction project.

"I'm going to be here to oversee the construction," Robb insisted. "She doesn't have to do it this time."

"Yeah, sure. I want that in writing."

Rachel thought that was a good idea. She recommended that I write out a contract, detailing under what conditions I would agree to sell the house. "Do you think you could do that?"

"Yes," I said, like a resentful child.

After leaving the therapist I felt defeated, made all the worse by Robb's suddenly sunny disposition beside me in the car. He'd been vindicated. "Gotta keep you on your toes. Gotta keep you on your toes," he said, patting my knee, which I quickly moved. "At least, when you're in the nursing home, drooling, you'll know your life was an adventure."

I snorted and looked out the window, wondering why our adventures had to include moving and whether Kim would define any of this as adventurous anyway. Stopped at an intersection I noticed a young, scrawny homeless man holding a sign, "Bad luck. Bad breaks. Can you help?" The thought that I could be spoiled crept into my head.

"Haven't I turned down a lot of assignments lately? Haven't I been at home with you guys more?" Robb asked.

"Yes," I said, again with an insolent tone of a scolded toddler. "You know I think you should have married someone more like you."

"No," he laughed. "We'd already have killed each other." He pulled the car into the parking lot of a store called Pinky's Pagers. A giant, inflatable pink gorilla was roaring from the rooftop. "Look at me," he demanded. "Look at me." I turned from the window. "Don't you think we're together for a reason?"

"Like what?" I asked gloomily.

"Like balance. Have you even considered that?"

"Great. I'm your ballast." I looked out the window again.

"Hey, look at me," Robb said touching my shoulder. I swiveled my head. "You've made us a family. And without you and the boys, there would be no reason to want to give up traveling." I tried to smile, but I couldn't help suspect I was being snowed. He asked me to trust him. He was sure a sale would end up being best for everyone.

I couldn't imagine how wrenching all of us from our home could be for the best. "I can't magically say, sure it's okay; yes, it's for the best. I need time to stop being mad at you and think."

That night I wrote up what I would want if we sold the house—Robb handling all the new construction; my not having to work any longer just to bring in money, which would mean I would never again have to write another relationship story for a women's magazine.

The next day I talked to my friend Alex, a college professor with a PhD from Columbia, who is as smart as anyone I know. I told her I didn't think I would end up in this kind of marriage, where I was supposed to just go along.

She was reassuring, telling me that her husband made a lot of the decisions in their family, which surprised me. "There are lots of things that mean more to him than they do to me."

"I feel like if I were a true feminist I would fight him on this."

"To what end? Do you want to fight just to win? So you win, then where are you? In an unhappy marriage? Alone? I love us as a family too much to fight over something that he cares about more than I do."

The following morning, coming home from dropping off the kids, I approached the house and, once again, marveled at its lines, the way the live oak beside it leaned out at the perfect angle. I stood at the side of the barn and touched the stones—stones the color of sugar-cookie dough with splotches of rust and gray. I wanted to pet the stones and tell the barn I was sorry. Then a thought came to me. As much as I loved the barn, I realized I wanted a *happy* home, versus this *particular* home. I could continue to battle him on the house sale and end up with neither the house nor my marriage. What I wanted was the happiness that goes on inside a home, which is so different from the structure itself. Robb was an amazing man and a good father; yes, he was difficult and exacting, but he was worth it.

Not sure if I was copping out or being realistic and mature, I solemnly told Robb to go ahead and list it with Skip. I tried to tell myself to leave this to fate, to trust Robb since he'd turned out to be right about the country. Maybe I'd have years left in the house.

"You're a saint," my mother said when I told her I'd agreed to sell, but that was hardly comforting. *Saint,* when applied to a woman, seems like a substitute for *fool.* Unlike my mother, I hadn't perfected the ability to navigate around a strong husband. But I had developed enough sense to know that when Robb Kendrick grabbed onto something there was a certain inevitability about it. Why prolong the pain and threaten the happiness of the kids? So much of who he was depended on not sitting still, I knew that. In sickness and health. And deep water. That's how our vows should have read.

"He is who he is," I told my mother. "Don't we all want our husband or wife to take our bad with the good?"

Just let go, I told myself the next morning while out on my run. Weegee was with me, his stride still long and beautiful. I pushed harder going up the hill toward the Campsite. Just let go. Just let go, I commanded myself. But I didn't feel any release. Only a stitch in my side.

CHAPTER ELEVEN

Mixed Bouquet

I *live in town Pula, state Croatia in Europa. This year we planted*
2000 plants of lavender, and we (my wife and son) want to plant
next year another 5000–6000 plants. We want to have lavender
farm and live only off lavender product. Surfing thru web I find
your site. Must tell you that reading about your experience gives me
strength to keep on. Every advice from you are welcome.

—MARIJAN JELENIC,
August 31, 2005

The season got off to a bad start with a lunch. In early May, I hosted
a luncheon to let other growers know we would be able to distill their lavender into oil that summer. Bert and his wife were among the farm owners
who came. Robb and I gave each grower a package, detailing how we would
charge for the distillation and giving them the option of letting us sell their
lavender oil on the wholesale market for a small commission. Bert and his wife
looked over the package thoroughly and asked questions about our capacity
and where we had gotten our equipment.

When I took the guests to see the distillation equipment, Bert mentioned that it was much bigger than his machine. Until that moment, I didn't realize that he had a distillery (though he swore he had told me) and never would have invited him had I known. Later in a newspaper article about the lavender fields in the Hill Country, I read that he too would be trying to contract with other growers to distill their lavender. He had every right to own his own equipment, but I couldn't help but feel he had only come to our lunch trying to collect information on a competitor's operation and pricing.

I called Bert immediately after reading the story to ask him if this was so, but I got nowhere with him. The only thing I accomplished was venting my frustration, which is almost always a dumb move.

"Well, I knew you were really mad when you dialed the phone," Robb said after I hung up with Bert. "Normally you'd get me—the bad cop—to make that kind of call."

As miffed as I was, I tried not to stew over Bert. I had other troubles brewing. Just before the start of the season, the owner of the health food store told me I couldn't put my flyers announcing our open dates in her store. I was stunned; I had always put flyers in her store. I was a loyal customer. Once when the store was running short of money, I'd helped her arrange a concert to raise funds so the unofficial town center for the non-Bubba crowd wouldn't close.

"From what I hear, you have a store there. That's direct competition with my store," she said coolly.

"Oh," I said, taking back the flyers I'd put on a rack near the front. "Okay. But I don't think of us as competitors. I think of us as working together. I always tell people to stop by here after leaving the field. I've even put you on our website as a place to eat in town."

"You just have so many more resources to advertise than I do, and I just don't think it's right for you to advertise in my store." I walked out of the store, hurt, and somewhat confused. I'd always felt that the people we were able to bring to Blanco helped all the businesses in town. I didn't like this new sharp-clawed aspect of the lavender business.

The bigger issue pushing me to the wine store on a regular basis that spring was the bloom. Or the lack of one. We hardly had any shoots coming up on the plants and there was no late freeze or drought to blame. It had actually been a gorgeous spring—lots of rain, not too hot.

"Maybe it hasn't been warm enough," Robb suggested. "Lavender needs lots of sun. Maybe it's been too cloudy."

"Okay, now you're sounding like Fred," I said. "It's not been hot enough. So now we complain when it's not hot enough?"

We called Jim, our extension agent, who told us that the mild, cloudy spring had put everything a few weeks behind. He suspected the clouds could be from farmers in the Yucatán burning their fields, with the smoke drifting up to Texas, blocking out our sun.

We decided to open the third weekend in May as planned and alert people on the website that the bloom would be late this year. Then we were just going to wait. And drink.

I laughed at the irony. I was now out every morning looking for the sun, the reviled Texas sun, praying for it to appear through the haze.

·

Do Not Even Think of Stealing This Sign," I wrote on a tag that I attached to a post holding up one of the signs for our lavender farm. "Observers are watching this spot." It was a silly bluff, but I had to do something. Since our first season we had lined the highway through the town and the smaller county roads with signs directing people to the farm. We'd never had any problem with them—until this year.

Before lavender season started, before we realized there would be a delay with the blooms, we'd rented a large billboard on the highway leading into Blanco from San Antonio to the south. Featuring our giant logo, the billboard invited people to come visit us during lavender season and beyond. We had decided to open our store every weekend, even after the official blooming season was over, to catch all the people coming through town who wanted to visit the farm and buy products. We were hoping the extra sales hours would compensate for the money we'd put into the store construction.

The billboard told drivers to turn left at the only stoplight in Blanco, and then to follow the signs, which we had placed in strategic positions. But Bert began putting up signs to his farm, which was closer to Blanco than we were. With his similar name and the similar typeface on his signs, there was confusion. How I regretted that I hadn't stopped him from using that name. A most unlavender-like hostility gripped me to think that our billboard and our years of building our name were helping Bert's sales.

I was even more livid when our signs started vanishing. As an emergency weekend replacement, I'd make a hand-lettered sign. Then during the week, a small print shop in Blanco would make me a proper one. But after two weekends of MIA signs, I attached my threat to the sign we were having the most trouble keeping. It was opposite a sign for Bert's farm, which remained unmolested.

After the sign across from Bert's disappeared one more time—despite my threat—we contacted the owners of the property along that stretch of road and asked if we could put up a permanent sign. Robb cemented a metal frame into a hole in the ground. A calligrapher in Blanco made a lovely sign on wood that we placed in the frame. "Let's see someone get that," Robb said after he'd finished installing it. Our sign never disappeared again, and we never found out the truth of what happened.

What got me hotter than that spring's timid sun was that Bert had more blooms than we did. I could see the back of his field from the parking lot of the local fertilizer store, and every once in a while I would drive through and take a peek. It didn't seem like a full bloom, but there was definitely a purple flush over the plants, which is what people wanted to see. This was actually his first year with a mature crop—his field was where ours was in 2001, when we had such a beautiful bloom. Maybe, I thought, the first bloom is always the biggest and best. But I really had no idea, which made it worse.

By the end of May, we had expected more blooms to appear, but they were still in hiding. Only about a third of the flowers from the year before decided to show—not even enough to allow cutting in the field. But as it got warmer and sunnier at the beginning of June I held out hope. I e-mailed Don Roberts in Oregon for an opinion on whether our bloom might come later now that the sun was out. Depressingly, he told me that our latitude probably had a specific blooming season and we might have missed our window that year. This made my stomach, which already felt like the home of a claw-sharpening cat, hurt even worse.

On the weekends, visitors would arrive hoping to see a field of purple—even though our website and our answering machine message specifically stated that the bloom was not full that year. Unlike two years earlier, when we'd had the bad bloom due to late freeze and drought, visitors this spring arrived with exact expectations of what the lavender should look like. They'd read descriptions and seen enough photos; reality in the dreamy lavender realm was as welcome as a thorn in a featherbed. Several people suggested we install a webcam to provide live shots of the field over the Internet, as is often done in leaf-peeping country. That seemed way beyond my technological capacity—and my budget.

I tried to take a light approach with those customers who huffed and steamed as if they'd been turned away from Elvis's reappearance. "I'm sorry but we just couldn't find a sunlamp big enough for the whole field," I'd say with a smile. Or, "You know it was a great spring for humans—nice and cool—but not for lavender." I offered free lavender lemonade to compensate for the disappointment. Many people drank the lemonade sitting at a table under a small live oak by the new store. Gus was not happy; he saw each glass poured as a dent in his savings account.

If all else failed, I would utter the two words that "real" farmers would use to console me: "It's farming." Which began to sound like the famous shrugged-shoulders of a movie line: "Forget it, Jake. It's Chinatown."

But I realized I was far from adopting such a nonchalant attitude. I would check the flowers once or twice a day, willing them to bloom, and get the entrepreneurial equivalent of stage fright every morning we were open, knowing I'd have to face unhappy people.

But not everyone was unhappy, thankfully. Visitors were enchanted with our new store and spent accordingly. Their consumption was helped along by the debut of our very own credit card machine, which immediately boosted sales. The extensive stash of products seemed to distract most from the sorry condition of the field, and so did botanical offerings that didn't depend on blooms for their appeal. Robb loved cactus and had planted agave and many spineless varieties around our house. In years past, when people had asked to take cuttings of the cactus or offshoots of the agave with them, we gave them away. "Cactus is the sourdough bread of plants," I would say. "One pad can make a whole garden after a while. Then you can pass a pad along so someone else can start theirs." This year, we had Juan pot cactus cuttings and agave offshoots, which sold briskly since our prices were far below what nurseries charged.

Even though our shelves were filled, I couldn't resist adding more products during the season. One weekend I greeted a woman in my typical manner. "Come on in, we have everything lavender you can ever imagine."

"Good!" the woman said with an eager smile. "I need lavender shave cream for my dad."

"Dang!" I said. "You just made a liar out of me. Okay, we have everything lavender you can imagine—*except* lavender shave cream. But you know what,

I'm going to get it." The following week I had my soapmaker create a lavender shaving cream just in time for Father's Day weekend.

The vineyard's lavender celebration and the accompanying driving tour was scheduled for the third weekend in June, and I had to pump myself up for what I knew would be two days spent like a politician in the vortex of a twenty-four-hour news-cycle scandal. Explaining, clarifying, soothing, apologizing.

"Welcome to the lavender-less Lavender Festival," I joked when greeting the six thousand visitors that weekend. I'd written up an explanation about the impact of the cloudy spring and the burning of faraway fields and posted copies on trees, tables, stone walls. I was hoping to avoid a thousand repetitions, with some success. I only had to give the spiel 990 times instead.

Late Sunday afternoon, as I was walking from the store toward the house counting the minutes till closing, I met up with the food writer from *Texas Monthly,* who was working on a story about whether the Hill Country was becoming Provence. She was citing the vineyards and olive orchards that were springing up and of course, the lavender. I had hoped to soon be herding people out the front gate, but her arrival meant I still had hours to go. I invited her up to the house, where we drank lavender lemonade and talked about the lavender, while Tasha closed down the shop. A month later when her story, "Stop and Smell the Lavender," came out, I laughed to read about myself.

"Out at Hill Country Lavender, owners Jeannie Ralston and Robb Kendrick had been praying to the rain gods to stop, to no avail: Their fields of lavender were green, not purple. 'It's the cool, wet weather,' Ralston said, looking a little frazzled."

"Frazzled?" I said to Robb. "And I thought I'd hidden it pretty well."

•

Don Roberts was right. The blooms never really showed themselves that season. Which meant there were no flowers for my dad and my brother to distill in the new equipment. Since my dad had already bought his airplane ticket, he came anyway in late June and got to experience the sorry situation himself. My brother Jeff joined us, and after a drive to the grocery store one day, he came back with a report on Bert's field. "I parked at the fertilizer place and did a little reconnaissance," he said. "I crawled through the grass and got a look at his lavender with these." He pulled out a pair of binoculars.

"Oh God!" I exclaimed. "How low we've stooped."

"There were people out cutting."

"There were?" I asked, heartsick since no one had been able to cut in our field.

"It wasn't a great bloom," my brother assured me. "Not as good as your first bloom. But definitely better than what you had this year."

"Definitely?"

"I'm just wondering what could be different about his field—maybe a microclimate since he's so close to the river. Or what he's doing different to the plants."

"I'd rather mow down the whole field than try to do something Bert Taylor was doing."

"No, I'm just wondering if there's anything we could do—fertilizer or bloom enhancer—to help the flowers along."

"Well, I can look into it." His suggestion made me squirm. I was already feeling guilty (Robb said it was because of my Catholic upbringing) that Daddy had invested $25,000 for the distillation equipment with nothing to show for it. Now, I felt that there might have been something we could have done to get a better bloom. That somehow I was responsible for its failure.

Jeff must have sensed my feelings. "But I do have a plan for Bert's place," he said with a wicked smile. "I figure if we spread salt on all the plants that would take care of them."

I rolled back in laughter—not just at the idea of it, but also the source. My brother is a devout Christian who has nothing but wholesome thoughts. It wouldn't have been half as funny if Robb had suggested the absurd sabotage.

•

The binoculars were so massive that they were mounted on a stand. If you tried to hold them, I was told, you couldn't keep them still enough. I stood on my tiptoes and peered through. After my eyes had refocused, I saw lush green trees and then a small woodshed high in the branches.

"What you're looking at is the enemy's Tower 7," the man behind me announced.

"Wow, that's one of them," I said, noticing a figure standing outside the shed.

"Now, I need to remind you that they can read your lips from there," the man said. He was speaking lockjawed, like a Connecticut Wasp.

"Okay, I'll be careful," I said as I looked closer at the figure. He was raising binoculars to look toward me. I covered my mouth slightly and said, "That guy is looking here now. Let me ask you, do you ever get the urge to wave at each other?"

I heard foot scraping and throat clearing behind me. "Uh, no, ma'am." I turned to look at the soldier, who was scowling. All right, I thought, don't make jokes with a Marine.

I was in a Marine watchtower on the infamous border between Guantánamo Bay and Cuban territory. Though Castro's threat had grown tepid in the past few years, the Marines acted as if nothing had changed since the Bay of Pigs Invasion. I climbed down from the tower, where Robb was shooting some photos of the Marine guards, and scribbled some lines in my notebook—a reporter's notebook, which was long and slim and fit perfectly in the palm of my hand and my back pocket.

Next to the gate that people going from Guantánamo to Cuba or vice versa used to pass through en masse, a film crew from Japan was shooting. Also along for the tour of the border was an NPR reporter, whose name I'd heard on the radio many times before, and a film crew from Australia, here working on a story about an Australian citizen who was a Guantánamo detainee.

As I stood at this historic intersection, I thought I must look like Katy had every time we walked through the door for twelve years. I was on the verge of panting with excitement; I was working on a serious piece of journalism again. I was in the throes of things—as I had been long ago when I reported for *Time* on the stock market collapse of 1987, or the abortion protests for *Life,* or the OJ murder in 1995 for *Glamour.* I was in a place I'd always wondered about since Robb and I had gone to Havana a few years after we got married. I found it strange and fascinating that America had been able to maintain this otherworldly toehold on this hostile island.

Robb and I were working as a team on the story, sent by *National Geographic.* After I wrote my story on Appalachia for the magazine thirteen years earlier, I swore I'd never work for it again. The editing process on that story had been horrific—something like being edited by the Kremlin, I imagined. Layers upon layers of bureaucracy had made the story almost unrecognizable to me. But a new editor was in charge, and the magazine was more streamlined. So, who was I to turn down the offer to go into the heart of a big news story for a prominent magazine, especially when I had been so long out of circulation on these types of issues? I didn't fool myself about why I was asked. Robb hadn't requested that I work on the story with him, but one of his favorite picture editors proposed the idea, thinking that a married couple would seem less threatening to the military, upping the chances of winning approval to go.

"They just wanted to make Robb happy," I would tell people who wanted to know how I'd gotten the assignment. "Send the wife down there with him." Denigrating my skills was a way to mask my own insecurities. I knew that I wouldn't be sent if they didn't think my writing and reporting were good enough, but still it rankled to realize that I'd essentially gotten the assignment because of who I was married to, not what I could do.

Military approval had arrived in the middle of lavender season, which gave me something new to worry about—getting myself together mentally to report such a difficult, controversial piece. It certainly would have helped to have a real, five-day workweek again, but instead I spent Mondays parked in the car studying books on Cuba while the boys took Spanish lessons and art classes in San Antonio.

At the same time, I was finishing up a fund-raiser for Miss P's school that was similar to the one Robb did for the Montessori school three years earlier. This one was bigger, however, and would end up raising more than double the money. Robb asked other *Geographic* photographers to donate to the school a scan of any image they chose, plus the rights to sell prints made from that image. Thirty-six responded, including some of the magazine's most legendary names.

Using the scans, we posted all the images on the school's website and via Paypal people were able to order and pay for prints on the Internet. The process was much more efficient than the fund-raiser we did for the Montessori school, and the publicity was more extensive. By sending out handsome press packs, we got coverage in local newspapers, photo magazines such as *Popular Photography* and *American Photo,* and in educational journals. We also exhibited prints of all the available images at Brieger Pottery, and had a swank opening night, complete with hors d'oeuvres and wine. "This doesn't feel like Blanco," a woman I knew from the film society said, as she spread a cracker with pate.

A week at the beach with my family at the beginning of July had been a welcome respite from all forms of pressure. The lavender store was still open on weekends, but I knew capable Tasha and her helpers, the Little Girls, could handle the traffic. While my parents drove back to their home in Tennessee with Gus and Jeb, Robb and I took off to Guantánamo together.

It wasn't a fun trip. Confronting scrawny, hopeless men who were confined indefinitely, possibly for life, was disturbing. As was the idea that some of these men might have planned September 11. I interviewed the detainee camp's head of security, a large man in a Hawaiian shirt and sunglasses, who I found disquieting. I would have preferred that our guy in security look less like a Miami drug dealer. We watched a plainclothes interrogator question a stocky Arab man in an orange jumpsuit. We saw detainees kicking soccer balls mindlessly against a fence during their biweekly half-hour exercise period and toured empty cellblocks, which, with their cement floors and bars, reminded me of a dog pound—a description that annoyed the military when it appeared in print. We saw the high-tech concrete jail where the most dangerous of all the detainees were kept. There was nothing remotely entertaining about what we saw and experienced. But I savored every moment.

Working with Robb once again as a reporting team took me back to our love-soaked article together in Fort Worth. I was thrilled to be hanging out with other journalists, talking shop, drinking beer, comparing notes on official bullshit, and bouncing impressions off one another. The compartment of my brain labeled "news reporting" hadn't atrophied, I was relieved to discover.

Though I'd never been away from the boys for longer than three nights, the six days I was in Cuba blinked by without the debilitating longing for them I feared. I knew they were in good hands, and even though I loved being a mother above all else, I knew I needed this trip, this kind of work. I can still play in the game, I thought on the flight out of Guantánamo, as the strange, scrubby patch of land gave way to the turquoise sea below and then to the U.S. mainland. At the Atlanta airport, I met my parents, who had driven from Tennessee to hand off the boys to me. I can still do this. It's not too late, I thought. I can't forget that, at one point in my life, I believed this was what I was meant to do.

CHAPTER TWELVE

Drying

I enjoyed my visit to your place last Saturday. You really started a great thing for Blanco. It must be satisfying to know you have been such a powerful influence to the whole town and area! Such a boost to the town's economy.

—Patricia Lane,
June 18, 2005

Hate it. Hate it. Hate it. Hate it. Hate it.

This is what I was thinking on a mid-September morning as I stood at my office window watching three strangers and Skip, our realtor, get out of their cars. Two weeks earlier, a young man from Austin had looked at the house alone, then came back with his father, an executive who'd recently retired. Skip had told us that the mother, who was now walking up with her son and husband, would be making the call, and all I could hope is that she would hate it.

Over the time that the house had been on the market we'd found that the people who liked it most didn't have the money to buy it, and the ones who had the money thought it was too rustic or unusual, or too big for a second or third home. Some potential buyers were put off because we were asking to rent back the house for at least six months so that we could build a guest-house near the Campsite. I was desperate that this woman now entering our screened porch would find fault somewhere.

"We should go out and meet them," Robb suggested.

"No, I'll meet them when they come over here," I said as I returned to my computer. I had spent the morning straightening and spritzing lavender air fresher in the bathrooms. I needed to get work done.

When the group entered the office, the mother was smiling. She seemed enchanted. Shit, I thought. Maybe I should tell her that the drawers on the old haberdashery counter we'd installed in place of kitchen cabinets don't open smoothly, that it hurts to walk barefoot on the catwalk, that she'll get tired of the stairs. Instead I forced myself to smile as I shook her hand.

Later that day, Skip returned with their offer for the house and ninety acres—twenty more than we originally intended to sell. They would allow us to rent till the end of June, so that we could build the house and have one last lavender season. It was all too perfect, and by the next day Robb had negotiated them up to near asking price.

"Okay, now what?" I asked petulantly as we sat at the dining room table with the signed contract in front of us. I was furious that the sale was actually happening. I knew it might, of course, but I'd hardly had time to wrap my mind around the possibility.

"We'll get the slab started in the back." Robb had been making his own drawings for the guesthouse, and he was going to act as the contractor since our dear Mr. Behrends had died soon after completing our barn. (I couldn't help but worry that we had done him in.)

"Ugh! Construction. The nightmare returns," I said, pressing my fingertips to my closed eyes till I started seeing orange whirls. "You know this is ridiculous." I turned to Robb, who was reading over the contract again. "I can imagine someday the boys telling people, 'Yeah, we had a strange childhood. One time we moved a quarter of a mile, from one part of our property to another.' Are we going to be the weird family who moves every couple of years?"

"Jeannie—"

"I mean, tell me now so I'll never get attached to another house."

"I don't know. Don't you want to be free to go where we want to go?" He'd put the contract down and reached across the table.

I didn't take his hand. "It's always where *you* want to go."

"I promise this will be good. It's the start of a new adventure."

"Hmmpf!" I snorted. "A new adventure in construction. A new adventure in stress." I got up to make myself more tea. "All I can say is this better fucking be the last time. This better make you happy. If I hear you complaining about the construction, or how you don't have enough money to do your personal work, I'll fucking freak out."

Robb was quiet as he walked toward me. I wasn't looking at him so I wasn't sure if he was angry or insulted. He stood close as I absently bobbed the tea bag in my empty mug, waiting for the water to boil, not wanting to meet his eyes. "Hey, do you think you could work another 'fucking' in there somewhere?" When I looked up, Robb was smiling. He was obviously too happy about the contract to fight.

"I mean it. I *fucking* mean it." I hit his arm once, then again. "God, you make me crazy."

·

The contract on the house had the same effect on me as finding an ant on my leg while lying in bed. Suddenly everything started itching.

"Watch out when Jeannie Ralston gets mad," Robb said playfully, as we drove into Blanco from a farm market three miles north of town. The market, called McCall Creek Farms, was owned by acquaintances—a couple, each from longtime Hill Country families. Their farmstand had become well-known for its vegetables, breads, and pastries. "We'll cut him off at every angle," Robb went on. "From the north, the south, the west. We'll squeeze him like an anaconda."

Robb was talking about Bert, who was starting to feel like my arch-rival, even though I liked to believe I was above such pettiness.

We had just finalized a ten-year lease with McCall Creek for a two-acre plot behind their farmstand. And in a few weeks—at the end of October, about the same time we'd close on our house—we would be putting eighteen hundred lavender plants in the field. I was still fantasizing that the house deal would fall apart, but in the meantime I knew we needed a plan for the lavender. The plan for our living quarters was to move to the guesthouse at the end of June, then on the Campsite itself construct the magnificent house Robb had been sketching ever since we'd put the barn on the market. It would be

Robb's project in every sense. As our therapist had suggested, I had written up an agreement, which he signed, that he would be the one overseeing the construction.

"It'll crush you to drive by your house every day with someone else living in it," predicted my mother, who was angry at Robb for making me move again.

I tried to envision that experience. Driving up the rise, seeing the house flick by through those skinny oaks, seeing the lavender field and the Thinking Tree—*my* Thinking Tree—the sharp slope of the tin roof, set off so perfectly by the creamy stone, knowing someone else's things and life were contained within. And then just continuing on, past the driveway, the pool and the windmill and our stone chicken house and vegetable garden. The idea made my chest heavy, but there were worse things, I tried to tell myself. At least we'll all be together, I thought, adopting that sentiment as my mantra to soothe me any time I started feeling swamped in bitterness or nostalgia.

"I guess I'm having a midlife crisis," Robb said to my mother over the phone one day. "Some men change wives, which I'd never consider. I just want to change houses." That had quieted my mother, his harshest critic.

"Just give me space someday to have my own midlife crisis," I told Robb. Even as I said it, I wondered if I hadn't already had one. The desperation to have a baby, the postpartum depression. Maybe that's what all of that was about.

Once that lavender field in front of the barn was no longer ours, we would need a crop of lavender in a different location to continue business as Hill Country Lavender. The house buyers were not purchasing the company too. Hill Country Lavender would be centered at the field at McCall Creek Farms, which should mature in time for the 2006 season. Robb and I agreed that even if we weren't selling the house we would have probably made a move like this eventually. We had both grown tired of the hordes at our house every season. Yes, I liked my party atmosphere, but thousands of people every weekend was beyond a party. It was more like Woodstock. Moving the lavender field would mean regaining privacy and getting priceless exposure. We'd be on the main highway through town, instead of four miles off of it. People wouldn't have to wind around through the backroads to find us and potentially get sidelined along the way by other lavender farms.

And that was a powerful impetus for starting a new location. I was still angry over Bert's siphoning off our customers—whether he meant to or not.

Our lavender farm would be on the highway and we'd catch people before they ever saw Bert's signs. Robb and I had already identified other places we wanted to lease—a field near a small vineyard on the south side of Blanco and one at an antiques market on a busy highway outside Fredericksburg.

"We'll have a little empire," Robb said, grinning.

I smiled too, a strangled smile to match my strangled heart. Nothing felt very light at the moment.

I knew Robb was teasing about the empire, but we could well be heading that way. A recent article in the *San Antonio Express News* had called us "the state's chief experts on lavender production and marketing." The writer also referred to lavender as a Texas industry—a designation that came much sooner than I'd anticipated when I first spoke of the potential at the Texas Department of Agriculture almost three years earlier. By my accounting, about one-third of the 120 people who had passed through our seminars (we were now giving two a year) had planted fields. Most in the Hill Country. Who'd ever have guessed that I would be considered an expert in anything—especially in agriculture, especially in an industry I'd helped create? If you never push yourself, you don't know these things, I thought. Or rather, in my case, if you don't have *someone* push you.

Though the empire Robb joked about appealed to me on one level, I also realized that so many Hill Country Lavender outposts would mean more work. I wasn't sure where we were heading with all this lavender and all these stores and no house. Everything felt up in the air, and my head was feeling crowded with competing desires—to use the free time the house sale would afford me to do more stories like Guantánamo Bay or to keep rolling with the lavender since it continued to feed my ego and our bank account.

·

Losing Sister was too much. Sister, who we'd gotten after Katy died, was our third dog tragedy in less than a year and the most disturbing because it was so senseless. Despite my sincere affection for my hometown, the way she was killed made me chafe at rural life once again, which is why one morning in mid-October I had proudly placed the bumper sticker not on the bumper, which seemed too low, but at a spot high up, right under the rear window of my new Honda Pilot SUV.

"I just love it," I said to Robb as I looked out the screened window of

Blanco's newest restaurant at my car parked outside. "A John Kerry sticker at a Texas barbecue joint."

Robb's eyebrows crashed together. "I don't think you need to go around flaunting that, not here," he said. "Remember you've got kids."

"Oh what do you think?" I asked as I put slabs of brisket on a bun. "Someone's going to attack us because I'm a Democrat."

Robb shrugged his shoulders and dabbed a napkin at the barbecue sauce on Jeb's face. "I just don't think you need to make such a big deal about it."

One of Robb's perversities was that while he took great joy in thumbing his nose at convention and any type of pretense, he was unusually timid about stirring up the political pot. At this point in my tenure in Blanco, Texas, I had no such hesitations. I returned from Guantánamo restless, then the house sold, then Sister was killed.

We'd taken in Sister, a foundling, a year earlier as a companion for Weegee. But without Katy, his lifelong partner, Weegee still seemed unsettled, and when we were skiing in Park City the previous March he had run away from the house—something he'd never done before.

Robb had flown home from Utah to look for him and eventually found him fifteen miles away. When we left for the beach and Guantánamo, we thought we'd taken sufficient precautions to prevent a repeat. But he'd figured out a way to slip off from Juanita. Two days later, he was found dead on the side of a highway. I grieved intensely for Weegee, maybe more than for Katy, but thankfully I didn't slip into a depression—this time I allowed myself time to mourn in full blubbering mode. I felt sure he had gone out looking for us both times he had run away and I couldn't bear the thought of him dying on the side of the road, wondering why we had left him. We buried him next to Katy, with his own cross.

Ever optimistic, we got another puppy and on one Saturday morning in September we discovered that both he and Sister were missing. We began calling for them, and soon we saw Mose, our new blue-eyed Catahoula puppy—Catahoulas are the state dog of Louisiana—running toward the house yelping and shivering. Robb took off with the boys on our new 4-wheel drive glorified golf cart to look for Sister. While I made pancakes for the boys on the griddle, I called all our neighbors asking if they'd seen Sister. In between calls, my phone rang.

"Do you own a little brown dog?" the man's voice on the other end asked.

"Oh yes, yes! Have you got her?"

"Yes, but . . ."

"Oh great. Thank God. I'll send my—"

"But I had to shoot her."

The world seemed to stop for a moment. In my mind, the pancakes stopped cooking. The steam from my tea froze in the air.

"You what? You *what?*" I yelled into the phone.

"I'm sorry, ma'am. But she was in my chicken coop."

"Is she . . . *dead?*"

"Yes, ma'am."

"She's dead! She's dead! You killed my dog?" I'm still not sure how I didn't reach through the phone to shake him. I stayed on the line only long enough to find out that he was the son of a new neighbor across the creek, a neighbor I hadn't met yet. I got in my car to look for Robb and the boys on the property. Once I found them, I threw myself into Robb's arms. "Sister's been shot. She's dead." If I'd had more sense, I would have checked myself around the boys, who started wailing. We all crumpled together. Gus pulled his blue frog-covered T-shirt over his face.

"Can we thue them?" Jeb asked between sobs. But the truth was there was nothing we could do. She'd been on their property. Her loss hit me hard because it was the fate I'd feared for our dogs ever since moving here. I hated the rough justice. Shoot first. Make calls later.

Robb went to the neighbor's to pick up Sister's body. He found out that the young guy had a small pen made of chicken wire for the birds. "This isn't a chicken coop. This is a snack box for dogs and owls and foxes," Robb said. "If you want to see how to keep your chickens safe, come look at our coop." Robb scolded him for not calling to tell us that the dogs were killing his birds. We would have gladly bought him a whole new flock and would have kept a better eye on the dogs.

"I hope you're not too upset," the guy said.

"This is going to be hard on my boys," Robb told him. "This is the first dog they picked out themselves."

When Robb recounted the story to me, I said, "You should have said, 'Did you see the name on her collar? *Sister.* That should tell you how upset we are. She was part of our family.' "

Robb tried to calm me down. "At least he had the decency to call us."

"Decency! I'm sure it's a crime to use that word around such a cold-blooded puppy killer."

I was still quaking mad about Sister's death when the Bush/Cheney signs started going up en masse again. A couple of weeks later I saw one at the driveway of Sister's murderer. Of course, I thought. It was then that I'd resolved to buy my bumper sticker. I didn't feel like hiding any longer. It was time that the people in Blanco know who (and what) I really was—and accept me or not. After I'd put it on my car, I called Mary Ellen in Austin. "I've officially come out as a liberal." We both cheered as if I had just released a dark family secret.

When we finished our barbecue on the afternoon of my bumper sticker's debut, we headed to the car. Robb noticed it first. A flat tire.

"Hmmm," he said. "That wasn't flat when we drove here." He poked at the tire, which was completely flaccid. "It wasn't a slow leak either."

"What happened to our tire?" Gus wanted to know.

"Maybe you drove over a piece of glass," I said, then met Robb's eyes. "You don't think . . ."

"I don't know. It's quite a coincidence, though. You put the sticker on. You park it right here so everyone can see it. Someone takes offense."

"No way. Sally used to drive around with 'Texas Democrat' on her truck," I protested.

"I'm just saying . . . it's best to be careful."

"Well, fuck them," I said.

"Mommy, you said a bad word!" Gus exclaimed, slapping his hand to his mouth.

"Sorry, honey. Mommy's just mad." I had started sounding like a goon off *The Sopranos* lately, I realized, as I herded Gus and Jeb back into the restaurant while Robb put on the spare.

"What are you mad at, Mommy?" Gus wanted to know as he sat down on my lap. Jeb stood on the bench beside me and twisted pieces of my hair on his finger. He used to twist his own hair this way, but had developed a bald spot on the crown of his head. We had to keep his hair buzzed to prevent further balding, and buzzed Gus's hair too so Jeb would have crew-cut company.

As we waited, I explained that some people might not approve that I like John Kerry for president. I tried to work in something about free speech.

"Is George Bush worse than Hitler?" Gus, our World War II history buff, asked just as Robb walked up.

"Jeannie, you'd better be careful what you teach him. You'd be really embarrassed if he said something like that in front of people around here."

"I didn't teach him that, and besides, it's just a question. I was going to tell him that of course he's not as bad."

Robb walked off to the bathroom to wash his hands while I put the boys in the car. "I'm not taking it off," I said to Robb when he got in the driver's seat.

The next day I took the tire to the service station in town. The mechanic showed me a slash in the side of the tire and patched it up. Ten days later, I had another flat, a different tire. How strange that after having no flat tires over the nine years I'd lived in Blanco, I had gotten two in less than two weeks.

I was undeterred. If anything, the flat tires made me more strident. About this time, I got an alarming e-mail from a woman who for some unknown— and frightening—reason had included me on her conservative mailing list. In the subject line, she'd written, "Thought for November." She sent a photo of Teddy Kennedy above a quote from Abraham Lincoln: "Congressmen who willfully take actions during wartime that damage morale and undermine the military are saboteurs and should be arrested, exiled, or hanged."

Normally I would have simply pushed the delete key, but I didn't feel so complacent. I was still itchy. This Lincoln quote seemed suspect so I e-mailed a friend who I knew was good at sniffing out Internet hoaxes. With information she sent back, I composed the following: "In 1866, after Lincoln's passing, the Supreme Court declared, in *Ex Parte Milligan,* that: 'The constitution of the United States is a law for rulers and people, equally in war and peace, and covers with its shield of protection all classes of men, at all times and under all circumstances. No doctrine involving more pernicious consequences was ever invented by the wit of men that any of its great provisions can be suspended during any of the great exigencies of Govenment.' "

At first I was going to send the e-mail only to the Kennedy hater. But the election was nearing and things were looking desperate. I changed it to "Reply All." I knew I could be starting a no-win online brawl with conservative kooks, but I pressed send anyway.

I soon got a response, sent to everyone on the list, from a name I didn't recognize. "Thanks and a tip of the hat to Jeannie for reminding us all of the meaning of liberty and the purpose of the US Constitution!" it read.

I wanted to hoot like a football fan with a painted face. I felt I'd won a victory against right-wing nuttiness, smack in the heart of Bush Country.

With my new attitude that I had lived in Blanco long enough, been "good" enough, to earn my right to speak, I used my platform at the film society to push a bit more. During October, I put together a slate of political films, including *Mr. Smith Goes to Washington* and *The Manchurian Candidate*. When we played *Citizen Kane* I took Gus, who had begun to like old movies too. I was determined that even if he wasn't getting regular exposure to the Met or MoMA, he would at least know his movies. I saved the film *Being There* for the Friday night before Election Day, hoping to make a point. Some people got it. "I love the movie," a woman wrote in an e-mail beforehand. "But I don't think I can come. Too close to reality, if you know what I mean." I had always assumed this woman was a staunch Republican.

Later, I would learn there were more Democrats in our midst than I'd ever realized. On election night, I went to what I hoped would be a celebration and saw several people from my church and the film society.

"You?" I said to a tough old ranching woman from church who had once told me about inseminating her own cows. She said she had stuck her whole arm up the cows' vaginas to release the semen. "I didn't know," I said to her at the party. "We need a secret handshake or something." Thinking of her with her arm deep inside the cow—an image that unfortunately came to mind every time I saw her—I demonstrated shaking hands with my left hand on my right bicep.

In January, enjoying my new role as an agitator, I put *La Dolce Vita* on the film society schedule just to see what would come of it. Some members protested. "Come on," I said. "You're not a real film society until you've done Fellini. We've got to push ourselves." During the movie—but especially during the orgy-ish scene at the end—I heard the door at the back of the theater shutting over and over. The members may have been able to take rural Texas decadence in *The Last Picture Show,* but not Italian debauchery. When the film was finished, I looked around and saw that only ten of the original thirty-four members remained in the audience.

"Now that we've done that, can we never do it again," one woman pleaded.

"All right, all right. Next week we're back to safe stuff—our African month. We'll start with *African Queen*," I said, as the ten people filed out. "But," I shouted after them, "you should be proud that you stuck it out through this. A lot of people cracked. But not us."

·

I'll say this for Bert. He had two good ideas.

The year before he had decided that Blanco should be declared "The Lavender Capital of Texas." He took his idea to the city council, which endorsed the new slogan. Then he asked our state representative to get the legislature to make it official.

He also thought the Blanco Chamber of Commerce should sponsor a lavender festival. By early 2005, when I got involved, a date in late May had been secured for the festival and at our first meeting, I lobbied to drop the name that Bert had proposed, Bloomin' Fest. First of all, the name smacked of the same kitsch that infected Fredericksburg, where shops and events are given silly names to reflect the German heritage of the region. Also, the name didn't say anything—not what kind of blooms, not where it was located.

"If the Blanco Chamber is going to get behind this, it ought to be the Blanco Lavender Festival—period," I said as I sat at the white table along with seven of the other growers in the area. "I think the goal should be getting more recognition for Blanco and connecting Blanco with the lavender."

From the first meeting, I was frequently asked to weigh in on plans for pulling the event together and found I had the most to say. None of the other growers, except Bert, had ever opened their fields to the public because their lavender hadn't fully matured yet. Some growers had been to a lavender festival in Sequim, Washington, and reported what type of activities and events they had seen. I felt as if I was the only one who hadn't been to Sequim, but I had never wanted to go. I wanted my ideas for the lavender to be my own, not cribbed from someone else's farm.

Because I was busy with the boys, our own lavender, my writing, and, tangentially, with the construction of the eco-friendly guesthouse (made from recycled Styrofoam and concrete blocks and featuring a composting toilet) that Robb was overseeing, I had no patience for long, rambling meetings and for inefficiency. One of the board members suggested several times that the farms pay a fee to the chamber to be included in the festival.

"No, that won't work," I said. "Without us, there would be no festival at all. You would have nothing to promote. We've put all the work into establishing our farms, which bring in business for the whole community, and I can tell you that Hill Country Lavender won't take any part in this festival if you try to charge us." With the threat of a festival without Hill Country Lavender, the board member backed off. But at the next meeting he brought up the idea once more; I could barely contain myself. "George, please don't insult us again!" I declared, which stopped the discussion.

In years past, I never would have thrown my weight around like some lavender, uh, monarch I guess, but I hadn't gotten to this point with the lavender to be hobbled by such pettiness.

·

As I looked around the room, the cafeteria of a junior high school in Fredericksburg, I realized that almost all of the forty farmers at the meeting had been through one of our seminars. It was the first gathering of the Central Texas Lavender Growers Association in February 2005, which was coming together at the same time as the Blanco Lavender Festival to promote lavender in the region. The group had wanted to call itself the Hill Country Lavender Growers Association, but having learned to be protective of our business name and newly possessing a trademark for it, I asked that the group find another title.

"So, we're hoping that we can put together a trail of all the lavender farms in the Hill Country," announced the head of the group, Susan, who had attended two of our seminars—one to learn how to grow it, the second to get marketing ideas. "We're looking for feedback from all of you." She paused and glanced at me. "Jeannie, since you're basically the mother of all this, can we start with you?"

"I think it's a great idea," I said to the group. "I can imagine a nice brochure that we get out before lavender season. Then all during the season people can find their way from one farm to another—not just on a festival weekend, but any time during the season."

Because I kept track of our seminar alumni, I knew the main lavender-growing region stretched over a nine-county area of the Hill Country. I truly believed that with more farms, the Hill Country would become better known as a lavender-growing area; this would attract more tourists and more business for everyone. But around me were reminders that others were more focused on getting their own part of the pie.

At the meeting sat the nursery owner from whom we had bought all our seedlings. After we began recommending the nursery, it went from sell-ing about one thousand lavender plants a year to fifty thousand. The owners' thanks to us was to start a lavender-farming conference that directly com-peted with the seminar we'd given for years. We had no advance knowledge of the conference until we received a mailing announcing the schedule of speakers—most brought in from California. I had no problem with the idea of a conference, but I thought it would have been nice if the owners had coor-dinated with us, their biggest lavender customers.

Also at the meeting was a seminar alumnus who had a lavender farm and store in Fredericksburg; she had complained bitterly to me a few days earlier that the state legislature was going to declare Blanco the official Lavender Capital of Texas. Her husband, a lobbyist, had learned about the pending res-olution. The state representative for Fredericksburg had told Blanco's repre-sentative not to even try introducing the resolution on the floor, because she would kill it. (Resolutions—nonbinding and inconsequential as they are—can be nixed by one vote.)

"Jeannie, you know better than anyone that lavender doesn't just grow in Blanco. It's unfair to single it out," the woman had said to me in a phone call.

"I don't know if it's unfair," I said after clarifying that I hadn't proposed the designation but did support it. "Listen, Fredericksburg has so much going for it already. You don't need another designation of this or that. Blanco as a town has decided to embrace the lavender and make it part of its identity. I don't see the Fredericksburg chamber doing that."

"But I don't think it's accurate," she responded.

"I believe Luling is the Watermelon Capital of Texas," I said, referring to a small town east of us. "That doesn't mean Luling is the only place in Texas that grows watermelon. It means Luling is the town that celebrates watermelons."

"Yes, but the wording of the resolution makes it sound as if Blanco is the *only* place it grows." After an hour on the phone, I thought we had worked out a compromise. I would have our representative edit the text to say that Blanco was "one of the areas in Texas" that grew lavender, but Blanco would still get its designation. It seemed we had avoided a showdown.

But a month later, the woman called me back. She was still angry, even with the new wording. "I thought we were going to change it to call the *Hill Country* the official lavender growing *region* of the state, instead of singling out Blanco," she said.

"No, we never decided on that," I said, telling her how *I* understood our agreement. We went in circles and at the end of our conversation she told me not to expect her state representative to ever let the resolution pass.

I was drained when I got off the phone, but I couldn't help but laugh. Could anything be more ridiculous—battling on the floor of the Texas legislature over a stupid slogan that didn't mean anything? What was all this lavender nonsense coming to and why was I in the middle of it?

"Because you're the Lavender Queen, honey," Robb said, after I'd asked that question out loud. "Remember?"

That little moniker didn't seem as charming as it did when Robb had first used it three years earlier. I could see that the lavender business I loved was becoming more complicated, more taxing, which made me truly sad. I called Jon, the vice-president of the Blanco chamber and Tasha's father, and told him the other side wasn't budging. Later Jon—who planned so much of the festival—worked out a solution. The legislature would pass a resolution calling the Hill Country the official lavender growing *region* of the state and the Blanco Lavender Festival the official lavender *festival* in the state.

"Fine, fine," I said when Jon called me to report. "Whatever works at this point." He added that the chamber had decided to keep on calling Blanco the Lavender Capital of Texas, with or without official sanction. "That's perfect. What can anyone do about it? Go get 'em," I said wearily.

The compromise didn't sit well with Bert. I almost felt pity for him. He had put such importance on that state designation—for some reason I couldn't imagine. But I stopped feeling bad for him a few weeks later.

The previous year, I had begun selling a lovely new book, *The Lavender Cookbook,* and decided to invite the author to conduct cooking classes at our farm for the upcoming Blanco Lavender Festival in May. When I called her, she informed me she had already been contacted by Bert and the owners of the vineyard, but no one had secured the date. She told me that she would go to whichever farm wanted to officially book her.

I could have snagged her right then, but after finding out how much she charged, and that we'd be responsible for her airfare and three nights' lodging, I had another idea. I called Bert and the vineyard owners to see if we could split her airfare and lodging three ways. Then she could visit each farm during the festival weekend, so that we all got the benefit of her classes. Bert and the vineyard owners were interested, and I was thrilled that we might be able to cooperate on this.

But Bert called me the next day to tell me he hadn't realized that his step-daughter had already booked the author to come to his farm, so he wasn't going to be joining forces with us after all.

I was stunned, and called the author immediately. She seemed as confused as I was but did offer a consolation. She would be in Texas in April—a month before the festival—and would do a cooking class for me then. I wouldn't have to pay airfare and only one night in a hotel.

I booked the weekend and proposed to the *San Antonio Express News* that a food writer do a story on the cooking class. "I'm just going to steal Bert's thunder," I said to Robb.

After advertising the event to our e-mail list, we had so many people sign up for the Saturday class that I added another on Sunday, with a different menu. To accommodate the class, we moved furniture in the upstairs of the barn and set up three tables, where the students could work and later eat. The menu on Saturday included veal scaloppine and artichoke hearts with pomegranate lavender sauce, stuffed peppers with lavender couscous and baby asparagus tips, and chocolate lavender meringue nests with strawberry compote. On Sunday, we made a brunch of corn crepes filled with scrambled eggs and apple sausage served with lavender cheddar sauce, sauteed cremini mushrooms with baby onions and lavender, and lavender apple rhubarb crisp with orange lavender cream.

Sunday's class was the most hectic because I tried to pack too much into one day. Just in time before we left it, our barn was going to be featured on an HGTV segment called *ReZoned,* about buildings that have been transformed from one use to another. On cooking-class Sunday, a film crew arrived at 6 a.m. to interview Robb before he headed west to the Panhandle to finish up his tintype project for the bank. The HGTV crew wanted to film the cooking class so they could talk about how our lavender business was honoring the barn's agricultural roots. I was eager to do this—even if it meant more stress having both events on the same day. I knew the national exposure would boost sales.

The previous fall when Robb was on a media tour for a book called *National Geographic's Greatest Portraits*—one of Robb's photos was on the cover—a CNN anchor asked him about his lavender farm, obviously having Googled him before the interview. I was livid that Robb hadn't said the full name—Hill Country Lavender—so that people could track down our website.

"You've become a media monster," Robb had said in his defense.

Maybe I had. The truth was that this year, 2005, I was still feeling intense pressure to make money even though I had no chance of saving the house. In previous years, our Hill Country Lavender finances had been mixed in with our other bookkeeping, so our profit margin wasn't always clear. This year we had opened a separate Hill Country Lavender checking account and Robb was closely following its health. I wanted to show him just how far I'd taken his idea, and maybe that I could do something better than him. I also hoped he'd regret selling if we had a whopping year.

To keep up cash flow and prepare for the time when the business wasn't centered at our house, we rented space in Tasha's parents' store, Brieger Pottery. We put our whole line of products in a special section of the store they gave over to us and hoisted a large Hill Country Lavender sign up on their storefront, right on Blanco's square. It was a symbiotic relationship—our reputation and online presence would attract people to their store; their location and loyal clients would help our sales.

That spring of 2005, the lavender sucked up more of my time than ever, mainly because of the lavender festival. Like it or not, I had become involved in every aspect, from finding sponsors to writing text for the website and brochures to figuring out how much wine to order for the gala growers' dinner on the Friday night of festival weekend. My main responsibility was, not surprisingly, press coverage. I sent out fifty press kits—including background information on Blanco and profiles of each participating farm—to media in the surrounding area and in the big markets of Houston and Dallas. In addition to many newspapers, two magazines, *Texas Highways* and *Southern Living*, signed on to do stories on the festival.

The time I gave to the festival—especially promoting it—was essentially charity work. Yes, I loved Blanco and wanted it to prosper as a town. I wanted it to have a more sophisticated image, which the lavender was already giving it. But I didn't really have time in my life for such extensive volunteer work. I needed to plan another moneymaker for Miss P's school; it was still struggling but fortunately hadn't gone the way of the Montessori school, which not surprisingly but heartbreakingly had closed at the end of 2004. The $20,000 from our earlier fund-raiser for Miss P was almost gone. But where was I going to find the time or energy to get more cash for her?

One night while I was doing my crossword puzzle in bed, I said to Robb, "You know what I'm fantasizing about?"

Robb turned from his magazine with an eager, hopeful look.

"Oh no, not *that*," I said. His face fell comically. "I'm fantasizing about living in a place where everything is already done. I don't have to worry about the schools. I can see movies anytime. There are nice restaurants." Even as I spoke, I realized I wasn't thinking about Austin. I knew Robb would never agree to live in a city again. I actually had no specific place in mind.

"You love your movies."

"But I'm thinking I'd rather be someplace where I could just be a worker bee. Someone could just tell me to bring cupcakes to the homeroom party. Or I could just watch the movies and not worry if the projector is going to work."

"It sounds like you're burning out."

"Burning out?" I stared at a fairly easy crossword clue but the answer wasn't coming to me. "Maybe I am. But that's not supposed to happen out here in the country. I'm supposed to be *relaxed*."

"You'd better not burn out yet. You've still got to get through lavender season."

"God help me," I said. It was late April and for weeks I had been frantically hovering over the field, keeping tabs on the weather, which was looking better than the year before. "A little more cloudy than usual," Robb diagnosed in early May when we were walking on the property with the boys, "but definitely not as bad as last year." The sun had blazed especially hot that day, and at 7 p.m. it still felt sweltering to me.

There were spikes coming out on the lavender plants, but even though this spring we'd fertilized the bushes, I still had an uneasy sense there weren't as many new stems as in the good seasons of the past. Our lavender plants around the pool were fat and filled with shoots—a taunting reminder of how all the plants should look. One afternoon, while Robb was tossing the boys in turn across the pool, I inspected the plants in the beds as if I might determine their secret for perfect blooms.

"You know, I don't think I can stand another season like last year," I said to Robb as I slipped into the water. "It makes me sick thinking that I'd have to find something to say to all those people. I just can't face the disappointment again."

"Don't worry so much," he said. "You've done everything you can."

·

Whereas Texas is known throughout the nation for the excellence and variety of its agricultural bounty and among the most distinctive and appealing of the crops grown here is the versatile herb known as lavender . . ." Our state representative was standing at the front of the ballroom in the Blanco courthouse, reading from a resolution declaring the Hill Country the official lavender growing region. We were at the Growers' Dinner, the night before the lavender festival opened. I was sitting with Robb sipping wine frantically, trying to calm down after the seating chart I'd made for the event was completely discarded, creating chaos when all the guests came upstairs for dinner.

"Whereas the decision by local entrepreneurs to grow lavender in the very heart of the Lone Star State has produced outstanding results," he went on, while I raised my glass to Robb. This was the compromise resolution—or the bastard resolution if you were Bert Taylor, who sat, unsmiling, at the table next to ours with the author of *The Lavender Cookbook*.

The next resolution, declaring Blanco the official lavender festival of Texas, was shorter and sillier in my mind, but I knew it meant something to many people in the room. "Whereas Blanco has long been known for its quaint town square and its beautiful environs, but in recent years it has also become known as a center for lavender growing . . ." When he finished reading, the 120 people—friends and family of the eight growers in the festival—applauded wildly.

"Well, we've been officially recognized by the state," I whispered to Robb. "Can we go now?"

"Yeah, our lives are pretty much over."

That weekend eight thousand people stopped by our farm. Some visitors stayed for hours—we offered classes on aromatherapy, notecard-making using pressed lavender, and lavender-wand weaving. (Lavender wands are a type of labor-intensive sachet from the Victorian times, made from stems of lavender intertwined with ribbons.) We also offered free chair massages, and I longed to indulge in one myself as I rushed around playing hostess wearing a purple hat someone had given me that read "Got Lavender?" while my staff wrote up sales in the store, which was often too crowded for me to enter.

I tried yet again to do a meal under my Thinking Tree. This time, I was going with the same menu I had used the previous September for a brunch during our Lavender Oil Festival, which had been a success. A friend catered the event, offering an assortment of baked goods and egg dishes—all with lavender included in some form. The highlight of the brunch, though, was the lavender mimosas. It hit me that alcohol was what these people needed to truly appreciate the food and the setting. That and some mood music—two violinists performed chamber music during the meal.

Our farm brought in more than $30,000 that weekend, and everyone— the chamber, the other farms, visitors the chamber interviewed for feedback— considered the event a success, despite the lack of a full bloom. But with that many people we were bound to have problems. On the Saturday of the festival, three elderly women fell in our field. I watched one woman go down like a just-tapped domino right in front of me. Her loss of verticalness was so sudden—one minute she was up; the next, kissing the dirt—that it might have been comical if it had happened to someone in any other age group. Luckily she only skinned her nose and hands and none of our toppling ladies broke bones or suffered serious injury. The face-plants were Robb's worst nightmare. He had long worried about someone getting hurt on our property and coming after us with a lawsuit.

That evening, a frantic Robb was out on his tractor in the fading light leveling the divots and rivulets out of the path between the parking area and the store. He made me post signs saying, Watch Your Step. Uneven Path. We were both relieved that there were no more casualties on Sunday.

On the Monday after the festival I got two e-mails from irate women who had eaten brunch under the Thinking Tree. Not only had our dogs gotten too close to them (we'd gotten another puppy to replace Sister), but we had used plastic utensils. The worst crime was our tablecloths—which included my beloved Provence purchase and others with lavender prints I'd found over the years.

"The setting under the oak was beautiful but to have tablecloths that had just been taken out of the dryer, never to have been touched by an iron and a little spray starch was unforgivable," one of the women wrote. The criticism stung because I thought I'd finally come up with a winning formula for the brunches. I wrote back, offering to refund their money, but neither woman answered.

"Some people love complaining," Robb said. "You know that."

"I know," I said, finding myself incomprehensibly close to tears. "I just thought people would like having brunch there. Why haven't I ever been able to make it work?"

"It did work," Robb reassured me.

"I just adore that tree. Don't they know they'll never be able to eat under it again?" The new owners of the house were not going to open the field to the public. "Don't they know nothing's going to be the same again." I began to wail like those childless cows I'd heard years ago in the middle of the night. We were a few weeks away from our move and it was beginning to dawn on me that the day was quickly coming when I wouldn't be waking up in this house.

•

At the end of one of our last days of the lavender season, we had a late surge of customers. I had sent Tasha and the Little Girls—though they were hardly little anymore—home at three, thinking I could handle the last hour by myself. Right before four, however, as I was totaling the sales for the day, three cars drove up, containing about ten people. The late arrivals milled around the store, picking up oil decanters, leafing through our growing book, discussing the thread count of the embroidered sheets.

"You can cut some flowers in the field, if you want," I said. I handed out scissors and buckets to the four women who wanted to harvest. I explained the drill—how to cut them and how to determine how much made up a bunch. (We had a new system; instead of estimating forty stems, I gave out twist ties and told them whatever fit into the twist tie was considered a bunch.) I called up to the house and asked Robb if he or Rachel could lend a hand in the store. Rachel was my older sister's thirteen-year-old daughter who was visiting from Tennessee to help with the lavender and the boys so I could prepare for the dreaded move. She had arrived with my father, who had come to distill, even though we only had half a cartful of flowers for him to work with in Blanco and frustratingly the plants in Mason were not mature yet. He and my brother Jeff were able to distill just enough floral oil for us to sell on our website and in the store at Brieger Pottery.

To help with the late influx, Robb came down from the house, and as I wrote out tickets and wrapped up products in lavender tissue paper, he talked to the customers, who were thrilled to meet the person who had started the lavender in the Hill Country. By the time the four women returned with their buckets of blossoms it was 4:30, a half hour past our usual closing time. They wanted each bunch tied with raffia separately. Robb volunteered to do it, but when he wrapped the bunches in tissue paper, he was in foreign territory. The paper ended up looking like it had a former life as mattress stuffing, but I successfully fought my urge to object.

"Robb, give them the drying instructions," I said, pointing to a sheet of paper with the headline Buy Once, Use Twice. It told customers how to dry the lavender after displaying it fresh, something I wrote up several seasons earlier after we grew tired of saying the same thing over and over. I also included written growing instructions with the lavender plants we sold for similar breath-saving reasons.

As I reloaded paper in the credit card machine, I called out to a woman looking at the soaps—all six varieties were handsomely displayed in antique baskets on a thin table in the middle of the room. "If you can't decide, we have a soap sampler with one of every flavor." I pointed her to a basket on a green-metal-and-glass display shelf. My soapmaker had come up with the idea of packaging together one small, matchbox-sized piece of each variety. The woman piled four of the samplers on the counter.

"Hey, we're having a sale on our hats over there," I said. We were down to eight of the painted hats, and since it was the end of the season I wanted to clear them out. "You should try one on." The woman put one on her head and went into the bathroom to look in the mirror. When she came out, she looked unsure. "Those were handmade in Haiti," I said. "Especially for us." Then I launched into an abbreviated version of how I ordered them. "So, they have good juju."

She put the hat down next to the soap samplers. "Will that be all?" I asked.

"Yeah, I'd better get out before I buy something else."

It was after five when everyone finally left.

"It certainly was worth that extra hour. Those ten people spent $582." I could feel Robb looking at me intently as I added up some more numbers. "And today's total is $3,622 and 15 cents." I lifted my head and smiled at him.

"What?" I said, when I noticed that he was still staring at me strangely.

"Is this how you want to spend your life?"

"What?" I repeated incredulously.

He asked if I really wanted to spend my life pushing for an extra $11 sale on a hat when I could be with my kids at the pool. Now that Robb had started saying no to more work, he had become almost evangelical about cherishing every moment of their childhood.

I didn't know how to answer. I'd never thought about it as my life, as forever. "I like coming up with new products. I like that we're making good money."

"This has never really been about making money, you know that," he said. But I *didn't* know that. I always thought he wanted to make as much as Daniel did in France. That seemed to be his goal. At least it seemed to be our potential.

"I don't know, then, what it's really about now. It's still fun, I guess. But it's different now; it's so friggin' consuming."

"That's why you need to decide."

"I don't know what you're saying."

What he was saying, it came out over several discussions in the next few days, is that he thought we should sell the lavender business too, not just the house. He thought we should be completely free. I was flabbergasted that he would even suggest a business sale after all we'd been through, but why I continued to be shocked by him I had no idea. He pointed out that the business had grown to a point where we either needed to sell it, or hire a full-time manager to run it, or I needed to quit writing, quit even trying to fit it in, or the illusion of fitting it in, and devote myself to keeping the lavender business growing.

I knew I didn't want to hire a manager. The only person I knew who could do it was Tasha, and she was still taking a full college load. No one else would be able to run it the way I would, plus managing a manager would be one more job for me. Quitting writing altogether seemed absurd. Earlier that year, I had attended a gathering of *National Geographic* writers in Washington, DC. I felt I was making progress again—slowly. I had always been a writer and knew I always would be. I didn't think selling something—even my own lavender—could ever satisfy the same way writing did, no matter if it weren't serious journalism, no matter if it were only a story about work-at-home moms or infertility treatments (fertility issues had become a favorite topic of mine for women's magazines since my own minor glitch).

When Robb asked me if I wanted to do "this" all my life, he was asking me to think about the lavender as a replacement for writing. I knew I could write all my life because I never got bored with it. Even if I got tired of a particular story, there was always another one to move on to.

I wasn't sure I could be only a businesswoman, a lavender farmer. The lavender had added so much, I knew. Layers to my life. The people I met, the satisfaction I got from growing something—a crop, a business—and discovering what I was capable of. It made living in the country more than bearable, it made it fun, stimulating. But I saw that my enthusiasm might be on the downward slope of my own bell curve. There were many areas I could branch into—our own line of aromatherapy, for instance. But when I stopped to consider it, the thought of going through another lavender festival—gearing up for it all year, worrying about the bloom—made me feel as if I'd eaten bad sushi. As did the idea of continuing my inane, useless rivalry with Bert.

I knew Robb was right about needing to make a decision. But how could I let go of something that had come to define me? I was a little celebrity in my little town, which had its own intoxicating power, no matter how wretched it was to admit that. The lavender had made me feel special, different. Even among media people. It had led to the last thing I thought I would have in the country—a life that was far from ordinary.

"You'll always have done what you did," Robb said during one of our conversations. "Even if you were to stop now."

"Let's think about it while we're gone," I finally said a few days after lavender season when we were in the midst of packing up the house. I was too emotional about leaving the house to fathom another loss. Every day I cried, either quietly to myself or violently with Robb, saying, "This is the last time we'll ever make chocolate chip cookies in this oven," or "We won't be hanging our stockings around this banister next Christmas," or "Remember when you and the boys made those tiny snowmen on the front steps here."

My decision was not to decide yet. On July 7, a week after we moved from the barn into the mostly finished guesthouse in the back, we were going with the boys to Mexico for five weeks to study at a language school in Guanajuato (more for Robb and me than the boys, who were already quite fluent thanks to Juanita). Robb and I would have nothing to tax our brains down there besides irregular verbs and the correct placement of personal pronouns.

Four days before our move, Robb was putting burgers on the grill near the pool. I was pouring wine for us and juice for the boys, who were doing what they called helicopter spins off the diving board. The sun was setting behind our windmill, which was churning and groaning merrily in a good breeze that was also making the T-shirts and jeans on our clothes line dance like marionettes. Long-fingered shadows stretched to the east, and the shade from the bigtooth maples we'd planted the year Jeb was born almost reached the western face of the barn. I had once imagined that the maples would be completely blocking the house from the afternoon sun once the boys were in college. Now, I would never see that.

I looked to the right of the barn, down the gentle slope to my Thinking Tree and the roundness of the lavender field—now, after being harvested, green like the rest of the vegetation around it. Robb followed my gaze, and casually touched my wineglass. But before I drank, he grabbed my forearm.

"Thanks," he said.

We looked at each other. I could have asked him, "For what?" But I thought I knew. Thanks for taking the ride with him. Thanks for the boys. Thanks for being willing—no matter how reluctantly at first—to continue the adventure. I let the wine slide down my throat. I felt it reach my stomach and spread out like a lava lamp from there and though I didn't know how I was going to survive the move, being wrenched from my home, I was with my family. The boys' squeals drifted through the air as they jumped again from the diving board. And I let go.

"Thank you too," I said.

Afterword

Smell is a potent wizard that transports you across thousands of miles and all the years you have lived.

—HELEN KELLER

"Lavender blueberry smoothies," read a sign on the health food store on the Blanco square during an early June weekend in 2006. "Lavender plants sold here," said another notice at the local florist. A banner flapping over the highway through town announced, "2nd Annual Blanco Lavender Festival."

Around the old limestone courthouse were booths and vendors, most decorated in purple and white, selling lavender cookies, mugs painted with lavender sprigs, lavender bath salts. Thousands of tourists, many licking lavender ice cream cones or wearing lavender-themed T-shirts or hats, coursed across the courthouse lawn in the 90-degree heat.

"Look what you started," said a man's voice behind me as I stood in front of the courthouse trying to absorb the magnitude of it all.

I turned to see my friend Roger, who was standing in his booth surrounded by his handmade wood bowls and vases. My eyes slid over the large straw cowboy hat that hid his white hair, and went straight to his short-sleeve shirt. It was amethyst. Deep amethyst. Not a color often seen on a Texas rancher in the full light of day.

"Look what you're *wearing*," I countered. "You better be careful who sees you in that. They might kick you out of the Farm Bureau."

"I know," he said as he guffawed cheerily, not unlike a small donkey, and pretended to look around for other members of the farming organization. "I just thought I'd get in the spirit of things."

On that weekend, it seemed as if the whole region had gotten in the lavender spirit. Eleven farms—all of which we had helped get started—were participating in the lavender festival, three more than the year before.

I raised my camera to take Roger's picture. "Robb's got to see you in this shirt. He won't believe it." Robb wasn't at the festival that year. He was at home with the kids and home was far away. We didn't live in Blanco any longer. I was here as a visitor, presiding over the operations at Hill Country Lavender, which we still owned, though it was now centered at McCall Creek Farms.

When we went off to Mexico, the idea was to revel in our break, then come back and build a main house on the Campsite. We'd already talked to architects about ideas for the house, which would incorporate the "million-dollar view," as one realtor had called the vista from that point. But while we were gone we were seduced by Mexico. Robb was freer, more relaxed than I'd ever seen him. The boys were already so fluent in their Spanish that after two weeks we took them out of the language school, which was too slow for them, and put them in a day camp with Mexican children, where they spoke Spanish so fast and confidently I thought for an instant they couldn't truly be my own American-born children.

"Do we really want to go back and build another house?" Robb asked one day while we were sitting on the porch of the home we rented in Guanajuato. Overseeing the building of the guesthouse on the back of our property, Robb had learned what I already knew. Construction was tedium hell. He pointed out that if we built the main house, we were probably going to be in Blanco until the boys finished high school. At six and eight, they would soon be too old to move easily. They would be deeply entrenched in their networks of friends and sports.

The boys had made the transition from our barn to the guesthouse with no apparent emotional damage (though only time and therapy will tell). They didn't cry or whine much at all—certainly less than I did—over leaving the only home they'd ever known. I thought they would at least miss the pool but only once did they ask to swim in it. When we told them it wasn't ours anymore, they never brought it up again—even though we drove by the pool every day to get to and from town.

"We're kind of at a crossroads right now," Robb had said in Mexico. "We're light on our feet. We've got money in the bank. The kids are still young." Robb proposed living in Mexico for a while. It would be the logical next step to ensure that Gus and Jeb became totally bilingual—a goal we had long had for them. I spent a few nervous nights considering the possibility, then said yes, with surprisingly little angst—especially after warning Robb to never expect me to move again.

Most people assumed that Robb had twisted my arm once more to make such a leap, but this time I was eager. Having already made my peace with the selling of the barn, I felt that my anchor—the barn—was cut loose. It seemed there was little besides the lavender to keep me in Blanco anymore. Yes, I loved the boys' school, but it required too much work and worry. In the back of my mind was the constant fear: Would it survive another year? I had good friends, but the ones I loved most were the type who would visit me in Mexico. If Robb had proposed such a move while we still owned the barn, I could never have agreed to such a radical step. But now I was free.

During our five-week Mexican vacation, we bought a very large souvenir, one too big to bring back to the States: A house in the colonial city of San Miguel de Allende, not far from Guanajuato. We found five established bilingual schools to choose from; there were elegant restaurants, art galleries, theater productions, and music festivals—all run for a large ex-pat community. Maybe most amazingly, there were two different forums for old movies and art films. This city—I'd actually be in a city, a small one, but still a city— seemed to fill all the criteria I fantasized about earlier that year. Who knew I'd have to go to Mexico to find culture again?

I was adamant, however, that we have a time limit for how long we would spend in Mexico. Two years at the most, I said. Our original plan for the lavender while we were gone was for Tasha to run the business for us since her college load would be lightening up, with our input from afar. But our plans always seem eminently alterable.

•

Before we left for Mexico in January 2006, Blanco gave us a parting shot, quite literally. It was right before Christmas and we had taken Robb's parents on a walk down to the creek so that they could see the property for the last time before we left. It was almost dusk and when I heard gunfire, I remembered we were still in hunting season. How could I have forgotten?

"Robb, let's go back. We're too close to the creek." We all turned around to walk back to the guesthouse. "I'll be so glad to not deal with hunting season again," I said to Robb's mother. "It makes me crazy. I'm just glad we've never had a problem."

When we got up to the guesthouse, we discovered that the shot we had heard earlier had been aimed at our dog Mose. He was bleeding from a wound in his back leg. We determined he'd been hit by a hollow-point bullet because it made a small hole going in, but blasted out much of his thigh muscle on its way out the other side. Miraculously, the bullet didn't hit a nerve, or bone, or his colon. The vet was able to stitch him up, and during our last week in the U.S., if anyone told me they were worried about our safety in Mexico, I responded, "Well, at least we won't have people shooting guns on our property line."

Mose made the trip down to San Miguel in the back of my car with a tube in his wound to drain off the excess fluid. While Robb drove down separately in his truck, Mose and I were joined in my Honda Pilot by our other dog, Rooster; our cats, Josie and Diego; Gus and Jeb; and Tasha's parents, the Briegers. "We were like Noah's Ark," I told my mom. "Two kids, two dogs, two cats, two friends."

We enrolled the boys in the best of the bilingual schools, one that seemed quite solvent, and again they seemed to roll happily—more or less—with the new arrangement their crazy parents had cooked up. I made a trip back to Texas in the spring to give a lavender-growing seminar—where we had a participant from France of all places, which brought the whole experience full circle for me—and later returned to take part in the 2006 lavender festival.

But Mexico is intoxicating. It didn't take us long to realize that we would be staying longer than two years. Robb and I were enjoying the novelty of synchronicity—both of us wanting to live in the same place at the same time. Tasha, who was about to graduate from college, wanted Hill Country Lavender for her own—despite being allergic and having a boyfriend, a local horse trainer, who hated the smell. (He calls lavender the "vile weed," and claims that he "doesn't trust anything that goats won't eat.") It made sense that Tasha should have the business if we weren't going to return anytime soon. She knew almost as much about lavender as we did, having sat in on all our seminars and lived through the joys and angst of the business with us. On her own she had set up a store at the new field at McCall Creek Farms, redesigned packaging, planned for the lavender festival, and come up with new products. After much tribulation and pangs of grief, we decided to sell it to her with her parents' backing, though we will always be connected to the business. I suppose I am something like president emeritus.

When I left the field at the end of the 2006 lavender festival, I melted into tears, hugging Tasha. It was my swan song as the head of Hill Country Lavender; I was feeling a mixture of pride and overpowering wistfulness. Pride in what we'd done and also in Tasha; it was as if I was seeing my valedictorian daughter off to college.

The staff at the farm that day, including the Big Little Girls, gave me a cheap tiara to poke fun at my Lavender Queen nickname. I keep the tiara in my office in Mexico, near the original framed pastel of people bent over cutting lavender in my field. The picture was the only part of the lavender business I couldn't give up. Sometimes I stare at it and touch the Thinking Tree in the corner of the painting, and run my fingers over the distant view of gray hills. I remember exactly how the breeze felt the day the painting was made, how it smelled. I remember the woman in the red pants and white shirt. I remember she bought ten bars of soap and took her hat off when she finished cutting, placing it over her chest as if the National Anthem was playing. She breathed in deeply with her eyes closed and told me this was her idea of nirvana. I still marvel at all we had and all we created in that patch of Texas.

I smile to myself when I think what the smell of lavender will mean to the boys once they are older. It won't be the smell of grandma's boudoir—which is what many people have told me it conjures up for them. I think it will be the smell of a Texas childhood spent entertaining thousands of people in the summer and watching their mother build something that changed her whole outlook as well as their community.

And to me, that aroma—which I never have tired of, not for a moment—will always be the smell of life. Real life. Sweet and complicated but never bland.

Still, my lavender days are not over. Four different people interested in growing lavender in Mexico have sought us out here for advice, and I've even given a mini-growing seminar *in Spanish* for some townspeople near San Miguel, who with the help of a U.S. charity are starting a lavender business to support the pueblo while the men are working in the States. I've researched the climate and soil conditions in the area, and just in case I ever feel too nostalgic for lavender, I've secured the domain name, www.sanmiguel-lavender.com.

Just recently, ten-year-old Gus came to my room in the morning with this news: "Mommy, I had a dream we had two lavender lemonade shops in San Miguel."

If I've learned anything from life so far, it is, you just never know.

ACKNOWLEDGMENTS

I would like to thank Richard Pine of InkWell Management for the two word e-mail that got this project under way and for everything after; to Libby O'Neill for her cheerleading; to Amy Hertz for her early and unhesitating embrace of the story; and to Christine Pride of Broadway Books for her careful, insightful edit and lovely sense of collaboration. Thanks to those who offered input as the idea and manuscript progressed: Franklin Ashley, my amazing college writing professor, Kate Holmes, Judith Massengale, Clare Ratliff, Susan Welchman, and Andrea Campbell. I am indebted as well to those who helped with the technical aspects of growing lavender as our farm evolved: Don Roberts, Jim Kamas, Pam and Frank Arnosky, Cathy and Mark Itz. I was blessed with a wonderful staff at the lavender farm starting with Tasha Brieger, my gal Friday (and Saturday and Sunday) and a dear friend, Megan Cox and Christina Ivy (my Little Girls), Lea Molina and Jeanna Davis. I also want to thank my friends, our lavender customers, and the town of Blanco, Texas (which will soon be the home of a business called Lavender Capital Laundromat), for their support of this unusual venture. Special appreciation goes to Jan and Jon Brieger for the many and varied ways they've been part of our lavender life, and to my parents for bringing me into a family that has been so encouraging, so loving and so much fun.

And always and sincerely thanks to the man who started it all.